NGOs, Political Protest, and Civil Soci

This book argues that non-governmental organizations (NGOs) have an important effect on political participation in the developing world. Contrary to popular belief, they promote moderate political participation through formal mechanisms such as voting only in democracies where institutions are working well. This is a radical departure from the bulk of the literature on civil society that sees NGOs and other associations as playing a role in strengthening democracy wherever they operate. Instead, Carew Boulding shows that where democratic institutions are weak, NGOs encourage much more contentious political participation, including demonstrations, riots, and protests. Except in extreme cases of poorly functioning democratic institutions, however, the political protest that results from NGO activity is not generally antisystem or incompatible with democracy – again, as long as democracy is functioning above a minimal level.

Carew Boulding is an assistant professor of political science at the University of Colorado at Boulder. She received her PhD in Political Science from the University of California, San Diego. Boulding's research focuses on how democracy works in younger democracies. She has published research on political participation, participatory budgeting, attitudes toward democracy, and government accountability. Her work has appeared in the *Journal of Politics, Comparative Political Studies, World Development, Latin American Research Review, Party Politics,* and *Studies in Comparative International Development.*

"Recent literature on the resurgence of protest in Latin America may have inadvertently reinforced the divide between protest politics and electoral politics. Boulding's first-rate analysis of NGOs' protest activity suggests that this divide is fluid rather than fixed. Her study makes an important contribution to the existing literature by explaining how the political context conditions the influence of NGO activity, and how this context, in turn, encourages NGOs to promote protests in some cases and voting in others. Boulding's study also provides a solid foundation about the effects of protest on new democracies, showing that protests are not always incompatible with the workings of young democracies. The methodological sophistication of her analysis is outstanding and well executed. Overall, Boulding has left a footprint on the contentious and comparative politics literatures."

– Moises Arce, Department of Political Science, University of Missouri

"Boulding has written an impressive and important book that offers a new way of understanding the role NGOs play in promoting political participation and political stability in young democracies. It weaves together rich empirical evidence from Bolivia, Latin America, and cross-national surveys to show that protests need not undermine weak democracies, but can strengthen them by giving citizens meaningful ways to express their grievances. This emphasis on contentious politics will energize a literature that tends to focus narrowly on voting and electoral politics."

– Claudio A. Holzner, University of Utah

NGOs, Political Protest, and Civil Society

CAREW BOULDING

University of Colorado at Boulder

CAMBRIDGE
UNIVERSITY PRESS

CAMBRIDGE
UNIVERSITY PRESS

32 Avenue of the Americas, New York NY 10013-2473, USA

Cambridge University Press is part of the University of Cambridge.

It furthers the University's mission by disseminating knowledge in the pursuit of education, learning and research at the highest international levels of excellence.

www.cambridge.org
Information on this title: www.cambridge.org/9781107659384

First published 2014
First paperback edition 2016

A catalogue record for this publication is available from the British Library

Library of Congress Cataloguing in Publication data
Boulding, Carew.
NGOs, political protest, and civil society / Carew Boulding.
    pages   cm
Includes bibliographical references and index.
ISBN 978-1-107-06570-3 (hardback)
1. Non-governmental organizations – Political activity – Developing countries.   2. Political
participation – Developing countries.   3. Civil society – Developing countries.   4. Protest
movements – Developing countries.   5. Democracy – Developing countries.   I. Title.
JZ4841.B68   2014
322.409172'4–dc23   2014002464

ISBN   978-1-107-06570-3   Hardback
ISBN   978-1-107-65938-4   Paperback

To my three amazing daughters, with gratitude
for the joy, balance, and focus you bring to me.
And to Aaron, my husband, for everything.

Contents

Figures

Tables

Appendixes

Acknowledgments

Writing this book has taken me through nearly a decade of change – finishing my PhD, becoming a mother, returning to my hometown of Boulder, Colorado, as an assistant professor, finding my footing and my voice as a scholar and researcher, and learning to balance a family of three young daughters and two exciting careers. My husband Aaron has been my partner the whole way, encouraging me to go for it, believing in me without fail, and joyfully sharing in our very full life. He inspires me to be the person, scholar, and mother that I want to be, for which I am very grateful.

I have my grandparents, Kenneth and Elise Boulding, to thank for making academia look like a good idea. I have early childhood memories of my grandfather lying in a hammock in the woods at their mountain cabin, holding a small tape recorder and dictating economics books, and my grandmother telling stories of exciting travels and fascinating people. Although no part of this process has felt remotely like lying in a hammock, it has been more rewarding than I could have imagined. I am grateful to my grandparents for setting such an example and hope one day to figure out how to spend more time in a hammock.

Luckily, I have also been influenced by folks with a slightly more realistic image of what an academic life would be like. Thank you to the many wonderful colleagues and professors at UC San Diego, including my adviser Paul Drake (whose regular encouragement kept me from dropping out of graduate school, I am certain), Emily Beaulieu, Gary Cox, David Cunningham, Scott Desposato, Melody Ellis Valdini, Clark Gibson, Maureen Feeley, Karen Ferree, Kathleen Gallagher Cunningham, Kristian Gleditsch, Peter Gourevitch, Steph Haggard, Susan Hyde, Miles Kahler, David Lake, Craig McIntosh, Alejandra Ríos Cázares, Phil Roeder, and Peter Smith.

I still have trouble believing the good fortune that brought me to the University of Colorado. I was thrilled to return to Boulder, but I never could have imagined I would have colleagues as smart, kind, and generous as they are. Jennifer Wolak, Jennifer Fitzgerald, and Vanessa Baird – you are amazing. Aysegul Aydin, Scott Adler, Krister Andersson, Andy Baker, Lorraine Bayard de Volo, Ken Bickers, David Bearce, David Brown, Steve Chan, Susan Clarke, Ed Greenberg, John Griffin, Joe Jupille, Moonhawk Kim, Amy Liu, Celeste Montoya, Anand Sokhey, Sarah Sokhey, Sven Steinmo, Jaroslav Tir ... what a department! Also at CU, the Institute of Behavioral Science has been a wonderful resource, providing a quiet "secret" office and a weekly working group where many of these ideas were developed.

This book has benefited from generous feedback at different stages from Moisés Arce, Fodei Batty, Damarys Canache, Thomas Carothers, José Cheibub, Matthew Cleary, Dan Corstange, Sarah Croco, Todd Eisenstadt, Thomas Flores, Karleen Jones West, Darren Kew, Sharon Lean, Daniel Moreno, Nancy Postero, Roberta Rice, Joel Simmons, Sidney Tarrow, Mariano Tommasi, Donna Lee Van Cott, Brian Wampler, and Deborah Yashar. Amaney Jamal and Claudio Holzner deserve special thanks for reading the whole manuscript and providing valuable feedback. I am thankful for the openness and generosity with which scholars in Bolivia shared their insights with me; in particular conversations with George Gray Molina, Ramiro Molina, Tom Kruse, and Xavier Álbo stand out. Many thanks also to my interview subjects in NGOs and government. My thanks, also, to Lewis Bateman and three anonymous reviewers for Cambridge University Press, who supported this project and gave valuable feedback for improving it.

Data collection for this project was supported by a Scholar Grant from the Center to Advance Research and Teaching in the Social Sciences (CARTSS) at the University of Colorado, and the research assistance of Maureen Donaghy, Raymond Foxworth, Duncan Lawrence, Shawnna Mullenax, Abby Nimz, and Lydia Van Vleet. Jami Nunez deserves special mention as my co-author for some of the research presented in Chapter 6 (drawn from our article published in *Latin American Research Review*). Also thanks to Lindsay Galway for creating the maps of Bolivia in Chapter 3. Funding for field work came from the Center for Iberian and Latin American Studies (CILAS) at the University of California, San Diego, and from the University of California Institute for Global Conflict and Cooperation (IGCC). Thanks also to the Latin American Public Opinion Project (LAPOP) and its major supporters (the United Stated Agency for International Development, the United Nations Development Programme, the Inter-American Development Bank, and Vanderbilt University) for making the data available. I am also grateful to the researchers at the World Values Survey and the Latinobarometer for making their data available.

There are two people who deserve so much thanks that anything written here seems inadequate. Irfan Nooruddin has been a constant champion of this book, a remarkable mentor, and a dear friend. Emily Beaulieu, my closest friend, has been a constant source of inspiration as we both navigated UCSD, then tenure-track jobs, having children, and writing books. This friendship has truly carried me through. Thank you.

Finally, I would not have made it this far without the support of my friends and family outside of academia. I am so grateful for my three incredible daughters, Sevilla, Maya, and Elise, who amaze and delight me every day. My family near and far deserve thanks for putting up with me through this long process, especially Mark and Patricia Boulding, Kathi and Wayne Grider, my Grandma Frances, my dear aunt Pam, my best friend Melinda, my sister Frances, and my brother Bjorn. Most importantly, thanks to my husband Aaron, for always believing in me and supporting me, and helping me keep perspective. My thanks start and finish with him.

All errors and omissions are, of course, my own.

1

Introduction

On Election Day in Bolivia the roads are full of people making their way to polling places, sometimes walking for hours in the blazing sun along the dusty roads of the high Andean plateau, or along muddy paths in the Amazon lowlands. Driving is prohibited for the duration of voting and the normally busy roads are strangely quiet without the usual din of motorized traffic. Occasionally official vehicles from the national electoral court or international observer groups fly by in a cloud of dust. People sell food and drinks by the side of the road, but most businesses are closed for the day. At polling places, people wait in line to vote, then spend time talking with friends and family before the long walk home. Despite the festival atmosphere of Election Day and relatively high voter turnout there are a number of reasons to suspect that elections are not living up to expectations in Bolivia.[1] Although Bolivia has held regular elections since the 1982 transition to democracy, political parties are weak and inconsistent, accusations of fraud are common, and corruption is pervasive. Public confidence in elections is low, and in many districts there is little or no real political competition.

In sharp contrast, protests in Bolivia have proved surprisingly effective at achieving political aims. Since 2000, protests have resulted in changes to tax policy and policies on subsidies, a reversal of a controversial plan to privatize water in one of the larger cities, and, most dramatically, the resignation of a democratically elected president. Protests have also been central to the political movement that ushered in widespread legislative and local electoral victories for the leftist political party *Movimiento al Socialismo* (MAS) and the election of Bolivia's first indigenous president, Evo Morales, in 2005 and again in 2009.

---

[1] This description is based on the author's observations of the 2004 referendum election in La Paz and the 2009 general election in Potosí.

Protest has become a common and effective form of political participation in recent years in Bolivia.

In this context of poorly performing – yet nominally democratic – institutions, non-governmental organizations (NGOs) play a puzzling role in mobilizing people for participation in both elections and in protest movements. NGOs are often credited with promoting democracy at the local level by encouraging political engagement, educating voters, and by strengthening the capacity of democratic institutions through advice and training. In Bolivia, however, it is clear that NGOs have also played key roles in mobilizing and organizing political protest movements. NGOs directly facilitated the first large-scale indigenous protests of the early 1990s, including the dramatic month-long march to the capital in 1990 (the "March for Territory and Dignity"). NGOs also helped organize protests surrounding the privatization of water in Cochabamba in 2003 (the "Water War"). More recently, NGOs were often involved in the wave of protests and blockades against the government of Sánchez de Lozada that culminated in the violent confrontations of the "Gas War" in La Paz and El Alto in 2003. These events marked a major turning point in Bolivian politics as the high levels of social mobilization and frequent street protests helped carry Evo Morales to an unprecedented electoral victory in the 2005 presidential elections. Morales became Bolivia's first indigenous president, and the first president to win more than 50 percent of the vote.

For many NGO advocates, these events in Bolivia represent a compelling story of change. NGOs, many with substantial international funding, have been working in Bolivia for decades, bringing resources to impoverished communities and empowering the poor, women, and indigenous people to participate in politics and make demands for a more responsive government. As a result, through very direct and contentious confrontation with the state, a project of major social change was initiated. For some proponents of NGO work, however, the close link between NGOs and protest movements represents an alarmingly contentious way to pursue the aims of social justice. For all the rhetoric in the foreign aid community praising local NGO activity, there is very little reference to protest or direct confrontation. Instead, NGOs are praised for strengthening democracy at the local level through education, citizen training, and dialogue – not through violent protest.

These events and debates in Bolivia are representative of larger issues across the developing world. What role do NGOs in developing democracies play in promoting political participation? And what does their impact on political participation mean for democracy? Bolivia is an instructive starting point for this discussion because it is a case of very high NGO activity, weak democratic institutions, and high levels of social mobilization and protest. In Bolivia these forces are shaping and defining political life, but the dynamics at play exist in all democracies in the developing world. The role that NGOs are increasingly playing in developing world democracies extends to democracies across Latin America and other regions of the developing world. In all of the newer democracies of the developing world, NGOs have taken on service delivery and advocacy roles, which have changed the ways in which ordinary people associate and participate in politics.

Is NGO activity strengthening democracy in developing countries? Or are NGOs threatening democracy by helping give voice to demands that resource-poor governments are ill-equipped to handle? To assess the role that NGOs play in newer democracies, this book focuses on two related questions about how NGOs influence political participation in developing democracies. First, under what conditions do NGOs encourage voting versus protest? And, second, what does protest resulting from NGO activity mean for weakly institutionalized democracies? Specifically, under what conditions is NGO activity likely to result in protest that is compatible with support for a democratic political system versus protest that is antisystem? The idea that NGOs might be encouraging political protest runs counter to much of the conventional wisdom on NGOs, which focuses on their role in training citizens to participate in democratic processes, bringing new resources to poor communities, or grassroots problem-solving. This book presents strong evidence that NGOs do facilitate political protest and contentious politics in almost every country in Latin America and in developing-world democracies outside of Latin America. There is little evidence, on the other hand, that protest is incompatible with support for a democratic political system. In fact, in nearly every country in Latin America, individuals who have protested report similar levels of support for democracy as non-protesters.

These questions address important unresolved tensions in both the NGO literature and the literature on political protest concerning the threshold at which political engagement crosses over into something more threatening. On the one hand, NGOs are praised for encouraging democratic political engagement at the local level by training democratic citizens and modeling productive, democratic conflict resolution techniques.[2] They are also praised for mobilizing activism on a wide range of social justice issues including the environment, human rights, economic policy, and many others.[3] On the other hand, NGOs have attracted criticism for many of the same activities, including activism that becomes disruptive or violent. For example, the violent protests in Seattle in 1999 led by NGOs protesting globalization attracted both supporters and detractors – some activists were energized by the high profile of the clashes and the media attention they received, but others were dismayed by the violence and confrontational tactics employed. Implicit in these analyses is the idea that

---

[2] For example, Bratton lauded NGOs as bolsters to civil society because they are often democratic and participatory (1989). Others more directly make the claim that NGOs train good democratic citizens (Reilly 1995).

[3] Keck and Sikkink pointed out this more contentious role for NGOs in attracting international attention to domestic political struggles, an idea that has greatly influenced both practitioners and scholars (1998).

at some point NGOs can go too far. That is, mobilization may generally be a good thing, but at some point it crosses over into the realm of unreasonable demands, violence, or instability.[4]

This divide is not just between moderate and radical observers of NGO activity. It points to a fundamental tension in the role that NGOs are thought to play in democracies in the developing world. NGOs – and civil society more broadly – help people mobilize and articulate their interests and demands to the state. NGOs build capacity for participation among the poor and traditionally excluded so that they can pressure governments in the developing world to be more responsive and more accountable. On one hand, this activity is thought to be good for democracy as it encourages participation and holds the government to account. But on the other hand, NGOs give voice to deep-seeded and widespread discontent that poor governments in the developing world may be ill equipped to address. By pointing out the failures of government, are NGOs strengthening democracy or undermining it?

The literature on political protest holds a similar tension. Some scholars see protest as a process through which oppressed people shake off their shackles and creatively and contentiously make demands on the state, something seen as essential for democracy to work. Protest is both an expression of important democratic freedoms and a sign that those freedoms are protected sufficiently that people are able to participate. For others, however, protest is seen as a precursor to wider conflicts, including violence, civil wars, and general political instability (Huntington 1968; Rose and Shin 2001). Again, implicit in these very different ways of thinking about contentious political engagement is a threshold. Up to a certain point, protest may be an important way of voicing previously excluded interests. Beyond a certain point, however, protest is viewed as a menace to political order, a dangerous burden putting strain on weak institutions. These different visions of the role of civil society mobilization in democracy represent fundamentally different conceptions of democracy. In one vision, democracy is essentially a set of rules for settling disputes, adjudicating disagreements peacefully, and establishing clear winners and losers through formal elections. In the other, democracy is essentially a contentious process of voicing political opinions.

This book addresses these debates by exploring how civil society mobilization works in newer democracies. Specifically, it seeks to identify the conditions

---

[4] The literature on civil society also shows this tension between contentious and moderate visions. For example, many of the seminal works on social cleavages and political parties saw parties as necessary for containing the unruly and polarizing forces of political engagement into more controlled interactions (Sartori 1976). Others characterized strong civil society as dangerous to effective policymaking or political stability (Almond and Verba 1963; Hirschman 1970; O'Donnell 1973). These authors rarely use the terminology "civil society" but are essentially talking about many of the same concepts of membership in organizations, and collective political behavior. See Bermeo (2003) for further discussion of how these early works inform the contemporary debates over civil society and participation.

under which NGOs are likely to promote protest versus voting, and some of the limits of where we should expect NGOs' facilitation of protest to be supportive of – or compatible with – a democratic political system. I argue that the critical factor that shapes the impact of NGO activity on political participation is the quality of democracy – in particular the degree to which elections are free and fair and offer opportunities to choose between political parties or candidates that reflect important issues and interests in society, and the overall confidence of ordinary people in elections as a tool for participation. Under conditions of poorly functioning elections, weak political parties, and low confidence in elections, NGOs encourage political protest. In other words, as the formal mechanisms for democratic political participation perform worse and worse, NGOs have an increasing effect on protest and a declining effect on voting. The inverse is also true. As democratic institutions perform better, NGOs have a larger effect on voting than on protest.

What does this protest mean for weakly institutionalized democracies? Even in cases of frequent protests, protest need not be incompatible with a democratic political system. In fact, in most countries that are at least minimally democratic, protest can be an important way of keeping electoral losers and others who are dissatisfied with the government as part of the policy debates as policymakers are forced to respond to protesters' demands. At some critical point, however, democratic institutions may perform so poorly that political protest is unlikely to continue being system supporting. There is real and important variation in the quality of democratic institutions between countries that qualify as minimally democratic. I argue that this variation in the quality of the process and performance of democratic institutions – especially the fairness of elections, the strength and coherence of political parties, and the degree of political competition – is the most important factor that shapes how NGOs influence political participation and the effect new political participation will have on support for a democratic political system.

WHY THIS BOOK?

The central finding of the book is that NGOs promote moderate political participation through formal mechanisms such as voting *only* in democracies where institutions are working quite well. This is a radical departure from the bulk of literature on civil society that sees NGOs and other associations as playing a role in strengthening democracy wherever they operate. Instead, I find that where democratic institutions are weak, NGOs encourage much more contentious political participation, including demonstrations, riots, and protests. Except in extreme cases of poorly functioning democratic institutions, however, the political protest that results from NGO activity is not generally antisystem or incompatible with democracy – again, as long as democracy is functioning above a minimal level.

This book offers an answer to the deep-seeded debate started by Huntington (1968) over whether the mobilization of civil society is a danger to stability and democracy (as Huntington suggests), or whether civil society is the necessary precondition for "making democracy work," as Putnam famously claimed (1994). By focusing on NGOs, which are newer actors that have changed the civil society scene in most developing countries, this book lays out the conditions under which civil society mobilization strengthens democracy and when it weakens it, which I argue is shaped by the quality of democratic institutions for participation.

I demonstrate that both Huntington and Putnam are wrong: Huntington for seeing civil society mobilization primarily as a threat to stability and to democracy and Putnam for seeing civil society as mainly fostering cooperative, moderate collaboration with the state. Instead, civil society in new democracies often facilitates contentious mobilization *at the same time* that it serves to legitimate support for democracy. But we can expect this relationship only in countries that are already democratic. Although NGOs are more likely to promote protest in countries with poorly functioning elections, they are rarely associated with antidemocratic attitudes as long as the country is above a minimal threshold for democratic performance.

The book offers a sharp contrast to the dominant view that civil society encourages moderate participation along the lines of peaceful activism, increasing voter turnout, and community problem solving – all of which should have a positive net benefit for democratic consolidation (Diamond 1999; Linz and Stepan 1996). International organizations and foreign aid donors have clearly accepted the premise that civil society is important for democracy: For example, the U.S. Agency for International Development (USAID) website states that the agency seeks to strengthen civil society so that individuals can "associate with like-minded individuals, express their views publicly, openly debate public policy, and petition their government" (USAID 2009). Similarly, the Swedish International Development Cooperation Agency (SIDA) describes civil society as important for promoting democracy because it "includes aspects such as tolerance, pluralism, social capital and trust, as well as respect for the opinions and desires of others" (SIDA 2007, 6).

Although there is a small and growing group of scholars who are much more skeptical that NGOs or civil society always play this role in the developing world, this project is one of the first to address explicitly the conditions under which NGOs in newer democracies strengthen institutional participation and when they are more likely to result in contentious behavior. Other work has pointed out that civil society is not always a pro-democracy force in authoritarian countries (Jamal 2007; Jamal and Nooruddin 2010; Rossteutscher 2010), but this book is the first to evaluate systematically how the quality of democratic institutions shapes the role of NGOs and civil society organizations in newer democracies.

The finding that the effect of NGOs on participation is shaped more by the larger context of institutional quality than by the specific actions of NGOs is also controversial. The vast majority of work on NGOs focuses on the individual organizations and how they operate, including attention to resources, local knowledge, capacity, and the type of activity in which the NGO is engaged. Although variation in the type of NGO may be tremendously important for some outcomes (ability to deliver services, for example), I find that NGOs also have large unintended consequences for participation that are influenced more by the context in which they are operating than by their specific activities. Although NGO scholars may certainly recognize the importance of context, the focus of the vast majority of work on NGOs has been at the level of the organization.

Similarly, much of the recent work on civil society in developing countries has focused on the type of organizations involved and how democratic they are. My work, in contrast, suggests that it is not enough to know how strong, or how democratic civil society is in a country to know if it will foster active engaged voting, or if it will encourage contentious political protest, or both. It is also essential to know what the institutional mechanisms for political participation are like.

Finally, this book offers a new and rigorous methodological approach to these questions. Both the literatures on NGOs and civil society have long been dominated by theory that has rarely been tested systematically. This book is the first to my knowledge to evaluate systematically the impact of NGOs and civil society organizations on participation in varying contexts of democratic quality.

THE SCOPE: DEMOCRACIES IN THE DEVELOPING WORLD

This book focuses on nominally democratic countries in the developing world because of the tremendous variation in the quality of the institutions that are called democratic and because it is unclear what the role for political protest is under these varying conditions. In 1978 nearly every country in Latin America was governed by an authoritarian regime. In a little more than a decade, by 1990, nearly every country in the region had competitively elected governments and could be considered democratic or semi-democratic. Similarly in other regions of the world, a move toward electoral democracy has been documented since the 1970s. In 2010, out of 194 countries and territories Freedom House considered 116 electoral democracies. The younger democracies in this group face some formidable challenges, including high economic inequality, high rates of poverty, deep social divides, and relatively weak political institutions compared to the older, wealthier democracies of Europe and North America. It has also become clear that transitioning to democratic government does not signal the end of contentious politics in the developing world. Instead, political protest and demonstrations continue to play a role in the politics of most democracies in the world.[5] Since Samuel Huntington first voiced concern over the stability of weak political institutions in the face of rapidly changing societies in *Political Order in Changing Societies,* there has been a fear that social mobilization may prove too much for young democracies (1968). Can young democracies with weak political institutions withstand the pressures of changing, politically mobilized societies? What happens to the dynamics of civil society when the state is unable or unwilling to respond to participatory pressure from civil society?

In many countries in the developing world, however, democracy has proved surprisingly stable even in the face of contentious political activity. In India, for example, stable democratic governance at the national level coexists with frequent ethnic riots at the local (Varshney 2003; Wilkinson 2006). In Latin America, democracy today is more durable and more extensive than ever before in the region (Hagopian and Mainwaring 2005), in spite of increasing political protests (Arce and Bellinger 2007; Bellinger and Arce 2010). And democracy has remained relatively stable in the face of new social movements organized in part around indigenous identity and social inclusion for the poor in Mexico, Bolivia, and Ecuador (Yashar 2005). Democracy has also persisted in the face of high levels of political protest in Brazil, Argentina, Peru, and Colombia. Even the countries that have experienced government instability have rarely seen the type of regime breakdown associated with instability before this current era of democracy (Pérez-Liñán 2007). In wealthy, established democracies political protest is rarely criticized as a threat to the regime, or as a threat to democracy. Rather, political protest is more often characterized as one of many ways that citizens make their opinions known and press for policy responsiveness. At the extreme, when protests turn violent and destructive, they are seen as a police problem – but rarely as a threat to the fundamental institutional order of democracy. In fact, protest is seen as a sign of confidence in the protections democracy guarantees for individual human rights and the lack of state repression that might discourage people from taking to the streets. In younger democracies, however, protest is frequently characterized as much more threatening, a sign of things falling apart, or a worrisome provocation for military intervention. At the very least, there is a recognized tension between participatory mobilization and stability of institutions (Rose and Shin 2001). Now that the "third wave" democracies are no longer in their infancy, it is becoming clear that protest is not always a sign of institutional breakdown in developing countries any more than in

---

[5] In 1981, 14.15 percent of respondents to the World Values Survey in developing countries claimed to have participated in demonstrations. In the second wave (around 1990), 18.37% reported demonstrating. In the third and fourth wave (around 1995 and 1999, respectively) those figures dropped to 13.48 percent and 11.06 percent. In the most recent wave (2005), the number has stayed at 11.03 percent.

developed ones.[6] There is, however, very little systematic empirical work investigating the conditions under which protest is compatible with support for a democratic political system.

THE ARGUMENT IN BRIEF

I argue that the organization of associational life (including membership in voluntary organizations, community groups, neighborhood associations, and contact with NGOs) – *combined with the larger context of how well electoral institutions work for ordinary people* – determines how people participate in politics and their attitudes toward democracy. NGOs, because of their growing presence in civic life in developing countries, play a crucial role in mobilizing people to participate in younger democracies, including promoting contentious politics that take unresponsive governments to task. This role is shaped by how well the formal institutions of participation and representation are working in a country, growing more contentious the worse formal institutions are. Because civil society organizations and NGOs help facilitate participation that is rooted in social issues, even very contentious political action that results often builds support for democratic systems as long as the system is reasonably democratic (and not systematically repressive). This participation, however, often takes a much more contentious form than advocates of NGOs and civil society have anticipated.

First, I explore the mechanisms through which individual involvement with NGOs and civil society organizations influence the decision to engage in political life. In practice, NGOs in the developing world do many of the same things that other voluntary associations do, but often with greater financial resources because they are more likely to be supported by international donors (Hulme and Edwards 1997). NGOs work in service provision (health care, sanitation, education, etc.) and they can work in advocacy (providing education, legal services, or directly lobbying the government). NGOs also often target their activities toward needy communities, bringing new resources to historically excluded populations. NGOs, by virtue of being problem-oriented organizations, also create new opportunities for association. Sometimes this happens directly, as when NGOs organize workshops and forums for communities to discuss issues, but it can also happen indirectly as people wait in line to get vaccines for their children, or obtain a driver's license, or any of the quotidian activities that occupy everyday life. Both the resources NGOs provide and the opportunities for association facilitate political participation much in the same way membership in other types of community organizations or voluntary associations is thought to: people who know each other, trust each other, and have some recognition of shared problems are more likely to decide to engage in political action.

---

[6] The term "Third Wave" comes from Huntington (1991) and refers to the spread of democracy in the developing world beginning in the 1970s.

Second, I show that the form participation is likely to take is more a function of larger contextual factors than of the individual ones. That is, I argue that a rich associational life facilitates political participation, but whether that participation takes the form of voting or the form of protest is shaped more by the context of how well democratic political institutions – especially elections – are functioning. People who are motivated to participate are more likely to vote when there is little fraud or corruption in the electoral process, when political parties represent meaningful choices, when there is real political competition, and when reasonable people have confidence that participating in elections might affect outcomes they deem important. These conditions are not fully met in any election, even in "advanced" democracies, but there is real variation in each of these factors that influences the likelihood individuals see voting as a meaningful activity. And, where elections are failing on some or all of these counts, a motivated person views contentious political action favorably.

I also argue that dissatisfaction with formal mechanisms of participation is not only a function of electoral fraud or corruption; it can also be a function of electoral outcomes. More specifically, failures of democratic governments to respond to the needs or interests of constituents can channel political participation into nontraditional and contentious forms of participation. For example, widespread dissatisfaction with formal voting can occur when elections are technically working fine but people have little confidence that electoral participation will produce substantive benefits. In fact, in some cases, the formal mechanisms of democratic governance may be functioning quite well, but the government is performing poorly in terms of meeting the real needs of citizens, or offering choices on issues that concern most people.

Based on this argument, this book explores four main hypotheses about how NGOs influence political behavior and attitudes toward democracy:

1. In minimally democratic contexts, I expect contact with NGOs to boost all types of political participation (voting and protest).
2. As the quality of democratic institutions declines, I expect NGOs to have an increasing effect on political protest.
3. As the quality of democratic institutions improves, I expect NGOs to have an increasing effect on mobilizing voter turnout.
4. Except in extreme cases of poorly functioning democratic institutions, the political protest that results from NGO activity is not generally anti-system or incompatible with democracy.

There are a number of possible alternative stories to the one I present here. For example, more active, politically interested people might simply be more willing to vote, protest, and contact NGOs. Similarly, it is possible that NGOs choose to locate in areas with high levels of need and high grievances, making it more likely that we would observe a relationship between NGOs and protest even if NGOs did little to mobilize protests. Although in some cases these alternatives may hold, overall NGOs have a robust independent effect on protest, even taking issues of selection and endogeneity into account. These issues of endogeneity and the direction of the causal relationships are ones that I return to in greater detail in each of the empirical chapters.

NGOS AND CIVIL SOCIETY: DEFINITIONS

The goal of this book is to explore the relationship between associational life in democracies in the developing world and political participation. I focus on the role of civil society organizations – particularly NGOs and membership associations – in shaping choices about how to participate in political action.[7] Focusing on NGOs in addition to other civil society organizations is useful for a number of reasons. First, NGOs have grown in number and in influence in developing countries since the 1980s, and have been targeted by foreign aid donors as visible, easy-to-reach organizations within civil society. Thus they often command substantial economic resources compared to other local voluntary organizations. NGOs are also frequently problem oriented and focused on reaching the poor or excluded members of society, making it more likely that contact with an NGO represents a real change in the associational life of many people (as opposed to a continuation of their normal civic life), and more likely that NGO activity will affect political participation.

Both the term non-governmental organization and the term civil society are notoriously difficult to define, so it is helpful to clarify their use here and how the two concepts relate. NGOs constitute a wide variety of non-governmental nonprofit membership and support organizations.[8] NGOs are organizations "characterized primarily by humanitarian or cooperative, rather than commercial, objectives... that pursue activities to relieve suffering, promote the interests of the poor, protect the environment, provide basic social services, or undertake community development" (World Bank 1989).[9] In developing countries, NGOs provide services ranging from local provision of health care,

[7] For an excellent summary of the literature that treats NGOs as part of civil society, see Mercer (2002).

[8] Hulme and Edwards (1997) use the term NGO only to refer to intermediary organizations that offer support to development and grassroots organizations (termed GROs). Carroll (1992) makes a similar distinction, but uses the term "community-based organizations" (CBOs). This project looks at the aggregate effect of all types of NGOs.

[9] There are also complicated and overlapping taxonomies of types of NGOs, starting with the division between "northern" or "international" NGOs (those based in a single developed country, but working in the developing world), "southern" NGOs (also called "indigenous NGOs," "third-world NGOs," or "domestic NGOs" and usually characterized as NGOs that are based exclusively in one developing country, though this distinction can be blurred by large amounts of "northern" money and influence). For southern NGOs, the distinctions become even more complex, trying to capture differences between grassroots organizations (GROs), which are based in local communities, and grassroots support organizations (GRSOs), which serve as intermediaries between local GROs and donors. There are also formal and informal networks between many of these organizations, including both GRO networks and GRSO networks (Fisher 1998: 4). The terms voluntary organization, associational organization, community-based organization, civil-society organization, and charitable organization are also all in use to refer to largely the same actors (Tvedt 1998).

sanitation, and housing services, to national-level research and policy advice. They also frequently act as intermediaries for foreign aid projects. Some NGOs have explicitly political goals, such as empowerment for women or the poor, while others choose to remain as politically neutral as they can. Some are tied to churches or religious organizations and others are secular. These organizations make up one important part of the fabric of civil society in any country. In the developing world, NGOs play a particularly important role, as they are the targets of international funding aimed at strengthening civil society and are often seen as intermediaries or facilitators for larger civil society. Civil society is a larger category and includes more than just NGOs: organizations such as community groups, clubs, churches, labor unions, and professional associations are also a part of civil society.

It is important to be clear on the differences between NGOs and other voluntary associations in order to understand the particular role that NGOs can play, and how they fit into the larger setting of civil society in a country. Unlike sports clubs, professional organizations, or neighborhood associations, NGOs are almost always problem oriented. NGOs are formed around solving problems of the environment, human rights, clean water, maternal health, housing, or poverty. And they often have international funding to support some portion of their activities. NGOs also target areas with high levels of need on their particular dimension of interest. An NGO working on poverty alleviation, for example, will set up programs in communities where poverty is a big concern. An NGO focused on water and sanitation may focus on either rural or urban communities in need, depending on the organization's strengths. Also, unlike voluntary organizations that rely on membership fees, NGOs are more likely to employ professional staff, and be required to show progress on a variety of metrics, including improvement in terms of the program goals or allocation of funds. Thus, on average, NGOs do more to reach out to people who are politically excluded than membership organizations do (Fisher 1998). Of course, robust associational life can exist in poor communities, but NGOs – in contrast to membership organizations – tend to bring in new resources to poor communities with a problem-oriented focus. New resources and attention to problems in the community create an environment where new political engagement is most likely.

Table 1.1 summarizes the key differences between NGOs and other membership associations, all of which can fall under the broader label of civil society. This table shows how these terms are commonly used, although in practice there is also a great deal of overlap between categories.

All of these types of organizations have grown in numbers and influence in the developing world over the last 100 years, but most rapidly since the 1980s. In 1909 there were fewer than 200 international NGOs in the world; in 1956 there were more than 1,000; in 2005 there were more than 20,000 (Union of International Associations' statistics cited in Werker and Ahmed [2008: 75]). Similar growth in numbers of domestic NGOs has been documented in

TABLE 1.1. *Comparing Civil Society Organizations: NGOs and Membership Associations*

	Civil Society Organizations	
	NGOs	**Membership Associations**
Definition	Non-governmental, nonprofit organizations primarily focused on humanitarian objectives	Voluntary, membership-based organizations involved in a wide range of activities distinct from government and business

Examples	International NGOs
	  CARE
	  Save the Children
	  World Vision
	  Catholic Relief Services
	  Amnesty International
	Local Service Provision NGOs
	  Health Care
	  Sanitation Services
	  Housing
	  Education
	Advocacy NGOs
	  Women's Empowerment
	  Capacity Building
	  Environmental advocacy
	  Indigenous rights
	Research NGOs
	  Policy advice
	  Think tanks
		Community Groups
		  Neighborhood Associations
		  Youth Groups
		Sports and Recreation
		Churches
		Labor Unions
		Arts or Music groups
		Educational Groups
		Professional Associations
		Consumer Organizations
		Charity and Volunteer Groups
		Advocacy Groups
		Social Movements

Note: There is substantial overlap in these categories as they are not mutually exclusive.

countries across the developing world, including Nepal, Bolivia, India, Tunisia, Brazil, and Thailand (Edwards 2009: 21). This growth in numbers can be attributed in part to the growing availability of foreign aid funds for NGOs involved in development projects. Since the 1980s, there has been a shift in foreign aid spending away from governments (many of which were plagued by corruption) toward NGOs. NGOs in the developing world have become the face of civil society for foreign aid donors seeking to promote democracy through strengthening civil society (Ottaway and Carothers 2000).

Considerable portions of both multilateral and bilateral aid are channeled through NGOs and many organizations have whole units devoted to strengthening ties with NGOs and building civil society. The World Bank, for example, involves civil society organizations through policy consultations, information sharing and training, grant making, and involving civil society in setting poverty reduction strategy goals. The World Bank estimates that 5 percent of its total annual portfolio (or about 1 billion dollars) is channeled to civil society organizations through grassroots development programs (World Bank 2006: xv). This effort to support civil society by collaborating with and funding NGOs and other civil society organizations is found across the major donors, including the U.S. and European aid agencies (Howell and Pearce 2002). Understanding how these diverse organizations affect political life is a challenging task. As these organizations become more numerous across the developing world, however, it is also a critically important one for many audiences, including international donors, developing-world government, academics, and NGO practitioners.

RESEARCH DESIGN AND PLAN OF THE BOOK

Understanding the complex connection between peoples' interactions in their daily lives and their choices about how to engage in political life is a difficult task. This book offers a new approach to investigating complex issues in comparative politics by directly testing individual, subnational, and cross-national implications of hypotheses and the interactions between levels of analysis. The book investigates the relationship between NGOs and participation both in rich context of Bolivian politics (through a subnational quantitative study of Bolivian municipalities and a qualitative consideration of the case) and across the varying contexts of democratic performance in Latin America (using multilevel models of individual and country-level factors affecting participation in eighteen countries), and finally in democracies in Asia, Africa, and Eastern Europe (again using multilevel models).

This research is rooted in the puzzling context of Bolivia, where NGOs have played an unusually decisive role in mobilizing protests. The initial goal of this research project was to understand the impact of NGO activity in the context of Bolivia, where democratic institutions are in place, but where issues of corruption, poor government performance, and frustration with the formal mechanisms of representation loom large. I realized that the context of government performance was key to understanding the effects of NGOs on political participation and on attitudes toward democracy, which pushed me to investigate local variation in the quality of democracy across the more than 300 municipalities in Bolivia. The theoretical perspective that I developed in the context of comparing NGO activity and political behavior across Bolivian municipalities has much broader implications. With Bolivia as a starting point, I then explore the effects of NGOs on political behavior across Latin America, focusing on how the impact of NGO activity differs as democratic political institutions perform better or worse. The results of this inquiry sparked further questions about whether the same relationships hold outside of Latin America in other developing-world democracies.

The result is a book that employs multiple methods of analysis to explore (1) the effect of NGO activity on voting and political protest across different contexts of responsiveness and institutional performance in developing democracies and (2) the consequences of political protest that is organized through NGOs and civil society in weak democracies. Empirically, I draw on an extensive array of data – from the individual, local, and national levels – to explore systematically the relationship between NGO activity and political participation. Part of the strategy here is to use a wide variety of data to get at a difficult empirical question – NGO activity is difficult to measure, as is protest activity, so the findings are (hopefully) more convincing if consistent across different measures. This book also seeks to explore the links between these levels in a systematic way, and to tease out individual, local, and national implications of the interaction between citizens and civil society organizations, including NGOs. Here I briefly detail the research strategies employed.

Subnational Analysis: Comparing Municipalities

Rather than relying on qualitative evidence alone for the informative case of Bolivia and treating Bolivia as a single case study, this project utilizes an original subnational dataset of Bolivian municipalities to offer a fully comparative subnational study of local level politics.[10] Subnational quantitative analyses offer several advantages. First, it greatly increases the number of observations, which is important for causal inference (King, Keohane, and Verba 1994; Snyder 2001). In Bolivia, for example, there are 327 municipalities, each of which has a mayor, a city council, and some number of NGOs working in the area. Comparing the effect of NGO activity over 327 municipalities offers a much better chance to understand the statistical significance of patterns than looking at country-level averages of twenty or so countries in Latin America, for example, or even the dozens of democratic countries in the developing world.

Second, especially in countries with large regional divides, very high inequality, or other large differences within the country, looking at national-level averages can be quite misleading. As Snyder (2001) points out, the problem of using national-level means in large-N cross-national analysis can be that very different cases are coded as the same, even though the underlying distribution of the variable may be quite different. That is, the same average can conceal very different ranges and distributions. This point has been of particular concern in analyses of Latin American countries, which are characterized by very high inequalities along income, urban–rural divides, asset ownership, and socioeconomic factors such as educational achievement.

---

[10] Municipalities in Bolivia are equivalent to U.S. counties in that the whole country is divided into contiguous municipalities. It is also an important unit of local government, including holding responsibility to administer funds under the 1994 decentralization reforms.

A final advantage of subnational data is the quality and comparability of the data collected at the municipal level in Bolivia. NGO activity is notoriously difficult to measure, especially at the national level where many different types of activities must be aggregated. There is no reliable cross-national dataset of NGO activity that includes local level NGO activities.[11] Because most of the theoretical arguments about NGOs expect their effects to be at the local level, this is a problem for cross-national analysis. Some attempts at measuring NGO activity cross-nationally have been attempted by using financial proxies such as aid allocation toward NGOs (Koch 2007; Nancy and Yontcheva 2006). Others have gathered data on international NGOs (Murdie and Bhasin 2011), or combined public opinion indicators with scores on freedom of association for a limited number of countries as a way of measuring civil society (Anheier 2004). Despite these efforts, there is no consistent, reliable source for measuring local NGO activity by country. There are similar challenges to collecting reliable data on political protest.[12] By definition protests are irregular events, and in many cases there is considerable risk for the protesters involved, both of which make gathering reliable data very difficult. Given these challenges, there is no easy way to construct a valid cross-national dataset of NGO activity and political protest.

To avoid these kinds of problems, I compiled an original municipal level dataset for Bolivia. This dataset includes measures of NGO project activity (available from a government registry of NGOs and their activities), incidences of political protest in the municipality, electoral results in national and local elections, and a variety of socioeconomic factors from the government census. I constructed the dataset over the course of several years, traveling to Bolivia in 2004 and 2007 to conduct interviews and meet with government officials at the National Electoral Court (*Corte Nacional Electoral* [CNE]), the National Statistics Institute (*Instituto Nacional de Estadística* [INE]), and the Viceministry of Public Investment and Foreign Financing (*Viceministerio de Inversión Pública y Financiamiento Externo,* or VIPFE) for the electoral, census, and NGO data. All three of the agencies publish much of these data in various formats, but talking to people at their offices in La Paz was very helpful for gaining a better understanding of how the data are collected. During these trips I also conducted interviews with people working at a number of NGOs, foreign aid agencies, and scholars in Bolivia. The data on political protest was coded from English- and Spanish-language newspapers.

Bolivia is an ideal setting in which to investigate the relationship between NGO activity and political participation under conditions of weakly performing democratic electoral institutions. Bolivia is a case where NGOs have had

---

[11] For example, The Union of International Associations maintains a database of international NGOs but not domestic NGOs.

[12] Some cross-national data on protest exists, including the Banks' Cross-National Time-Series Data Archive (Banks 2010).

a clear and important role in facilitating political protest, under conditions of less than responsive political institutions. The work of experts on Bolivian social movements agrees. Nearly every study of social movements in Bolivia points to some role for NGOs in the massive protest movements that have shaped recent political life in Bolivia (Lucero 2008; Postero 2007; Postero and Zamosc 2004; Van Cott 2005; Yashar 2005). The subnational analysis offers solid evidence for the argument presented here – that the context of how well people perceive electoral institutions to be functioning for them influences how they choose to participate in politics. Even at the local level, the context of local elections shapes the effect of NGO activity: where elections are competitive, NGOs tend to encourage voting, but in municipalities with little or no competitive choices in local elections, the relationship between NGOs and political protest is strongest.

Multilevel Models: Individuals and the Functioning of Democracy

The relationships between NGO activity and protest suggested by the study of Bolivian municipalities beg the question of whether NGOs play this role in other contexts and whether these relationships hold at the individual level. Thus, the larger empirical framework utilizes individual-level survey data and country-level variables in multilevel statistical analyses to explore how contact with NGOs affects individual political behavior differently in different countries, which vary in the degree to which democratic political institutions are performing well. Multilevel statistical models are an ideal way to test for the kind of conditional relationships I argue are essential for understanding the effects of membership in civil society organizations or contact with NGOs on decisions about how to participate in politics.[13]

Specifically, I turn to public opinion data from the Latinobarómetro and World Values Survey to explore the relationship between individual contact with NGOs and membership in civil society organizations on voting and protest behavior. Then, using a variety of indicators of the quality of democratic electoral institutions (including evaluations of how free and fair recent elections were, the extent to which political parties represent stable interests in society and have been around for more than a single election, overall confidence in the electoral process, and the degree to which elections offer real

---

[13] Multilevel data structures exist when one level of analysis is nested within another unit of analysis and data exist for both (Steenbergen and Jones 2002). For example, an individual may be more likely to vote if he or she has more education, has personal interests at stake in the election, or is strongly partisan (all individual level characteristics). At the same time individuals may also be influenced by factors in their community such as the level of campaign advertising in their media market or whether it was snowing on Election Day (community-level characteristics). The goal of modeling multilevel structures is to account for variation in a dependent variable at the lowest level by taking into account relevant variables at both levels (Steenbergen and Jones 2002).

choices to voters[14]), I evaluate how the individual determinants of voting and protest change under different national-level contexts. I find strong corroboration that individuals who have contact with NGOs are more likely to participate in protest and that this relationship is not limited to the Latin American context, but is in fact quite widespread in the developing world.

In sum, at many different levels of analysis and using different measurement techniques, I find a strong relationship between NGOs and political protest that increases in strength as the quality of democratic institutions declines. Municipalities in Bolivia with active NGOs are more likely to experience protest, especially if elections are uncompetitive. Individuals across Latin America and other parts of the developing world are more likely to protest if they have had contact with an NGO – and more so in countries with high levels of fraud, corruption, or weak political parties.

Chapter Outline

The book proceeds as follows. Chapter 2 lays out theoretical expectations about how NGOs influence political participation in developing democracies. First, I discuss the literatures on social capital, civil society, and NGOs focusing on the tension inherent between NGOs' role as activists and their role as bolsters for local democracy. Second, I detail the ways in which resources and opportunities for association provided by NGOs lower the costs of all types of participation. Third, I argue that the critical factor for understanding the effect NGOs have on political behavior is the context of how well democratic institutions are working. I offer a broad understanding of democratic quality that encompasses both the quality of elections themselves (electoral fraud), but also the deeper issues of political party organization and the extent to which elections represent a choice between alternatives that people care about. Finally, I consider the implications of NGO and civil society-led protest for attitudes toward democratic political systems, concluding that although protest may not be what most proponents of civil society expected, it rarely leads to antidemocratic attitudes. Instead, protest may be a critical way for conflicting opinions to be voiced in democracies where formal institutions are not functioning well.

Chapter 3 presents results from a new subnational dataset on protest, voter turnout, and NGO activity in the more than 300 municipalities in Bolivia. These local-level data offer strong evidence confirming a link between NGO activity and increases in political protest in municipalities. More interestingly, NGOs also stimulate voter turnout, but only in municipalities with close elections. Likewise, the strongest relationship between NGOs and protest is found in municipalities with little or no political competition. This is compelling evidence that citizens make decisions about how to participate that are based at

---

[14] For more detail on the measures used, see Chapters 4 and 5.

least partially on perceptions of effectiveness: where voting is seen as effective, NGO activity increases voting, but where voting is seen as ineffective, NGOs facilitate political protest.

Chapter 4 explores the conditions under which contact with NGOs and membership in associations leads to voting versus political protest across eighteen Latin American countries. I employ survey data from the Latinobarómetro combined with country-level measures of the quality of democratic institutions as a way to evaluate the effect of individual contact with NGOs on voting and protest behavior under differently functioning electoral mechanisms. This chapter presents evidence of a strong link between individual contact with NGOs and all types of political participation across eighteen Latin American countries. Counter to much of the conventional wisdom on NGOs and civil society, contact with NGOs is a much stronger and more consistent predictor of protest than of voting. In fact, in *every* country in the survey, there is a clear link between contact with an NGO or civil society organization and participation in a variety of protest activities, including authorized demonstrations, unauthorized demonstrations, land invasions, riots, and blocking traffic. More interesting, the link between NGOs and political protest is strongest in the countries where people have little confidence in elections, where political parties are unstable or fail to represent programmatic issues, or where election fraud is common. NGOs have more of an effect on voting in countries where elections are seen as meaningful mechanisms for expressing interests and making demands on the state.

In Chapter 5, I explore the effect of membership in civil society organization on protest and voting outside of Latin America. Using data from the World Values Survey, I find strong evidence that associational membership is linked to political protest around the globe, and that membership has a stronger effect on protest the more troubled the democratic institutions are. Where elections are seen to be working well, membership in associations tends to increase voting but in countries where elections are fraught with fraud, or where government in plagued by corruption, membership is strongly connected to protest activity. This chapter makes several points. First, it shows that the empirical relationship described here is not limited to Latin America – and not just driven by the presence of activist NGOs in Latin America. Rather, the findings in this chapter support the idea that the causal mechanism linking NGOs to protest is largely indirect associational effects, not direct mobilization – and that the context of electoral institutions is critical for understanding the effect NGOs are likely to have.

Chapter 6 returns to the case of Bolivia to consider how civil society affects attitudes toward democracy in weakly democratic contexts. How does civil society affect support for the political system when formal institutions are in crisis? Rather than seeing civil society as inherently pro-democratic and stabilizing or antidemocratic and threatening to stability, I argue that civil society can build support for democratic systems at the same time it facilitates contentious political engagement and criticism of the government. Civil society is likely to strengthen support for democratic political systems as long as it is active in mobilizing participation and as long as the government remains above a minimal threshold of democratic practices (most importantly, that opposition voices are not systematically repressed). This chapter explores these arguments in the context of the dramatic social mobilization and political upheaval in Bolivia between 2000 and 2010, and then through an analysis of individual level data from Bolivia in a year of extreme institutional crisis: 2004. Even during this year of crisis, Bolivians who are members in civil society organizations hold higher levels of diffuse support for the political system than nonmembers. Members are more supportive and even among those who have recently participated in protest. Civil society, however, is not associated with higher support for government during the crisis. Despite extremely high levels of mobilization, extreme dissatisfaction with government, and evidence that membership in associations actively facilitates political protest, civil society continues to be positively associated with support for the political system. Chapter 7 concludes the book.

2

NGOs, Mobilization, Participation, and Democracy

After decades of growth in the developing world, non-governmental organizations (NGOs) today are at an uneasy crossroads between competing visions of democracy. In one vision, NGOs are the cornerstone of stable moderate civil society in developing countries, working to foster the type of strong civil society that makes "democracy work" according to Putnam (1994). In the other, NGOs are part of the growing movement of participatory democracy, building capacity among the poor, giving voice to long-excluded popular sectors, and clamoring for radical change to the status quo. These very different perspectives point to a tension in the goals for civil society in democracy more broadly. Is civil society important because of its role in mobilizing people for social change? (In which case protest may be a central role.) Or is civil society important because it socializes people to participate in politics through institutionalized and controlled pathways: voting, writing letters, signing petitions? (In which case mobilizing protest might be seen as unexpected.)

This tension is particularly explicit in the discussion of the role NGOs play in building civil society in new democracies. On one hand, NGOs are credited with actively strengthening democracy at the local level by promoting political engagement and training citizens in the democratic process. The assumption here is that given the chance and the appropriate resources, NGOs would help foster the type of strong, liberal, democratic civil society that theorists have identified as a boon to democracy in developed countries. On the other hand, NGOs are lauded as the cornerstone of socially progressive activism in developing countries, advocating for indigenous rights, environmental issues, human rights, women's rights, and a host of other causes. In this role, NGOs are firmly labeled as activists. They mobilize people to pressure the government in a variety of ways, including demonstrations and political protest.

Very little attention is paid to the tension between these dual roles for NGOs, or the conditions under which one is more likely than the other. The conventional wisdom offers clear expectations that NGOs and civil society should be good for promoting democratic participation and strengthening democracy, but most of these theories implicitly assume the existence of a well-functioning and responsive state. Explorations of civil society tend to be more concerned with the ability of citizens to organize themselves and make their demands on the state known than with the state's ability to respond. What happens to the dynamics of civil society when the state is unable or unwilling to respond to participatory pressure from civil society? What is the relationship between civil society and political participation under conditions of institutional crisis in democracies or semi-democracies?

The extant view on how NGOs influence political participation has been established through several different research streams: (1) studies of civil society, (2) studies of associational life and social capital, and (3) work specifically focused on NGOs in developing countries. The first analyzes civil society as the "third" sector of society, distinct from states, markets or the private life of the family and tends to focus on comparisons of the density, organization, or nature of civil society as a whole across countries or across time (Edwards 2009). Work on social capital and associational life, in contrast, tends to focus on how individual involvement in different types of organizations influences attitudes toward government, other people, and problem solving strategies (Warren 2001). Finally, a growing body of work focuses explicitly on the role of NGOs in the developing world, often drawing from theories developed by scholars of civil society and social capital, but frequently with a more policy-oriented or activist focus in mind.

These three interrelated research agendas make for a large and unwieldy literature, but offer general consensus that civil society (including NGOs and other associations) is good for democracy in a number of ways ranging in importance from a minor role in facilitating democratic participation to serving as a necessary precondition for democracy to work (or survive) at all. Although the bulk of this literature is largely optimistic about civil society, the tension between several of the roles civil society organizations are thought to play in young democracies remains largely unresolved. Civil society is thought to facilitate active engagement with political life, boost participation, train democratic citizens, solve collective action problems and prepare citizens to make demands more effectively on the state. Civil society – and the social capital it generates – is necessary for holding governments to account and for demanding better performance (Putnam 1994). The dominant view is that civil society encourages moderate participation along the lines of peaceful activism, increasing voter turnout, and community problem solving – all of which should have a positive net benefit for democratic consolidation (Diamond 1999; Linz and Stepan 1996). Little attention is paid, however, to the ability or willingness of the state to respond to such demands, and little discussion of how the motivated, well-connected citizen of a strong civil society reacts to a political system that is ill prepared to respond to new demands.

Recent evidence from developing countries has also brought these relationships into question. First, it is not clear that civil society always favors democracy. Work on associational life in non-democracies has shown that civil society can actually strengthen authoritarian regimes through many of the same mechanisms – building trust in government and channeling participation into controlled pathways (Jamal 2007; Jamal and Nooruddin 2010; Rossteutscher 2010). Second, there is some concern that civil society may not always be a moderating influence. In particular, civil society may help exacerbate ethnic divisions within society, sometimes with violent outcomes, by making it easier for ethnic groups to mobilize and compete with each other (Olzak 1994; Olzak and Tsutsui 1998; Tsutsui 2004; Tsutsui and Wotipka 2004). At the extremes, strong civil society may be incompatible with weakly democratic political institutions (Huntington 1968).

This chapter lays out my theoretical expectations about how NGOs influence political participation in developing democracies, focusing on the conditions under which NGOs lead to voting versus protest and the conditions under which NGOs build support for a democratic political system versus undermine it. I argue that NGOs offer many of the same resources and opportunities for association in younger democracies that civic groups do in wealthier, older democracies. As a result, they tend to facilitate political participation by freeing up time and resources for political activities. NGOs also create opportunities for interactions between people that make it easier for political parties and social movement organizers to mobilize people to participate. Although some NGOs have long held promoting political engagement among their goals, many more seek to remain politically neutral and focus on service provision such as health care or economic assistance. I argue that because the political ramifications of NGO activity are largely unintentional – facilitated through resources and associational opportunities – even apolitical NGOs are likely to have some mobilizing impact.

There are, however, key differences in the role NGOs play in facilitating political participation in developing democracies compared with the role of civic groups in the United States and Europe. The context of democratic quality varies greatly in developing countries – even among countries that meet a minimal definition of democracy. Many younger democracies experience frequent problems with election fraud, corruption, and poor government performance (Keefer 2007). I argue that this context of democratic quality shapes the form that civil society mobilization takes, ranging from moderate activities like voting to much more radical protest participation. Specifically, in weakly democratic countries, where democratic institutions are present but not working well, NGOs tend to promote political participation that is seen as more effective than voting – including contentious political action such as street protests and demonstrations. Since there is wide variation in the quality of democracy in the developing world, NGOs can promote very different types of political participation under different conditions of democracy.

I argue that both protest and voting behavior can best be explained by looking at the role of NGOs and membership in associational life, combined with
attention to the context of how well institutional mechanisms for participation
are working along the following lines: the degree to which elections are free
and fair and people have confidence in them, the degree to which elections represent real choices to voters, and the degree to which political parties represent
important policy differences. I define the quality of democratic institutions in
terms of both formal adherence to the rules of democratic process (free and
fair elections, lack of blatant fraud, etc.) and the broader set of institutions
that make elections meaningful, including the extent to which political parties
represent important interests in society and the level of political competition.

Finally, this chapter considers how this link between NGOs and protest in
weak democracies matters for democratic stability and support for democracy
in these countries. Despite concerns that contentious political engagement may
be a threat to the stability of weak democracies, I argue that as long as minimal
democratic openness is maintained, the inclusion of contentious voices rarely
undermines support for democracy. That is, except in cases where the government systematically or violently represses protests to the extent that the system
can no longer be considered democratic, even contentious political participation tends to build support for democratic political systems by giving voice
to discontent. Contrary to the conventional wisdom, NGOs often promote
contentious political action, especially in democracies with the weakest institutions for formal participation.

THE "THIRD SECTOR"

Civil Society

Conceptually, civil society is the largest of the categories under discussion here –
both voluntary associations and NGOs are among the many organizations that
make up the fabric of civil society. Civil society also includes less formal interactions between friends and neighbors that might not be captured in formal
surveys of organizational activities, including things like how willing neighbors
are to talk to each other about problems or conflicts, the density of social
networks outside of the family, and attitudes toward conflict resolution. Civil
society in this view "contains all associations and networks between the family
and the state in which membership and activities are 'voluntary' – formally registered NGOs of many different kinds, labor unions, political parties, churches
and other religious groups, professional and business associations, community
and self-help groups, social movements and the independent media" (Edwards
2009: 20).[1]

---

[1] Civil society can be defined as "the sphere of institutions, organizations and individuals located
between the family, the state and the market in which people associate voluntarily to advance

The conventional wisdom strongly asserts that a strong civil society is important for democracy in a number of ways. First, civil society helps social-ize people to be better democratic citizens, both by teaching and modeling productive conflict resolution techniques, and by training people how to par-ticipate in elections (Booth and Richard 1998). As part of this role, civil society helps mobilize people to participate in politics. As Edwards and Foley (2001: 6) write, "civil society gives identity and voice to the distinct interests and diverse points of view characteristic of modern society; it stimulates public debate and presses government for action on a thousand and one matters of public interest." In new democracies, this role is thought to be particularly important as "civil society contributes to the development of new democracies by mediating between citizen and state, articulating citizen interests to govern-ment, inculcating democratic norms, and constraining government by stimulat-ing citizen activity" (Booth and Richard 2001: 43).[2]

Second, civil society is thought to improve the performance of government by taking on a number of public and quasi-public functions. The associations of civil society "aid efforts or directly act to heal the sick, counsel the afflicted, support the penniless, educate both young and old, foster and disseminate cul-ture, and generally provide many of the necessities and adornments of a mod-ern society" (Edwards and Foley 2001: 5). Inherent in this conception of the role for civil society is a notion of the limits of the ability of the state to provide these functions, which might reasonably result in lack of confidence in the gov-ernment. The role that civil society might play in pointing out the weaknesses, however, is rarely discussed.

Associations and Social Capital

There is a related research agenda focused on the role of associational life in generating social capital and trust, both of which are seen as essential for making democracy work well. This work, which has its roots in the work on civic culture (Almond and Verba 1963) and sociology studies of social capi-tal (Coleman 1988, 1994), was launched into high gear by Putnam's com-pelling study of the importance of associational organizations (NGOs among them) in Italy. Studies of social capital tend to focus on the benefits accrued

---

common interests" (Anheier 2004: 22), or "an intermediate associational realm between state and family populated by organizations which are separate from the state, enjoy autonomy in relation to the state and are formed voluntarily by members of the society to protect or extend their interests or values" (White 1994: 379). Diamond (1999) adds another definition: "The realm of organized social life that is open, voluntary, self-generating, at least partially self-sup-porting, autonomous from the state" and "bound by a legal order or a set of shared collective rules" (221).

[2] Others also point to a role for civil society in facilitating political participation, including: (Conway 1991; Nagel 1987; Rosenstone and Hansen 1993; Verba and Nie 1987; Verba, Nie, and Kim 1979; Verba, Schlozman, and Brady 1995).

to individuals and societies through associational membership, which builds social capital,[3] increases trust between citizens, and helps people solve collective action problems that can inhibit full participation in democracy.

This conception of how membership in associations influences attitudes and behaviors of individuals and groups of citizens launched a wave of research using survey evidence on membership in associations to test a variety of hypotheses about the effect of membership on a wide variety of outcomes including "civic engagement, national-level economic growth, returns to human capital, fertility, local economic development, neighborhood stability, housing quality and levels of crime, government-community relations, juvenile delinquency, and organizational effectiveness" (Edwards and Foley 2001: 5).

Most of the empirical work on social capital draws on survey data from established democracies in Europe and North America,[4] but there is a growing body of work exploring these concepts in developing countries. For example, a number of recent studies seek to evaluate the effect of social capital on development outcomes (Grootaert and Bastelaer 2002; Isham, Kelly, and Ramaswamy 2002; Krishna 2002). Others have begun looking at the effects of social capital on institutional performance in new democracies, finding that the concept travels well and explains interesting variation (Anderson, 2010; Tusalem, 2007).

Non-Governmental Organizations

Drawing on the theoretical perspectives offered by scholars of civil society and social capital and inspired by the growing numbers of NGOs working worldwide, a related body of work focused on NGOs in developing countries and the role they play in building social capital and civil society has developed. The specific literature on NGOs is most concerned with which types of NGOs are most effective, how foreign aid funding changes local dynamics, and the role that NGOs can play in strengthening civil society as part of democracy promotion efforts.

NGOs and voluntary associations have become key providers of services for health and social welfare in all regions of the world, and now constitute a huge global industry (Salamon and Anheier 2004). NGOs are credited with a wide range of desirable outcomes, both directly through their actions, and indirectly through the role they play in building a strong, democratic civil society. So, as

---

[3] Putnam defines social capital as "features of social organization, such as trust, norms, and networks, that can improve the efficiency of society by facilitating coordinated actions" (1993: 167).

[4] For example, in *Voice and Equality*, Verba et al. show that patterns of civic life are strongly related to political participation in the United States (1995) and multiple recent studies investigate various mechanisms for these relationships, including trust (Braithwaite and Levi 2003; Brehm and Rahn 1997; Hetherington 2005; Newton 2001), and the type of associations people join (Coffe and Geys 2007).

NGOs work to reduce poverty, they also improve democracy at the local level (Clark 1991) and they promote social mobilization and community engagement (Alvarez 2009; Bebbington and Thiele 1993; Fisher 1998; Korten 1990). They are often characterized as the cornerstone of strong and legitimate civil society in developing countries (Bratton 1989; Clarke 1998a; Lambrou 1997; World Bank 1989), and they contribute to the kind of civil society that can act as a counterweight to authoritarian governments (Clark 1991; Diamond 1999; Mercer 2002).

There is debate over whether NGOs function as part of civil society (as foreign aid donors clearly hope and expect) or their reliance on international funding has cut them off from their local roots, making them fundamentally different from more grassroots organizations. NGOs that are dependent on donor resources may tend to support donor interests over local communities (Hudock 1999; Hulme and Edwards 1997; Kamat 2002; Mendelson and Glenn 2002; Meyer 1995). Skeptics argue that NGOs, despite claiming to be local organizations with access to local knowledge and influence, are often grant-seeking organizations more focused on pleasing foreign aid donors than on community issues (Hulme and Edwards 1997). In this view, we should be skeptical that NGOs make much of a real difference at all. In some cases, this is undoubtedly true. The image of a well-appointed NGO office in a capital city, staffed with well-paid professionals, but having very little impact on the ground, is unfortunately a familiar one.[5] There are also many organizations that do real work with the funds that they receive. Because NGOs often are a channel for entirely new resources – foreign aid dollars, for example, that would not have a conduit to some poor communities without the help of NGOs, even very inefficient NGOs may deliver some new resources to local communities.

More Critical Views

Despite the fairly rosy view of civil society and associational activity offered by the bulk of the literature, there is a growing body of research that takes a much more critical view. Several critics have pointed out that Putnam and much of the research he inspired take a universally cheery view of civil society organizations, ignoring the "uncivil" side of well-organized societies, including violence and persecution of minorities (Armony 2004; Berman 1997; Levi 1996).

There is mounting evidence that the context and the content of associational life matter as much as its existence. For example, associations under authoritarian regimes can reinforce patron–client ties to strengthen the authoritarian regime – just the opposite of what many advocates of NGOs as bastions of

---

[5] Both Bob (2005) and Henderson (2002, 2003) make the case that the foreign aid process provides incentives for organizations to aggressively market themselves to donors, sometimes at great costs to their core mission.

democracy would expect (Jamal 2007). Jamal and Nooruddin (2010) demonstrate that social capital in the form of interpersonal trust has quite different effects under different conditions of democracy. When democratic institutions are performing well, interpersonal trust leads to more support for democracy, but under less democratic conditions, trust does not have the same democratic utility – that is, in authoritarian regimes, more interpersonal trust does not translate into more support for democracy. This conditional relationship, which is supported with empirical evidence from the World Values Survey, suggests that the organization of social interactions and the resulting levels of social capital may have very different effects depending on the level of democracy or effectiveness of government institutions.

Others have criticized the idea of applying the logic of civil society in developed countries to developing countries based on differences between the types of associations found in developing countries. Many NGOs and nonprofit sector organizations in the developing world (especially in Latin America) came of age under authoritarian or corporatists governments, which often used NGOs as part of the official associational life of the regime (Wiarda 2003). Other NGOs were created with the explicit goal of promoting democracy and bringing down authoritarian regimes. Both of these relationships to the state are very different from the role we imagine NGOs playing in liberal established democracies where they occupy a third realm relatively free from state interference.

More disturbingly, some have suggested that civil society may actually *increase* the propensity for violence in developing countries. Focusing mostly on the role of large international humanitarian NGOs in conflict zones, several studies point to a link between NGO activity and violence through structural factors in the aid process (Uvin 1998) or through the diffusion of global norms of human rights, often through international NGO (INGO) activity, making it easier for ethnic groups to mobilize, increasing competition between ethnic groups and leading to more ethnic violence and nonviolent ethnic protest (Olzak 1994). This idea is supported by a large study of ethnic protests that shows protest is more likely in peripheral countries with more memberships in international organizations (Olzak and Tsutsui 1998). Newer research on the relationship between international human rights NGOs and protest confirms that some INGOs appear to be directly facilitating violent protests (Murdie and Bhasin 2011). Similarly, associational membership in some contexts can be linked to violence (Backer, Bhavnani, and Bodea 2010).

Some of the early work on NGOs pointed to a possible connection between NGOs as activists and NGOs as social movement organizations, focusing on the way that international NGOs influenced local NGOs to become more outspoken and radical (Clark 1991). More directly, some work implies that NGOs organize protests on behalf of the poor (Covey 1995; Korten 1990) and can use mass advocacy as one of many strategies to influence the state (Fisher 1998: 114–117). A few case studies link NGOs and protest in developing countries, for example Thailand (Dechalert 1999; Devine 2006; Schock 2005), the

Philippines (Clarke 1998b), Poland (Ekiert and Kubik 2001), and Kazakhstan (Luong and Weinthal 1999). Other work on NGOs directly emphasizes the role of NGOs as activists. For example, Keck and Sikkink (1998) describe the role of NGOs primarily in terms of activism – both training people how to organize effectively as activists and making connections between local groups and international groups in order to put pressure on governments in the developing world to promote social change.[6]

This discussion illustrates the underlying tension in the literature on NGOs: Are NGOs doing more to stabilize democracy and encourage moderation, or are they doing more to mobilize people in the contentious effort to fight for social change? The remainder of this chapter addresses this question, first by considering the mechanisms through which NGOs mobilize all types of participation, and then by considering under what conditions NGOs encourage contentious political mobilization as opposed to participation through voting.

The tension between the argument that NGOs are good for democracy because they mobilize people to be critical of the government versus the argument that NGOs are good for democracy because they build support for democracy points to a clear need for a better theory of how NGOs affect political participation – and how the context of government performance changes the role that NGOs take. The next section discusses the mechanisms through which NGOs boost political participation before moving on to consider how the quality of democracy influences the likelihood NGO activity will result in voting, protest, and support for democracy.

VOTING, PROTEST, AND CIVIL SOCIETY

Studies of voter turnout and studies of political protest abound in the social sciences, so it is helpful to clarify what new is being offered here, and what gap is being filled in the existing literature. I argue the advantages of studying protest and voting together, rather than as unrelated phenomenon, and consider the relationship between these very different types of participation. Although protest is sometimes characterized as a sign of things falling apart, most often protest is a form of political engagement and is more likely among politically active people (Booth and Seligson 2009). There are, however, considerable differences in the costs to the individual associated with these different types of participation. With this in mind, I review the existing literature on the determinants of voting and protest. Although we have learned a great deal about what makes individuals more willing to participate and a great deal about how the political context shapes participation in developed democracies, there

---

[6] A more radical critique offered by Petras and Veltmeyer (2011) takes issue with this point, arguing instead that many NGOs became the "Trojan horses" for state-sponsored neoliberal reforms, filling in the gaps where services were cut and making it less likely that people would protest unpopular reforms.

is very little systematic work that explores the interaction between individual and contextual factors in the democracies in the developing world – where the variation in the context of institutional performance is arguably much greater than in wealthier, older democracies. With a few notable exceptions, the study of voting and the study of contentious politics and protest have largely been undertaken as part of very separate conversations.[7] This project intentionally takes the study of voting and political protest as different aspects of the same phenomenon of political participation in order to explore the determinants of a fuller spectrum of political action and the conditions under which NGO activity is most likely to lead to one versus the other.

Voter Participation

Voter participation is one of the few areas in political science where we have some definite answers: In the United States and other developed democracies, research has revealed a great deal about the types of individuals who are most likely to participate and the institutional and structural factors that influence overall participation rates in elections across countries. As Verba, Schlozman, and Brady famously summarized, people fail to participate "because they can't; because they don't want to; or because nobody asked" (1995: 15). That is, people either lack the resources to participate, the motivation to participate, or they are not sufficiently networked in their political community for anyone to recruit or mobilize them.

Resources make it possible to participate. Wealthier people are more likely to participate because they can afford the time and energy needed. Across the United States and Europe survey studies regularly demonstrate that more affluent, more educated and older individuals participate at higher rates than poorer, less educated and younger people (Rosenstone and Hansen 1993; Verba, Schlozman, and Brady 1995; Wolfinger and Rosenstone 1980).

Resources appear to be a necessary condition for participation, but time and money alone do not explain most of the variation in who chooses to participate – not all wealthy people vote, and plenty of poorer people do. To understand why some people participate in politics, it is essential to understand who feels motivated and how people are recruited or mobilized into political activities. The research here also points to some clear answers: people are more motivated to participate when the stakes are high for them, either because they have direct personal stakes in an electoral issue, strong preferences over outcomes, strong identification with candidates or parties in the race, or a strong sense that voting is an important civic duty (Rosenstone and Hansen 1993).

---

[7] Some important exceptions include (Anderson and Mendes 2006; Goldstone 2003; McAdam and Tarrow 2010; Norris 2002).

People also participate more when they feel that their participation matters for the outcome in question. Although the small chance of any particular vote being decisive in an election has long led social scientists to puzzle over the irrationality of voting at all (Downs 1957), there is real variation in the extent to which people feel that their vote matters. People with high feelings of political efficacy – either in the sense that they trust their own opinions matter, or in the sense that they think their vote matters – are more likely to vote than those who feel undervalued or that the election is a lost cause (Balch 1974; Craig 1979; Craig and Maggiotto 1982; Lane 1959). Put differently, "working in a campaign or signing a petition involves some sense that the cause is not hopeless (even if the particular effort is). Participation is a waste of time if one does not believe that one's efforts make a material difference to political outcomes. Those who have confidence that their participation will make a difference are more likely to act than those who lack that basic confidence" (Rosenstone and Hansen 1993: 16).

These factors help describe the type of person who is actively engaged in politics. But how do people *become* involved? Usually, the answer lies with their nonpolitical life, including their social ties, their community network, and their connections to associations and civil society. These networks create opportunities for people to be asked to participate, opportunities for recruitment and mobilization through both formal and informal channels. People with strong ties to their community are both more likely to participate and more likely to convince their friends and families to do so. As Rosenstone and Hansen explain, "membership in social networks makes people responsive to mobilization. Social networks, that is, convert direct mobilization into indirect mobilization" (1993: 27). That is, "by working through social networks, political leaders need not provide selective incentives themselves, need not coax, cajole, and persuade people to take part. Social networks do it for them. Family, friends, neighbors, and co-workers echo leaders' call to action, and participants respond to please their neighbors and co-workers and to honor their obligations to friends" (29–30).

The organization of private life also affects who participates in politics and who is excluded. In particular, gender inequalities in participation can be explained largely through gaps in nonpolitical participation (Burns, Schlozman, and Verba 2001). Men, compared with women, are more likely to work outside the home and gain skills and resources for political activity through their interactions at work (2001: 9).

Outside of individual factors, we also know a number of institutional and contextual factors shape political participation. In explaining cross-national variation in participation, most agree that countries have higher turnout rates where voting is compulsory (Blais and Aarts 2006; Blais and Carty 1990; Blais and Dobrzynska 1998; Franklin 1996, 2004). Electoral rules also matter. Countries with proportional representation (rather than plurality rules) tend to have higher turnout (Blais and Carty 1990; Franklin 2004; Jackman and Miller 1995; Norris 2002; Powell 1980; Radcliff and Davis 2000). Other factors, including the organization of the party system, the number of political parties, the level of political competition, and specific features of how elections are run are also thought to matter, although there is less firm agreement on how these shape cross-national participation rates.

It is clear that factors at the individual level, including time, money, ties to other people, interest in politics, and a sense of political efficacy matter for who votes. It is equally clear that features of the overall political system, including formal institutions, also matter. Most of the academic studies of voter turnout have focused on cross-national comparisons of advanced democracies or turnout in the United States, with relatively little attention paid to turnout in developing countries, although a growing number of studies has begun testing theories of voter participation in developing countries, including in Latin America (Fornos, Power, and Garand 2004; Boulding and Brown, 2013) and Africa (Kuenzi and Lambright 2007). Voting is an obviously important act of democratic participation, but people in democracies also participate in much more contentious ways, including a wide range of protest activities. Who participates in protest? Do the same factors that shape voter participation make all forms of political activity more likely?

Social Movements and Contentious Mobilization

Unlike voting, protest does not occur on a regular election calendar. Instead, protest can include isolated one-day events or long-term protest movements involving multiple actors, strategies, and targets. Protest behavior includes sit-ins, hunger strikes, mass demonstrations, labor strikes, picketing, marching, shouting, blocking traffic, and occupying public spaces. Compared to voting, protest can also be much costlier to the individual, bringing risks ranging from fines to imprisonment to outright violence. Because of these differences, protest has often been studied as something quite distinct from voting. Many of the factors that encourage voting, however, also encourage more contentious political engagement. In particular, access to resources, a sense of political efficacy (belief that the protest might be an effective way to achieve political aims), and contact with associational networks all make it more likely that a person will protest or vote.

Access to resources facilitates protest in much the same way as voting – people with more time and money are better able to shoulder the burden of participating either at the voting booth or in the streets. Social movement scholars have long pointed to the availability of resources as an important factor in determining when and where aggrieved people are able to overcome barriers to collective action and organize a protest (Zald 1992). This research has developed from an early focus on grievances and relative deprivation (Gurr 1970) to a recognition that resources and tools for overcoming collective action problems inherent in group activity were important for predicting which of a multitude of grievances in the world lend themselves to organized political action (Meyer and Tarrow 1998; Tilly 1978; Zald and McCarthy 1990). Thus, even though poorer or less privileged groups may have stronger incentives to protest, protest is unlikely where resources are extremely scarce because few tools are available to mobilize people and solve the inherent collective actions problems associated with individuals taking risks for collective benefit (Edwards and McCarthy 2004; Gamson 1990; Tilly 1978).

The idea that resources are important for protest is supported by survey research. Despite longstanding assumptions that protesters are the malcontents of society, Jenkins and Wallace (1996) find that educated professionals (especially the technical intelligentsia and private sector intellectuals) are more likely to protest than the working class (in Europe and the United States). Moreno and Mosley (2010) make this case in the context of recent protest mobilization in Bolivia and Argentina, demonstrating that protest in these cases is not the result of "disaffected radicalism" but has become a common form of participation across class lines. Protest, however, sometimes appeals to a different demographic than does more traditional political participation. We know from survey studies of social movements in the United States in the 1960s and 1970s that young, well-educated, secular, African American supporters of postmaterialist values were more likely to protest and engage in high levels of conventional participation. Women, youth, and the less educated are more likely to be "protest specialists," choosing protest as their sole form of participation and avoiding more conventional participation (Barnes and Kaase 1979).

Like voter participation, people are more likely to protest when they are networked with other protesters, or have contact with organizations in civil society that connect them with social movement mobilizers. Newer research on individual-level predictors of protest show that being asked to protest by a friend or relative is an important determinant of protesting (Schussman and Soule 2005), and that high levels of interpersonal trust (Benson and Rochon 2004; Kaase 1999; Valencia, Cohen, and Hermosilla 2010) make protest more likely. Because protest is not governed by the election calendar, a great deal of research on social movements has explored the structural explanations focus on how the larger political context shapes the likelihood that protest movements form, how they mobilize supporters, which claims they pursue, which tactics and strategies they employ, and their chances for successfully influencing policy (Meyer 2004).

More recently, the focus has shifted to the idea of political opportunity structures that make movements more or less likely (for example, a decline in repression, new divisions among elites, or an increase in enfranchisement of a previously excluded group) (Tarrow 1998). This approach began with Charles Tilly's (1978) work on mobilization in Europe, focusing on opportunities for mobilization and state repression. These concepts proved useful in explaining social movements in the United States (Eisinger 1973; McAdam 1999), but received more criticism as "more and more aspects of the links between politics and movement formation emerged" and the concept "tended to balloon" (Tarrow 2011: 28). Opportunities and context clearly shape the rise and fall of protest cycles and movements, although there has been some disagreement over how best to operationalize the large variety of potential opportunities in empirical research (Gamson and Meyer 1996). Drawing on this perspective, I focus on the ways in which the quality of democratic institutions for participation influences protest events.

NGOS, RESOURCES, AND ASSOCIATION IN DEVELOPING DEMOCRACIES

Instead of social clubs and civic groups, much of the fabric of civil society in developing countries comprises NGOs. The literature on voter participation and social movements both suggest that how people interact in their daily life – what types of associations they join, how often they attend meetings of community organizations, how they interact with their neighbors – is an important determinant of how they will choose to engage in political life. In developing democracies, NGOs often fill this role. The next section lays out the debate over whether this role for NGOs tends to strengthen or undermine democracy.

I argue that NGOs stimulate participation through at least two distinct mechanisms: (1) providing resources that can be used for political organizing and (2) associational effects as NGOs facilitate interaction between members of the community. Both of these things can facilitate political participation, but tell us little about how participation will be channeled or directed. In this section, I first lay out the direct effects of NGO activities in terms of bringing in resources and creating opportunities for association. I then turn to the importance of the context of how well electoral institutions are functioning for understanding how new participatory potential is channeled into action.[8] Finally, I discuss how contentious participation affects attitudes toward democracy and support for the political system.

First, NGOs bring some level of resources to a community. Resources, whether they are financial, educational, or infrastructural, can make participation easier. Reducing financial strain for individual community members means they may have more time for political activities. Likewise, better infrastructure can translate into better access to political events, as it is easier for people to travel and participate if roads are passable. Other resources common to NGOs, such as telephones, computers, fax machines, and vehicles can also be used to

---

[8] A number of studies from developed countries (mostly the United States) demonstrate an empirical link between associational membership and participation in protest activities (Lim 2008; McVeigh and Smith 1999; Schussman and Soule 2005; Sobieraj and White 2004; Somma 2010; Useem 1980) but there are few works that test these relationships systematically in the context of democracies in the developing world.

facilitate political organization and participation. In some cases NGOs work on activities that are directly related to lowering the costs of political participation, such as offering transportation to and from the polls on Election Day. In other cases, the resources provided may free up time and energy for political activities in much more indirect ways by alleviating some immediate concerns over getting enough to eat, getting health care for a sick loved one, or providing some other social service. These are intentionally wide-ranging examples, but the point is that any influx of resources into a community can facilitate political participation, especially in resource-poor contexts where many NGOs direct the bulk of their efforts.

Second, NGOs provide space for people to associate and interact with one another.[9] Although resources are widely assumed to increase the likelihood of collective action (Eisinger 1973; McAdam 1999), it is also agreed that "the simple availability of resources is not sufficient; coordination and strategic effort is typically required in order to convert available pools of individually held resources into collective resources and to utilize those resources in collective action" (Edwards and McCarthy 2004: 116).

One important mechanism for translating resources into collective action is the social capital generated through association. Whether the organization is providing health care, educational services, or community organizing, they engage community members in interactions. As people gather together – regardless of their purpose – some degree of social capital is gained simply through organized, repeated interaction. This idea has deep roots in the literature on social capital and civic culture (Almond and Verba 1963; Clarke 1998b; Putnam 1994). NGOs, whether they are providing small business training, lobbying for women's or indigenous rights, providing health care, or building houses, all involve local interaction between NGO workers, neighbors, and others in the community. By spending time together, talking, and working toward a common project, people build trust in each other. Communicating shared grievances in this kind of setting paves the way for political action as increased trust helps address the collective action problems inherent in mobilization.

People who interact over shared problems build trust with one another, as they learn which neighbors are reliable, which neighbors are well informed, and which are not to be trusted. Opportunities for association also allows for better access to information, especially if combined with high levels of trust. Just having regular opportunities to interact means that people are more likely to be talking about common grievances or political issues, and they are more likely to be well informed about policies or issues that might affect them.

NGOs open an office, provide some service (vaccines, legal advice, agricultural services, or micro-credit loans, for example), and people in the community

---

[9] Fisher (1998) describes this as the "spillover effect" of NGO activity. As associational activity increases, people trust each other more, understand each other more, and see their common problems, all of which helps solve the complicated collective action dilemmas that can hinder mobilization.

gain two benefits: the direct resources of some sort, and the indirect increase in the chance to associate. If we think of political participation as an action with both costs and benefits attached, both of these side effects of NGO activity make it marginally easier for people in a community with NGOs to participate politically. Specifically, voting and political protest both take time that could be devoted to other things. For the very poor, free time can be scarce as more immediate concerns such as finding a way to feed the family take precedence over issues such as voting or demonstrating. Resources provided by NGOs may free up time and energy for political participation by alleviating pressure in other areas of life. The opportunities for association, likewise, can lower the costs to participation by facilitating stronger ties between neighbors (making it easier for people to help one another with things like childcare, for example). Associative ties can also increase the perceived benefits of participating. If you know that most people in your community are voting, or protesting it is more likely that you will find a way to participate too – both because it might seem more likely that the participation will have an impact, and because there might be social pressures to join in.

As people become more connected with one another, and empowered through positive interactions with their neighbors, they are more likely to tackle difficult problems facing their community. In other words, as more organizations bring more people together, participation in politics is likely to increase. These effects can be intentional – in fact, many NGOs in developing countries see this type of work as central to their mission of education, empowerment, and outreach. NGOs can serve as training grounds for democratic behavior, encouraging people to participate in decision making, compromise, and democratic practices such as voting. It can also be an *unintentional* side effect. Even NGOs that actively seek to remain apolitical still promote interactions among the people they serve.

To illustrate the ways in which even ostensibly nonpolitical NGOs can promote protest activity, consider this scenario. NGOs began working with indigenous communities in the Amazon in the early 1970s, offering educations programs, and legal assistance in the struggle to gain legal territorial rights to ancestral lands. Through the 1980s, NGOs brought resources and opportunities for association – both within isolated communities and increasingly between them. By the early 1990s, the demand for change was high, and the tools were in place for mobilization. In 1992 members of many different indigenous groups joined together in a month-long march from the lowlands up the mountains to the capital city of La Paz. Without the support of NGOs, it is difficult to imagine this protest occurring (Healy 2001).[10]

The resources and associational opportunities that NGOs bring to communities lower the barriers to individual political participation. If people fail to participate "because they can't; because they don't want to; or because nobody

---

[10] This case is presented in more detail in Chapter 3.

asked" (Verba, Schlozman, and Brady 1995: 15), then NGO activity often makes it more likely that people can participate and that they might want to. But the presence of an NGO in a community also increases the chance that a political party or social movement might ask for participation. The more densely networked a community is, and the more organized and willing to participate its members are, the more likely that they will be targeted by political organizations seeking to mobilize supporters (Rosenstone and Hansen 1993). Having a few more resources, knowing your neighbors a little better, having a clearer sense of shared political problems and feeling motivated to participate in politics might make voting more likely, but it also most certainly makes protest more likely as well.

MOBILIZATION AND QUALITY OF DEMOCRACY

What impact do NGOs have on political participation in the many countries in the developing world that are considered democratic but also have serious problems with electoral fraud, corruption, and generally weak democratic institutions? I argue that where elections are seen as flawed, fraudulent affairs that have little chance of resulting in real change, people are more likely to see protest as an effective alternative – or at least as a complementary strategy to voting. By facilitating political participation in general, NGOs under those circumstances are more likely to encourage protest behavior than voting.

Another way to think about the role of NGOs is that they make participation more likely – they increase the likelihood that people will decide to become politically active, but that tells us very little about what type of political action people will choose to engage in. How that potential is translated into action is shaped by how well the political institutions are functioning. Where elections are seen as an effective mechanism for citizens to express their interests and preferences to the state, voting is a better option. In this scenario individuals who are well positioned to participate should find voting a good option, and political parties and social movement organizations are also likely to focus their mobilizing efforts on elections. However, we know that in developing countries elections are frequently less than perfect.[11] When elections are not seen as an effective mechanism for communicating to the state, I expect NGOs to do more to stimulate political protest. People may protest out of frustration with elections, or they may protest in addition to voting as a way to protest flawed electoral processes. In both cases, the greater the perceived problems with elections, the more likely that mobilized motivated people will take to the streets.

[11] In fairness, elections anywhere are less than perfect, including elections in wealthy "advanced" democracies. The point here is that the variation in performance of democratic electoral institutions is greater.

In more formal terms, the decision to vote and the decision to protest can be thought of as a function of the probability that participating will result in the desired policy, weighted by the benefit of the policy (or how important it is to the individual), less the cost of participation. In other words, people are more likely to vote when they (1) care about the issues in the election, or the choice between candidates, and (2) think that doing so will increase the probability they get the policy outcome they desire. However, if the process is viewed as flawed, one can imagine a double reluctance to participate, both because voting may not be instrumentally useful in getting you your candidate, but also because participating in a "rigged" election feels unfair and frustrating. Protest is always more costly, but may in some circumstances have a higher chance of being effective, and thus be the more attractive option.

Political parties and social movement organizations also respond strategically to the context of quality of democracy in choosing how to direct their mobilizing efforts. Political parties, for example, often help mobilize protests and boycotts around elections that they view as unfair or fraudulent (Beaulieu 2014). In this sense, protest and voting can be complementary strategies, with elections providing focal points for both protest and voter mobilization. Where confidence in elections is high, protest can still be a reasonable and effective strategy. Where elections are flawed, however, voting becomes less attractive relative to protest.

The effectiveness of protest at achieving policy aims is another consideration. Where protest is commonly believed to be an effective tool for pressuring the government, it is a more attractive option for the same reasons of efficacy: people like to participate in ways that seem to make a difference. Where protest is viewed as largely symbolic or ineffective, it is less likely to attract as many participants. Protest and voting can also be used strategically in concert with one another. Many protests are, in fact, organized around elections (Beaulieu 2014; Tucker 2007). Protesting and voting, then, should not be seen as alternatives to one another, but as choices in a range of participatory options. At the extreme of frustration with voting, people might reasonably abandon electoral participation altogether, but in many instances people who are willing to participate are willing to participate in many different ways.

Defining Quality of Democracy

I have made the case that NGO activity is likely to do more to promote voting under conditions of well-functioning elections, and more likely to promote protest under conditions of poorly functioning elections. But what does it mean for elections to be functioning "well"? I argue that for the formal institutions for participation to be functioning well in a democracy, ordinary people must have confidence that both the process and the outcomes at stake in the elections are reasonably fair. Multiple factors affect public confidence in electoral processes and outcomes, including (1) the visibility and prevalence of election fraud, (2) the extent to which political parties in elections represent stable and rooted interests in society, and (3) the confidence that ordinary people have that elections might affect outcomes that they care about.

First, for people to see voting as a reasonably meaningful option for channeling their political energies, they must have some degree of confidence in elections, political parties, and the political system. Confidence in elections can be undermined in a number of common ways in developing countries. Most obviously, where election fraud is rampant, people have little reason to expect their vote to count in real and substantive ways. Fraud can consist of obvious violations such as vote-buying and voter intimidation, but also can be accomplished through a nearly limitless menu of creative electoral manipulations. In his review of studies of election fraud, Lehoucq concludes that election fraud

can reduce turnout, contribute to cynicism, and therefore fabricate enough votes to tip the scales in one party's favor. Because electoral fraud can be decisive in close races, its ultimate cost may be that it undermines democratic stability. Regardless of whether fraud is decisive, it encourages incumbents and opponents to discredit elections and their outcomes. Precisely because it is so hard to determine the efficacy of ballot rigging, electoral fraud and its denunciation corrode the democratic body politic. (2003: 249).

In some cases, frustrations with elections can be directly linked to street protests. For example, Eisenstadt (2002) demonstrates that as political parties in Mexico increasingly began to utilize electoral courts to settle disputes over elections, street protests declined. That is, as people began to have more faith in the formal institutions, protest became a less attractive option. Election fraud can also serve as an important focal point for political protests, helping people overcome collective action barriers to protest by drawing clear attention to flaws in the political system, making large-scale protests more likely (Tucker 2007).

Election fraud and outright corruption are not the only problems. In some cases, elections run more or less without procedural problems, but fail to offer meaningful choices between candidates, or political parties – or, more fundamentally, fail to offer credible alternatives to the status quo. Under conditions where people have few expectations that voting will change anything of substance in their lives, protest becomes a more appealing mechanism for expressing interests and opinions to the state.

Second, elections must also provide some real choice between candidates, political parties, or policies. Choice in this sense is a function both of how competitive elections are (Is anyone voting for the opposition? Is there a real choice to be made?) and a function of political parties. In highly fragmented and weak political party systems, there can be little accountability from election to election or stability of policy platforms, making it much more difficult for voters to link parties and candidates to real policy issues (Mainwaring and Scully 1995). Political parties that are stable, moderate, socially rooted, and long-lasting offer a much better chance for effective elections than parties that are weak, short-lived, and centered on candidates rather than issues.

In specific cases, the problems of poor electoral institutions are most likely abundantly clear: fraud, lack of real choices, corruption, etc., but the range of possible problems with electoral institutions is nearly infinite. I am less concerned with pinning down just what constitutes a free and fair election and more concerned with the conditions under which people feel satisfied that electoral tools are meaningful for expressing their needs and preferences to the state. In sum, we can safely say that elections will be more attractive venues for political participation under conditions of stable, moderate political parties, relatively free and fair elections with little obvious fraud, and real choices on the ballot, and high voter confidence in elections. In contrast, the more people see elections as rigged, political parties as weak, and little effective choice on the ballot, the more unattractive elections will be, even to people who are motivated to participate politically. Table 2.1 describes what election fraud, political competition, political parties, public opinion, and government response to opposition look like in strongly democratic countries, weakly democratic countries, and countries that are nondemocratic.

It is important to emphasize that the weaknesses in democratic processes and outcomes that I describe here can all occur in countries that most experts would label as democratic. In fact, I argue that this variation within democracies is crucial for understanding the impact that changes in associational life (including the growth of NGOs) are likely to have on political participation and the democracy more broadly. I have argued that NGOs and civil society facilitate protest where the institutional mechanisms for participation are flawed, and promote voter participation where elections are working well. In the following section, I consider the implications for democracy. If associational participation makes protest more likely in weaker democracies, does it also threaten democratic stability?

CIVIL SOCIETY, MOBILIZATION, AND ATTITUDES
TOWARD DEMOCRACY

The role of NGOs in mobilizing contentious political activity in weak democracies speaks to a much larger debate over whether the mobilization of civil society is a danger to stability and democracy (Huntington 1968), or whether civil society is the necessary precondition for "making democracy work" (Putnam 1994). If NGOs and civil society organizations help to channel political

TABLE 2.1. *Democratic Variation within Democracies*

Factors that Affect the Quality of Institutions for Participation	Range of Democratic Quality		
	Strongly Democratic	Weakly Democratic	Nondemocratic
Election fraud	Little or no fraud; few accusations of fraud; very little chance fraud determines election outcomes	Some credible reports of fraud; unlikely fraud determines election outcomes	Widespread credible reports of fraud; good chance election results affected
Political competition	Open competition over issues that people care about	Limited political competition; competition not focused on policy issues of importance; exclusion of some important interests in society	Repression of opposition political parties; political competition restricted by the state
Political parties	Long-term political parties competing on stable policy platforms	A mixture of new and old parties; some policy issues represented	Single party rule
Public opinion	High public confidence that elections matter in peoples' lives	Widespread doubt that elections ever matter	No elections; authoritarian elections
Government response to opposition	Opposition actors and viewpoints respected	Conflict between opposition and the state, up to and including protests	Direct repression of opposition actors and viewpoints, including violently

participation into contentious political action when elections are not working well, is the resulting protest likely to strengthen democracy by providing an outlet for previously excluded interests?[12]

I argue that neither Huntington nor Putnam accurately explain the role of civil society in weaker democracies. Huntington is limited by seeing civil society mobilization primarily as a threat to stability and to democracy; and Putnam

[12] See Hirschman (1970).

for seeing civil society as mainly fostering cooperative, moderate collaboration with the state. Instead, civil society in new democracies often facilitates
contentious mobilization *at the same time* that it serves to legitimate support
for democracy. But we can expect this relationship only in countries that are
already democratic. Although NGOs are more likely to promote protest in
countries with poorly functioning elections, they are rarely associated with
antidemocratic attitudes as long as the country is above a minimal threshold
for democratic performance.

How does the mobilization of contentious political participation affect
attitudes toward democracy and support for the political system? There are
two opposing viewpoints: those who see contentious mobilization as destabilizing or threatening to democracy and those who see contentious participation as a path for voicing grievances and engaging with the state that builds
overall support for the democratic system. Huntington provided an early and
clear articulation of the instability hypothesis. He argued that rapid social
mobilization would lead to political instability if not matched with sufficient
political institutionalization (1968). Early theories of political protest often
characterized protest as indicative of societal breakdown, usually brought
about by modernization. Protest was almost always characterized as fundamentally in opposition to democratic politics (Kornhauser 1959; Lipset 1960).
In this view, mobilization builds demand for change that weakly institutionalized states cannot handle, leading to frustration with the system as a whole
and revolutionary threats. More recently, the argument has been made that
strong civil society can help citizens become more critical of poorly performing democracies by helping citizens more accurately asses their government's
failures (Moehler 2008; Norris 1999). An analysis of civic education programs
in the Dominican Republic, for example, showed that those programs actually
reduced trust in political institutions as people became better informed (Finkel,
Sabatini, and Bevis 2000).

The more optimistic viewpoint sees civil society as a strongly positive
force for democracy: training democratic citizens, building support for democratic processes and institutions (Diamond 1999), and building social capital that improves accountability and institutional performance (Putnam
1994). In this view, protest mobilization can be seen as an increasingly normal part of political participation, and not something that should be viewed
as inherently antisystem (Booth and Seligson 2009; Moreno and Moseley
2010; Norris, Walgrave, and Aelst 2005). Protest might even be a sign of
democratic health, as contentious action under repressive regimes can be
much riskier.

Rather than seeing civil society mobilization as inherently dangerous or
inherently good for democracy, I argue that the civil society can bring contentious issues to the forefront in very combative ways without undermining
support for the democratic system – as long as the government remains above
a threshold for democracy. A precise threshold is hard to define, but some

clear violations would include direct repression of opposition leaders or political parties, violent suppression of peaceful protest activities, and postponing elections. In cases where the government response can no longer be characterized as democratic, mobilization may also become antisystem (although it is harder to say that it would be antidemocratic in these cases since the system itself is no longer democratic). In particular, government response to contentious opposition can itself shape attitudes toward democracy. In cases where the government actively represses the opposition, or violently suppresses protest activity, it is much more likely that protests may take an antisystem stance.

In the majority of democracies, however, even very contentious conflict with civil society is unlikely to promote antisystem attitudes for several reasons. First, people often protest with a reason, and protests that are facilitated through socially rooted organizations or issue-oriented organizations are rarely without cause. That is people are protesting often because of real inequalities and grievances including low wages, political injustice, lack of public services, lack of public safety, or labor issues. Where inequalities are high and the formal institutions of democracy have done little to change long-term patterns of social injustice, civil society mobilization can take some radical forms, including large-scale protests that are very disruptive to everyday life. The alternative, however, is not that people are content with the formal institutions of democracy. Rather, large-scale protest can give people a voice on issues that were excluded from formal policy discussions or institutionalized debate. Even as civil society may facilitate more critical views of the government and more contentious methods of expressing political opinions, both are forms of political engagement (Booth and Seligson 2009).

Although protest is clearly less predictable and less controlled than voting, protest plays an important role in any democracy – but a particularly important one in democracies that must govern highly unequal or socially divided societies. In particular, political protest is a mechanism for those groups in society that lost the most recent election or otherwise feel excluded from formal democratic processes to continue to make their interests heard as debates and discussions over policy occur. The type of protest that comes out of strong associative ties between citizens in democracies where electoral institutions are weak is more likely to be productive for democracy than damaging because it engages discontented voices into conversation with government.

Put differently, contentious civil society mobilization is most likely to be compatible with support for democratic systems under the following conditions: (1) when civil society is active in facilitating political participation and (2) when the government response to protest does not involve systematic repression of opposition voices. Where protest is viewed as an effective form of participation that is useful for influencing policy changes, it is also more likely to build support for democracy. Protest can be an organized outburst of frustration with the status quo, but it is also often an important means of political engagement.

HYPOTHESES, SUMMARIZED

Several testable hypotheses follow from this discussion, both at the group (municipal or country) level and at the individual level. First, I expect that if NGOs provide resources and a forum for people to meet and talk, we should expect NGO activity to be associated with an increase in political participation, including contentious political action (Hypothesis 1). Resources and opportunities for association, both of which make obtaining accurate information easier and provide tools for overcoming collective action barriers to participation would be just as useful to a person, political party, or social movement trying to organize neighbors to march in the streets against an unpopular policy as they would be useful for trying to rally support for a candidate in a local election.

In trying to understand the conditions under which NGOs are most likely to lead to protest versus voting, I argue that the quality of democratic institutions is the most important factor that shapes when NGOs are more likely to promote protest, on one hand, or voting on the other. Individuals who have contact with NGOs under conditions of strongly democratic institutions are more likely to vote than their counterparts who have not had contact with NGOs;

Individuals who have contact with NGOs under conditions of weakly democratic institutions are more likely to protest than their counterparts who have not had contact with NGOs (Hypothesis 2). Again, the quality of democratic institutions refers to the extent to which elections are free and fair, the extent to which political parties are well organized and represent real interests in society, the degree of political competition, and overall confidence in elections by average citizens.

This argument also has implications for the type of protest that is likely to arise from NGO activity. Up to a certain point, there is little reason to suspect NGOs of generating antisystem or antidemocratic protest, even if they are facilitating the introduction of interests that are difficult to accommodate into the existing political system. As long as democratic institutions are functioning above some threshold, the engagement of new interests can continue to be compatible with a democratic system. In democracies, NGOs can simultaneously facilitate protest and build support for democratic political systems (Hypothesis 3). At some point of poorly functioning institutions, however, it becomes much more unlikely that providing resources and opportunities for association will lead to support for the political system. Table 2.2 summarizes these hypotheses.

TABLE 2.2. *Hypotheses*

Hypothesis 1	Individuals who have contact with NGOs are more likely to participate in politics, including contentious participation.
Hypothesis 2	Individuals who have contact with NGOs **under conditions of strongly democratic institutions** are more likely to vote than their counterparts who have not had contact with NGOs; Individuals who have contact with NGOs **under conditions of weakly democratic institutions** are more likely to protest than their counterparts who have not had contact with NGOs.
Hypothesis 3	In democracies, NGOs can simultaneously facilitate protest and support for democratic political systems.

CONCLUSIONS

This book points to the powerful role that NGOs can play in facilitating protest in developing democracies where the electoral mechanisms for participation are weak. NGOs, because they frequently command greater resources and target them toward people who have been historically excluded from electoral politics are positioned to change political participation even more than more grassroots, domestically rooted civil society organizations. However, the larger insight here is that attention to civil society (including NGOs) is essential for understanding political participation – particularly in the context of developing countries where the institutional mechanisms for channeling political ideas and interests in society into policy have serious flaws. The predictions offered here are clear: when elections are obviously flawed or failing, membership in civil society organizations and contact with NGOs will encourage and facilitate contentious political action.

Non-governmental organizations matter a lot for political participation, contrary to what some skeptics might think. And they matter in both direct and indirect ways. Both directly mobilizing and indirectly providing resources and opportunities for association facilitate political participation. NGOs are not just "paper organizations" or feeble substitutes for more homegrown, organic civil society. In fact, because they bring more substantial resources than voluntary associations in poor communities (and because they actively target resources toward populations with scarce resources), they have a bigger effect in changing the dynamic of political participation than other civil society organizations, which tend to reinforce divisions within society because those with resources are more likely to be well organized in the first place, more likely to have time to organize voluntary organizations, and more likely (in most places) to participate in politics.

The research presented in the following chapters offers strong evidence that this relationship holds true empirically at multiple levels of analysis, including subnational comparisons of municipalities in Bolivia, cross-national comparisons in Latin America, and across other developing countries in the world. Chapter 3 explores variation in NGO activity and participation at the local level in Bolivia. Chapters 4 and 5 move to the broader context of cross-national comparisons in Latin America (Chapter 4) and developing democracies outside of Latin America (Chapter 5). Finally, Chapter 6 returns to the case of Bolivia to explore the relationship between civil society and attitudes toward democracy under conditions of contentious mobilization.

3

Local NGO Activity and Its Consequences in Bolivian Municipalities

In October of 2003, columns of colorfully dressed protesters marched down the winding road into La Paz, the capital city of Bolivia. Indigenous groups, labor groups, miners, students, retired workers, and neighborhood associations converged on the central government plaza to demand the resignation of President Sánchez de Lozada. These marches, which came after weeks of growing tensions between the state and popular sectors, became increasingly violent. In a series of confrontations over several weeks, nearly 100 people were killed in clashes between protesters and the armed forces, and finally the president was forced to flee the country.

The vice president, Carlos Mesa Gilbert, took over the presidency with a promise that he would not continue to use force against the protesters. However, after several months of continuing protests and roadblocks, he declared the country "ungovernable" and tried unsuccessfully to resign. In June of 2005, with the country paralyzed by continuing strikes and roadblocks, Congress accepted Mesa's resignation, sparking a constitutional crisis over succession, which ended with hurried new presidential elections. In December of 2005, Evo Morales, the charismatic former head of the coca-growers union and an important leader in the popular uprisings, was elected as the first indigenous president in Bolivia's history.

By all accounts, non-governmental organizations (NGOs) played a key role in mobilizing people for these protests, both directly and indirectly. Most of the key social groups involved in the demonstrations – indigenous groups, labor unions, miners, student groups, and retired workers – have a history of strong links to NGOs, who for several decades have brought significant new resources to underprivileged communities and groups in Bolivia. More directly, radio

Parts of this chapter were published in the *Journal of Politics* with the title "NGOs and Political Participation in Weak Democracies: Subnational Evidence on Protest and Voter Turnout from Bolivia" (Boulding 2010).

station run by a prominent women's NGO in the adjoining city of El Alto was instrumental in organizing the protests by broadcasting plans to coordinate the day's marches and demonstrations. The NGOs and social movements involved also have strong ties to the new political party of Evo Morales, *Movimiento al Socialismo* (Movement Toward Socialism), known as MAS.

For the proponents of NGOs, this was seen as a major victory for democracy and representation of traditionally excluded groups in Bolivia. Following unprecedented levels of NGO activity in Bolivia, and growing links between NGOs and social movements, the indigenous majority in Bolivia finally won the presidency and a majority of the seats in Congress. However, NGO critics see the same series of events as evidence of the potentially destabilizing effects of NGOs and civil society mobilization. The protests and demonstrations effectively brought the country to the brink of crisis, brought down several presidencies, and carried a new brand of populist leader to the head of state. In either case, this role for NGOs is a surprising one, and very different from the common image of NGOs as pillars of moderate, democratic civil society.

These dynamics in Bolivia are representative of larger issues across the developing world. As the number of democratic countries in the developing world has grown, so too have uncertainties about how democracy works in countries with weak governments, weak economies, and a history of conflict between state and society. These questions of accountability and governance have become increasingly central for developing countries, foreign aid donors, and academics. NGOs increasingly find themselves at the center of these debates. What role do NGOs in developing democracies play in promoting political participation?

In this chapter, I first offer a qualitative analysis of the role NGOs have played in supporting and facilitating the rise of several important social movements that have transformed Bolivian politics – often through the sustained use of protest tactics. This discussion, which is based on secondary sources and my own interviews with NGO workers, government employees, foreign aid workers, and activists during trips to Bolivia in 2004, 2007, and 2009, makes several points.[1] First, by tracing the history of NGO involvement in Bolivia since the 1950s, I show that NGOs have influenced participation in both direct and indirect ways with profound consequences for electoral politics and protest mobilization, particularly in the 1990s and 2000s as social mobilization reached unprecedented levels. Second, NGOs are strategic in their actions, focusing efforts where impact is high and shifting tactics toward more direct efforts to

---

[1] Before beginning formal research for this project, I also spent six months in Bolivia in 2000 during which time I volunteered with an NGO running a home for children in La Paz and witnessed first hand the beginning of the protest movements that would change the shape of Bolivian politics beginning with the "Water War" in Cochabamba in 2000 and culminating with the "Gas War" of 2003, the resignation of President Sánchez de Lozada, the dramatic year of protests in 2004, and the election of Evo Morales in 2005.

build capacity for participation when opportunities present themselves. Finally, I discuss how two very different types of NGOs have both facilitated political participation, first focusing on development NGOs that provide services, and moving on to the indigenous rights NGOs that played important roles in the social movement mobilizations of the lowland indigenous movement and the highland indigenous movement. These cases clearly demonstrate that NGOs have facilitated protest in a number of important ways and that the impact of NGO activity is largely shaped by the broader political context.

The second part of this chapter presents the results of a quantitative analysis of the relationship between NGO activity, political protest, and voter turn-out at the municipal level between 1999 and 2004 in Bolivia, bringing a new local-level dataset on NGO activity, voter turnout, and political protest to bear on the question of how NGOs influence political participation. This analysis systematically tests the relationship between NGO activity, measured using organizational counts of NGOs registered with the national government, and two different forms of political participation: voter turnout from local election returns and political protest coded from both English- and Spanish-language news sources.

Exploring these relationships with local-level data from Bolivia offers several advantages. First, NGO activity is essentially a local activity, but it has previously been very difficult to find local level data on NGOs and political participation in developing countries. Second, this dataset includes two time periods, 1999 and 2004, allowing for better causal inference than a snapshot of variation between municipalities. The political context of events in Bolivia during these years provides an ideal setting in which to examine the effects of NGOs in a weak democracy more systematically. Between 1999 and 2004 there was widespread frustration with the effectiveness of local elections, following disappointment with the major constitutional reforms devolving authority and revenue to the municipalities in 1994. Most importantly, there is also wide variation in the performance of democratic institutions at the local level, allowing for a good subnational test of the conditional impact of NGOs on participation.

The quantitative evidence confirms what the case material from Bolivia suggests: NGO activity in this weakly democratic setting is strongly associated with protest activity. Municipalities with high NGO activity witnessed increases in protest activity on average across the country. More crucially, even within this weakly democratic country, the relationship between NGOs and political protest is strongest in the municipalities where democracy is performing the most poorly (as indicated by the absence of political competition). Only weak evidence is found for a relationship between NGOs and voter turnout. This chapter shows that even at the local level, the tools of civil society that we rely on to motivate people to vote can also lead to protest.

The impact NGOs have on participation works through both direct and indirect mechanisms. Some NGOs do turn to actively organizing protest, but protest can also be an unintended consequence of NGO activity for other organizations. Regardless of their specific activities or political inclinations, NGOs provide both resources and opportunities for association, which makes gathering information and overcoming collective action barriers to political participation easier and more likely. Table 3.1 illustrates the wide range of activities that NGOs in Bolivia are involved in. Some, such as health care, basic sanitation and housing, are largely focused on service provision – offering pre-natal screenings, vaccines, or dental care, working on drinking water systems or building houses, for example. Others are more specifically focused on issues of building institutions and strengthening representation for certain groups. Some NGOs work directly with municipalities on issues of transparency and capacity, or with community groups to try to strengthen civil society and bring new voices into participation.

It is my contention that most of the activities in this wide range of possible NGO activities do something to facilitate political participation – at least on the margins. Both the organizations focused on services and the ones focused on community building bring some level of resources to a community, and increase the chance that people will be talking about problems in the community. Assuming all else is equal, this should facilitate political participation. In settings where the institutional mechanisms for democratic participation are seen as flawed, two things may happen. First, activist NGOs are more likely to turn to unconventional tactics to gain attention and press for political change, and more likely to devote resources to mobilizing participation. Second, at the level of individual citizens, if contact with an NGO encourages them to participate, they are more likely to engage in protest and demonstrations if voting is seen as ineffective. In this view, the relationship between NGO activity and political participation is a conditional one: the effect of NGO activity on participation is conditioned by the quality of the electoral mechanisms in place.

NGOS, CIVIL SOCIETY, AND PARTICIPATION IN BOLIVIA

NGOs have a complicated and involved history with the Bolivian state, social movements, and international donors. In the following sections, I first discuss the history of NGO activity in Bolivia since the 1950s, focusing on the growth in size and scope of NGO work and the changing dynamics between NGOs, the Bolivian government, and popular sectors. This discussion makes clear that NGOs are important actors in the politics of Bolivia, despite their efforts to remain "non-governmental." Second, I discuss the very different types of NGOs working in Bolivia (development NGOs vs. activist NGOs) and detail how they have affected political participation, both directly and indirectly. These case studies illustrate the multiple ways in which NGO resources and associational space facilitates political participation, both intentionally as the result of direct mobilizing, and unintentionally as the result of bringing new resources to previously isolated communities. Finally, the story of the relationship between

TABLE 3.1. *NGOs in Bolivia by Sector and Subsector*

Sector	Subsector	Number of NGOs	Number of Projects
Agriculture	Farming	136	327
	Agro-Industry	32	49
	Forestry	59	103
	Livestock	76	138
	Fisheries	11	15
Legal Assistance	Legal Advice	6	12
Communication	Roads	10	11
	Alternative Technologies	18	24
	Press	3	6
	Radio	14	17
	Television	6	8
Education and Culture	Culture	36	64
	Adult Education	52	92
	Special Education	31	60
	Occasional Education (Workshops)	34	46
	Formal/ Regular Education	56	112
Energy	Electricity	13	15
	Solar Power	8	13
Institutional Strengthening	Municipalities	61	109
	NGOs	23	67
	Other Organizations	80	226
	Prefectures	3	3
Environment	Biodiversity Conservation	27	59
	Natural Resource Management	35	62
	Environmental Improvement	55	76
	Zoning (Territorial Demarcation)	12	18
Mining	Cooperatives	9	19
	Other	7	11
Small Industry/ Handicrafts	Handicrafts	45	65
	Small Business	42	74
	Small Industry	17	27
	Textiles	32	51
Health	Dental Health	15	18
	Maternal Health/ Birth	9	12
	Prenatal Health	14	18
	Control de crecimiento y desarrollo	20	33
	Cancer Detection and Prevention for Women	2	2
	Drug Addiction and Mental Health	7	9

(*continued*)

TABLE 3.1. *(continued)*

Sector	Subsector	Number of NGOs	Number of Projects
	Sexually Transmitted Diseases and HIV/AIDS	13	17
	Acute Illnesses (cholera)	13	17
	Acute Respiratory Illnesses	4	4
	Essential Medications	12	18
	Traditional Medicine	11	13
	Other Illnesses (tuberculosis, Chagas disease, malaria)	36	78
	Family Planning	12	66
	Immunizations	8	9
	Services for the Disabled	6	8
	Health Education	50	90
	Indigenous Health Care	9	14
	Oral Health	4	7
	Sanitation	5	7
Basic Sanitation	Drinking Water	47	77
	Waste Disposal	8	9
	Human Waste Disposal	29	43
Housing	Self-Construction	11	15
	Construction	10	11
	Repairs	10	22
	Urban Planning	3	6

Source: VIPFE (2006).

NGOs and political participation in Bolivia shows that the impact NGOs have is largely conditional on the broader political context. NGOs help mobilize people into the type of participation that is seen as most effective – sometimes electoral participation, sometimes protest, and sometimes both.

NGO Activity in Bolivia, 1950–2010

NGOs have been working in Bolivia since the 1950s when funding became available from the United States through the Alliance for Progress, which focused on non-state development groups as part of its program to promote democracy and economic development in Latin America. The Catholic Church also promoted NGOs and provided funding in the 1950s and 1960s as part of a new focus on helping the poor. In the 1970s, a second group of NGOs were formed in opposition to the military dictatorship. These more radical organizations formed ties with *campesino* and labor groups, radical miners, and leftist sectors of the church. During this period ties were also formed between NGOs and some political parties, most notably the *Movimiento de la Izquierda Revolucionario* (MIR), the Revolutionary Movement of the Left.

The number of NGOs working in Bolivia rapidly expanded beginning in the early 1980s. In 1982, after decades of authoritarian rule, Bolivia became a democracy. This political opening coincided with a new worldwide focus on the possibilities offered by NGOs. The United Nations called the 1980s the "NGO decade" and development thinkers lauded NGOs as a new hope for development. Following these trends, bilateral and multilateral donors increasingly directed foreign aid funds to non-governmental projects. In Bolivia, neoliberal restructuring of the government and the economy, including cutting back on state social services and privatizing many state-held industries, created a huge new demand for NGO services. Growth in the number of international NGOs also took off during this time.

The state, with the support of international donors, instituted an emergency relief effort to mitigate some of the worst hardships associated with the New Economic Policy that reduced government social spending. The Social Emergency Fund, or *Fondo Social de Emergencia* (FSE), gave NGOs an important new role. The government of Paz Estensorro, realizing that NGOs could help administer the funds that flowed in from international donors (and that the existing state bureaucracy was inadequate) worked directly with NGOs for the first time (Postero 2007). The FSE changed the relationship between NGOs and the state. First, it represented the first time that NGOs were working in direct partnership with the state, rather than working independently or as organized opposition. Second, it sparked a new kind of professionalization among NGOs. Along with the task of administering larger sums of money came opportunities for training, and the necessity of learning the language of the foreign aid bureaucracy, including accountability progress reports and glossy brochures.[2] Finally, NGOs spread their projects beyond the major cities delivering services to remote rural areas that previously had little access to resources.

There was a clear increase in the number of NGOs working in Bolivia during these years. Figure 3.1 shows the numbers of NGOs that formally registered with the government over time. Beginning in 1980, there is a clear upward trend. This trend may be somewhat exaggerated, as some NGOs that were already working in Bolivia decided to formally register once more government funds were available, but the trend matches similar data on the huge growth of the number of NGOs working in developing countries worldwide (Werker and Ahmed 2008). The figure here distinguishes between Bolivian NGOs and International NGOs, but this is somewhat misleading. Nearly all of the Bolivian NGOs are at least partially funded with international resources, either

---

[2] For a more detailed discussion of the pressures inherent in the relationship between NGOs and international donors, see Boulding (2012).

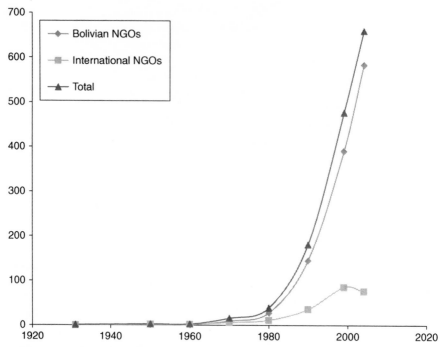

FIGURE 3.1. Growth in NGOs in Bolivia, 1931–2004.
Source: (VIPFE 2004)

through official development assistance programs such as USAID programs or World Bank projects, or by working with international NGOs as affiliates. The Bolivian government, which publishes the registry, makes an effort to point out that the vast majority of NGOs are not international to deflect criticisms of dependence on foreign aid. Thus, although certainly some NGOs have strong activist roots, many of the NGOs working in Bolivia have an explicit mandate for providing social services or administering development projects.

Following the NGO boom of the 1980s, the next major change in the role of NGOs in Bolivia came in the mid-1990s with the Law of Popular Participation[3] (LPP), which dramatically reshaped relationships between state and society in Bolivia. The LPP was passed in 1994 as part of sweeping decentralization reforms implemented under president Gonzalo Sánchez de Lozada.[4] The reforms restructured local government by offering transfers from the federal budget and mandating participation of civil society groups, which opened

---

[3] *Ley de Participación Popular.*
[4] Sánchez de Lozada's first term was 1993–1997. He is the same president who, in his second term (2002–2003), was forced to resign following the violence and popular protests of October 2003.

up opportunities for NGOs, who rushed in as advisors. Sánchez de Lozada (popularly referred to as "Goni") hoped these reforms would streamline and modernize the Bolivian government and economy by following the neoliberal prescriptions of privatizing state-run industries, decentralizing governance for more efficiency at the local level, and liberalizing internal markets.

Municipalities, which previously existed under Bolivian law, but without much uniformity across the country, became the focus for the newly decentralized political structure. The idea was that if administrative units were more local, they would better incorporate the highly dispersed population living in very rural areas. Municipal lines were redrawn to include both urban and rural areas and to cover the whole country, effectively making municipalities the smallest administrative unit of government. New responsibilities for health care administration, education, sanitation, and infrastructure were placed at the municipal level.

In addition to shifting budget resources[5] to the municipal level, the law also sought to build more formal ties between local governance and the existing civil society, which already formed a dense network of community ties. The law specifically addresses traditionally underrepresented groups in Bolivia, naming specific rights of bilingual and bicultural education and establishing a new program for recognizing property rights for traditional lands. More importantly, the law includes provisions for incorporating civil society, including indigenous groups, into the decision-making process at the municipal level. In largely indigenous municipalities, municipal governments can designate indigenous submayors, who ensure representation of their communities on the oversight committees and allow for more autonomy within the indigenous communities.

During the negotiation and drafting of the new law, there was an intense debate between those who thought civil society representation should be based on territory and those who thought it should be based along functional or corporatist lines (Van Cott 2000: 155). In the end, territorial representation won out, in the form of territorially based social groups given the generic name *Organizaciónes Territoriales de Base* (OTBs), or Territorial Grassroots Organizations, made up of representatives of different groups within each municipality. These groups were indigenous groups, neighborhood committees, and *campesino* organizations. In practice, the OTBs are made up of approximately 12,145 indigenous and *campesino* communities

---

[5] Resources under the LPP are distributed according to a population-based formula, with 20 percent of the national revenues redistributed to the municipalities. This was also a big change. Before the LPP, 75 percent of revenues went to the central government, 10 percent to municipalities, 10 percent to departmental development corporations, and 5 percent to the universities. Under the LPP, in part to mitigate the effects of shifting resources away from the three big cities (who had long received a lion's share of revenue), the 10 percent from the department development corporations was reallocated to the municipalities (Van Cott 2000: 156). Municipalities also received the authority to collect local taxes on property, transactions, vehicles, and alcohol.

and between 4,000 and 8,000 neighborhood committees (Molina Monasterios 1997: 213).

The function of the OTBs under the law is to provide checks and balances to municipal governments. NGOs often played an advisory role in helping OTBs organize and articulate their demands. The OTBs select members of an oversight committee (*comité de vigilancia*) according to local or traditional custom. The oversight committee then has formal authority to work with the municipal councils on budget and policy decisions. This was a major change as it incorporated traditionally excluded groups into the formal political process in a direct way, and allowed for recognition of indigenous social organization and leadership within the democratic process. Oversight committees also have the responsibility of communicating the priorities of community organizations to the municipal government. This process, called Participatory Municipal Planning (PPM) was established with the help of NGOs (Kohl 2003a).

Some have been very critical of the implementation of these reforms, how the new requirements have forced indigenous communities to change their leadership structures and identities, and the role of NGOs as ubiquitous advisers – and very powerful actors – in the new system (Kohl 2003a; Postero 2007). Indigenous groups "had to organize their own villages to make diagnoses of their needs, to attend meetings where budgets were discussed, to make arguments backed by rational arguments, and to speak a particular kind of bureaucratic jargon defined by the new law. Because these skills were not held by a majority of the supposed beneficiaries of the law, the state and municipalities relied heavily on NGOs, often funded by international organizations, to carry out the widespread training necessary to 'educate' citizens about how to access their new rights" (Postero 2007: 167–168). Good or bad, there is little doubt that the reforms of the Law of Popular Participation opened up important new roles for NGOs in mobilizing and channeling popular participation and interactions with local governments.

Links between NGOs and Political Participation in Bolivia

Although some NGOs gained a more formal role in mediating political participation at the local level with the reforms of the LPP, the overall impact of NGO activity on political mobilization must be understood in the context of the highly organized and diverse set of civil society organizations already at work in Bolivian society. Despite Bolivia's high levels of poverty, sparsely populated rural areas, and low levels of economic development, NGO activity was never filling an associational vacuum. Instead, NGOs brought new resources to extremely poor communities and provided associational space that dovetailed with well-organized (if very poor) existing civil society groups, boosting their ability to mobilize people into political activity. Militant union organizations, miners groups, community organizations, neighborhood associations, and social movement organizations have played a strong and evolving role in mobilizing political participation in different ways across the highly varied geography of Bolivia. These organizations have also adapted to changing demographics as poor people have migrated from rural areas to urban areas and changing political circumstances as Bolivia cycled through military coup, civilian rule, and the transition to democracy in 1982. In fact, "Bolivia has the highest density of militant social movements of any country in Latin America, including high levels of mine and factory worker participation, community and informal market vendor organizations, indigenous and peasant movements, and public employee unions (Petras and Veltmeyer 2011: 169).

For example, in the city of El Alto, which is populated mainly by people who have migrated from rural areas, many people maintain strong ties to their rural home communities, and are organized into neighborhood associations, which in turn are coordinated through the Federation of Neighborhood Organizations (*Federación de Juntas Vecinales* [FEJUVE]). These organizations often organize protests to demand services and form tight alliances with political parties (Arbona 2008; Kohl, Farthing, and Muruchi 2011). Because many of these organizations had a long history of contentious political engagement with the state (ranging from militant resistance to military regimes to protesting economic policies under civilian rule), protest has long been viewed as an effective tool for participatory action. NGOs in El Alto often cultivate close ties with the neighborhood associations as they tackle community level development projects (Kohl, Farthing, and Muruchi 2011).

Since there are hundreds of NGOs operating thousands of projects in Bolivia, it is helpful to describe some examples of the work that NGOs do in Bolivia, the relationships they have with social movement protest organizations, and the impact they have on the political participation choices of ordinary Bolivians. Most NGOs working in Bolivia are focused on development issues (including health, education, water, sanitation, or fighting poverty). Some NGOs are explicitly more focused on contentious social issues than others. For example, many health care NGOs have tried to maintain a neutral attitude toward politics in order to continue providing services under changing political climates. Other NGOs, however, take issues of social justice, human rights, indigenous rights, and the claims of indigenous social movements as the core of their mission. All of these organizations can be categorized as development NGOs, but not all of them are activist organizations in the sense of directly mobilizing people or lobbying on policy issues. Both of these types of organizations facilitate political participation by providing resources and opportunities for association.

Development NGOs
Many development NGOs in Bolivia were founded in the late 1980s and early 1990s focusing on development services following the very difficult economic years of the 1980s. This focus on service provision, which was supported and funded by international donors, often quickly led to questions of political

capacity building. Many organizations that started out working on services for the poor found themselves pulled by new opportunities opened up by the Law of Popular Participation, which included provisions for NGOs to serve as advisors to municipalities drafting development plans. This role, which involved direct relationships with local governments, raised the issue of whether NGOs should also focus on encouraging political participation in the communities being served.

For example, the director of a mid-size NGO based in Santa Cruz described this tension in his organization, which began as a small NGO focused on hunger and nutrition. When the LPP was passed, this NGO had already built a solid reputation working in one municipality. Other municipalities then invited the organization to help out with similar problems of health care, clean water, food, and other services. At this point, the organization struggled with whether its primary goal was to provide services or help communities organize to improve things on their own. Faced with this tension, the NGO changed its focus to more directly include attention to capacity building among citizens. By 2007, the organization was trying to move away from directly administering services, and more to capacity building and strengthening citizen participation. The vision of this organization, according to the founder and director, is "to strengthen citizen participation, not just help out the state" by providing services the state has failed to provide. Although the LPP opened up opportunities for NGOs to expand, it also put them in the uncomfortable position of feeling torn between constituents and "discomfort at the idea of just acting on the orders of the municipalities." Citizens in the community also began to demand a different type of services. Instead of just wanting food and water projects, they also wanted training on how to make their demands to local government. In the case of this Santa Cruz-based NGO, these tensions resulted in a big change in the priorities of the organization. In 2005, the NGO wrote a new strategic plan focusing on three sectors: (1) economic development, (2) human development, and (3) building institutional capacity, with an eye toward helping the communities take more responsibility for their own problems, including making more organized demands on the state.

This example illustrates the complicated dynamic between NGOs, citizens, and political participation. Although the NGO started out with the idea of providing services without directly engaging in politics, both NGO workers and citizens soon saw the problem of poor economic development as a problem of poor political "capacity." The project of *capacitación* or "capacity building" then became central to the work of the NGO. The demand for capacity building partly reflects the strong organizational ties already existing in many communities in Bolivia. Unlike many poor communities elsewhere, in Bolivia it is quite common for people to have strong ties with one another, including women's groups, cooperatives, unions, neighborhood groups, and the like. Development NGOs bring resources – both financial and organizational – to poor communities across Bolivia. They also navigate a tricky middle ground between serving citizens as service providers and helping build capacity among citizens to make demands on the government themselves.

NGOs and the Indigenous Movements in Bolivia
Other NGOs in Bolivia have always seen their role as one of facilitating mobilization and helping poor or excluded groups fight for recognition of their rights and improvements in their living conditions. There are relatively fewer of these organizations compared with the more typical development NGOs, but the impact of these more activist NGOs on the social movements and protest movements in Bolivia has been important – particularly for the indigenous social movements. The role that NGOs played in the formation of the lowland indigenous movement is perhaps the clearest example of the impact of NGO resources and mobilizing on political participation. The NGOs that began working in indigenous communities in the amazon lowlands of Bolivia in the 1970s brought resources that connected different communities that had previously had very little contact with one another. The indigenous people of eastern Bolivia, live in isolated communities, sometimes with very little contact with the rest of the country, and very weak penetration of the national government. Overall, the eastern indigenous groups had extremely few resources to direct toward political organizing or mobilization before the arrival of NGOs. In addition, owing in part to the opportunities presented by the Law of Popular Participation, and the move to fund organizations focusing on *ethnodesarrollo*,[6] NGOs in the lowlands gravitated toward projects of community building or *capacitación* (capacity building), which directly seek to promote political participation.

Beginning in the late 1970s, a new international focus on the rights of indigenous peoples was gaining momentum. The United Nations held a conference in 1977 on discrimination against indigenous peoples in the Americas. International NGOs helped facilitate transnational indigenous federations across the globe, and alliances were created across international borders to put pressure on governments for more equitable policies and recognition of indigenous rights (Keck and Sikkink 1998). In Eastern Bolivia, this new international context coincided with dramatically changing demographic pressures as new immigrants from the rest of Bolivia began to flood to the Eastern lowlands, threatening traditional lands.

In the late 1970s, an NGO called *Apoyo Para el Campesino-Indígena del Oriente Boliviano* (APCOB, Support for the Peasants-Indigenous People of Eastern Bolivia) began organizing meetings between several lowland indigenous groups of the Chiquitano and Ayoreo Indians (Postero 2007, 49). Over several years, these meetings grew to include the Guaraní, Guarayo, and Mataco Indian groups as well. Another NGO, a Jesuit organization called the *Centro*

---

[6] Ethno-Development, or development projects focused on maintaining ethnic indigenous identities.

de Investigacion y Promocion del Campesinado (CIPCA, or the Center for Research and Advancement for Campesinos), began working to support various efforts at regional federations of indigenous people focusing on development issues and cultural projects (Postero 2007). In 1979, a Guarani Federation called *Asamblea del Pueblo Guarani* (APG, Assembly of Guarani People), was founded with the institutional support of CIPCA.

In 1982, CIDOB (the Indigenous Federation of Eastern Bolivia or *Confederación de Pueblos Indígenas del Oriente Boliviano*) was officially organized to represent the indigenous movement of the eastern lowlands on the national political scene. Since the earliest organization of CIDOB the main objectives have remained constant: (1) legal recognition of indigenous territories; (2) legal recognition of indigenous organizations and traditional authorities; (3) improvement of economic conditions, health, and education; and (4) respect and protection for indigenous cultures (http://www.cidob-bo.org/). As one of the major social movement organizations in Bolivia today, CIDOB continues to receive institutional support from NGOs.

The timing of the mobilization of CIDOB into national politics, following only a few years after engagement by NGOs who brought significant new resources to the cause suggest that the NGOs in this case played more than a sideline support role. Rather, it is difficult to imagine how these particular groups of indigenous people could have mobilized as an organized force in national politics without the resources and facilitation of NGOs. It is also important that the type of NGO that targeted indigenous groups in the eastern lowlands tended to be focused on the activities that are most likely to boost participation, make connections between communities, and facilitate mobilization.

Another example to illustrate this point is the involvement of an NGO called *Centro de Promocion Agropecuaria Campesina* (CEPAC, or Center for the Promotion of Peasant Agriculture) with the indigenous communities around Santa Cruz de la Sierra.[7] CEPAC is a Bolivian NGO that began working in several indigenous communities in 1990, offering literacy training programs and programs targeting hunger and poverty alleviation. In 1992, CEPAC shifted its focus from standard development programs toward *capacitación* or capacity building, a type of community organizing that was seen as very desirable by international donors. According to one of the founding directors, this shift in strategy was driven in part by the availability of international funding for such projects (author interview January 2007). In 1993, CEPAC applied for and received a grant for "institutional strengthening" from the international

---

[7] For a colorful description of the role that NGOs played in the "capacity building" of the eastern lowland indigenous movement, see the 2005 memoir of NGO worker William Powers, titled *Whispering in the Giant's Ear: A Frontline Chronicle from Bolivia's War on Globalization.* Power details his role working for an NGO called FAN (*Fundacion Amigos de la Naturaleza* or the Foundation for Friends of Nature) that was central in the organizing of the Amazonian tribes.

NGO International Working Group on Indigenous Affairs (IWGIA) providing $13,000 to fund five general assemblies, paying for all transportation, food and lodging for delegates (crucial since most delegates could not afford to travel on their own). Over the next few years, the group met frequently to discuss problems, goals, and strategies, and make connections. The grant also funded an investigation of Guarani conditions conducted by four young Guaranis doing surveys (Postero 2007: 71).

Even though there were some disputes over whether CEPAC shared its funding for indigenous groups as well as it could have, the groups realized that outside funding was available and, with training from NGOs, learned how to frame their needs in terms that were interesting and appealing to international donors. For better or worse, with the development of new sources of funding came a whole new set of rules for procuring it. The new organizations trying to obtain funding for tackling problems in the indigenous communities became mired in flow charts, project proposals, and all the bureaucratic paperwork that is designed to improve accountability in aid relationships. But the new resources that followed represented a dramatic change in the organizing capacity of the indigenous groups.

Indigenous Movements in the Andean Highlands

In contrast to the lowland indigenous movement, the Aymara and Quechua Indians of the Bolivian highlands had access to more organizational resources prior to NGO engagement. The types of NGOs that targeted the highland indigenous communities were also more mixed in their orientation, including some NGOs focusing solely on service provision and others with a strong emphasis on community development and capacity building. The highland indigenous movement did experience a spike in both influence and participatory activity following the big influx of new NGO activity in the 1980s, and both NGO involvement with the indigenous communities of the altiplano and the intensity of the mobilization as a social movement have continued to rise in recent years.

The most powerful organization in the contemporary indigenous social movement before the rise of the MAS was the *Confederación Sindical Única de Trabajadores Campesinos de Bolivia* (CSUTCB). The CSUTCB as a formal organization has its roots in the 1970s. The precursor of the CSUTCB, a para-statal organization called the *Confederación Nacional de Trajabadores Campesinos de Bolivia* (CNTCB) was an important actor in the pact between the military and campesinos. By 1979, the CSUTCB had come into its own as an organization to express the rights and needs of indigenous *campesinos*. The first conference for campesino unity was held in June of 1979, sponsored by the labor union organization the COB and including representatives of the Kataristas (an early indigenous rights group) and other labor groups, and the CSUTCB was formed. Although the name of the organization invokes images of class consciousness more than indigenous identity, the CSUTCB was clearly an Indian organization, with the image of an Aymara leader as their symbol (García Linera 2004).

As this timeline and the name of the organization suggest, the line between the labor and indigenous movements is not always clear. Postero calls the CSUTB the "strongest segment of the labor movement" and does not characterize the organization as primarily indigenous (2007:137). However, García Linera, the author of a book on the contemporary Bolivian social movements, clearly argues that the CSUTCB is an indigenous movement primarily, but with ties to organized labor. He cites that even though the CSUTCB was organized out of the COB, from its inception it laid claim to the historic traditions and identity of indigenous people in a way that the COB and other labor organizations avoided. In more recent years, as the radical Aymara nationalist and former Katartista guerilla fighter Felipe Quispe took over leadership, the indigenous nature of the organization was unquestionable.

The legacy of connection with organized labor, and more importantly, the organization of many highland indigenous communities into hierarchical syndicate structures, already linked to national movements, meant that the highland groups had both organizational experience and capacity prior to the involvement of NGOs that the lowland groups lacked. Thus, although there is strong evidence that NGOs played a role in facilitating some of the new mobilization, it is less clear that these groups would not have mobilized without NGO assistance. However, the highland indigenous movement, like their lowland counterparts, benefited from the new international focus on indigenous issues from organizations like the United Nations and international NGOs, and the subsequent flow of NGO resources to highland *campesino* communities.

This history and organizational capacity allows for very effective mobilizing. For example, García Linera (2004: 167) describes the internal sanctioning within the CSUTCB as being very strong. There is a moral obligation for all members of the community to participate combined with punishments for the families of those who shirk. Sanctions can range from fines to public punishment, according to community traditions.

The types of NGOs that worked with indigenous communities on the altiplano were more mixed than those that worked with the lowland Indians. Following the neoliberal reforms that cut government services during the 1980s, many NGOs stepped up to help administer the funds of a new Social Emergency Fund (FSE), providing basic services such as food and health care to mitigate the worst of the effects of the neoliberal reforms. These NGOs did not have the same political goals of boosting participation and community involvement as others did; however, capacity building NGOs also existed. In particular, several prominent NGOs work with women to encourage economic independence and political involvement.

The different branches of the indigenous rights movement in Bolivia coalesced in dramatic fashion in 1990, when lowland Indians staged a dramatic and highly visible march from the lowlands to La Paz. This march, called the

Marcha por Territorio y Dignidad (March for Territory and Dignity), was joined by Andean groups and represented the first coordinated, national protest of indigenous groups as a unified actor. NGOs, whose work with indigenous groups may have made the mobilization possible in the first place, also played a key supporting role in facilitating the protest, offering legal advice for protesters and support services throughout the march (Healy 2001).

During the 2000s, both electoral and protest strategies came into play as the reforms of the LPP opened up an electoral forum for competing over new resources at the local level and as social movements turned to increasingly widespread protests to influence policy at the national level. NGOs continued to play a supporting role, both directly in some of the social movement organizations and indirectly by bringing resources to the communities in which social movements were organizing. The protest march of 1990 was the precursor of the larger mobilizations that would become commonplace in the early 2000s, and eventually help bring about the election of Evo Morales, Bolivia's first indigenous president, in 2005.

The examples offered here show that a variety of different types of NGO activity have influenced political mobilization in Bolivia, especially in recent decades as Bolivian social movements have gained in power and the political reforms of the Law of Popular Participation have opened up different opportunities for popular action. In the case of many NGOs that focus on development issues like health care and nutrition, political capacity building came as a secondary goal – sometimes even an unintended one. But for some NGOs, like the organizations that work to empower and build capacity among indigenous communities, political action has long been part of the goal of their work. More importantly, the type of political participation that NGOs facilitate seems to be a function of what is working well. As the reforms of the LPP brought new resources to local governments, many NGOs stepped up their involvement with local governments and electoral strategies for change. When the reforms of the LPP failed to live up to the high expectations they raised, popular protest became more common. In the next section, I explore how NGO activity (of all types) influences political participation on average across all the municipalities in Bolivia, using a new dataset of NGO activity, voter participation, and political protest.

QUANTITATIVE ANALYSIS: NGOS, PROTEST, AND VOTING IN BOLIVIAN MUNICIPALITIES

Bolivia is a good place to systematically test the relationship between NGO activity and political participation (both voting and protest) because it has high levels of NGO activity and wide variation on political participation. Bolivia is an established democracy since its transition from authoritarian rule in 1982, but one with significant flaws, including high levels of corruption and popular dissatisfaction with democracy. As discussed above, the major constitutional

reforms under the Law of Popular Participation in 1994 decentralized authority to the municipalities, transferred funds to the municipal level, and mandated participatory budgeting and oversight by local organizations.[8] NGOs
played an important role during the implementation of these reforms, often
acting as advisers to the local governments during the planning phase, assist-
ing with organizing oversight organizations, and educating citizens about their
rights to participate in the new processes (Kohl 2003a).

The 1999 municipal elections were the first regularly scheduled local elections following the initial implementation of the reforms. Despite widespread
optimism that decentralization would bring dramatic improvements in terms
of poverty reduction and political accountability, reforms instead achieved
mixed results. Problems with financial management and corruption continued,
and the demand for real change was largely unmet (Kohl 2003a).

During the years between 1999 and 2004, Bolivia experienced a growing
crisis of governance as political protests frequently shut down the capital and
other major cities. Several major incidences of protest, including the "Water
War" over privatizing the city of Cochabamba's water supply in 2000 and
the "Gas War" of 2003 brought political protest to the forefront as an important strategy for participation. Both of these events were large-scale protests
around specific issues (although the multiple groups that joined the protests
were not always united in their goals or their tactics). Neither of these events
are included in the data analyzed here (the data on incidences of protest for this
project cover the years 1999 and 2004, intentionally omitting these flashpoint
events), but they are important to mention as part of the changing climate of
Bolivian politics as ordinary citizens increasingly felt alienated from the political process and contentious politics became normalized as a frequent part of
daily life across the country.[9]

Survey responses show that the average Bolivian in 2000 and in 2004 had
between "little confidence" or "no confidence" in political parties, the national
congress, the police, the president, or the judiciary. The mean response to a
Latinobarómetro survey question asking respondents to rank their confidence
in each institution from 1 for "a lot of confidence" to 4 for "no confidence" is
between 3 and 4 for each institution in both the 2000 survey and the 2004 survey. Bolivia during theses years is an exemplary case of democracy under strain,
or weak democracy struggling to live up to the promises of its institutions.
Unfortunately, for many Bolivians, this was also a time of crisis of confidence
in the democratic institutions that had promised great reforms and had failed

[8] The LPP allowed for greater access to resources for NGOs in the municipalities in Bolivia, and
promoted the formation of new NGOs to take advantage of the newly mandated role for NGOs
in municipal budget and governance procedures. The national mandate for providing resources
to NGOs across municipalities makes for a better test of how NGOs affect participation by
reducing the potentially confounding selection problems of NGOs locating in areas with higher
levels of discontent.

[9] An individual level study of protest in Bolivia in 2004 finds that people who have personal experience with corruption are more likely to protest (Gingerich 2009).

to deliver. Thus these years lend themselves very well to an evaluation of the effect of NGOs on political participation in the context of poorly performing electoral mechanisms: Bolivians felt little confidence that even if voting were to lead to reforms, those reforms would lead to real and lasting change.

Data and Research Design

I explore the relationship between NGO activity and political action using an original dataset on NGOs, election results, and political protest at the municipal level from Bolivia. Specifically, I test whether a change in the number of NGOs working in a municipality is associated with either a change in the incidences of protest in the area, or a change in voter turnout rates. First, two different sets of regressions are estimated to test the effect of changes in numbers of NGOs on changes in voter turnout and political protest over a five-year period from 1999–2004. The first uses change in voter turnout as the dependent variable and the second uses change in incidences of protest as the dependent variable. Given the overall context of Bolivia during these years, in which the national political environment is one of weak democratic institutions, I expect a strong relationship between NGOs and protest, but a much weaker effect on voter turnout.

Second, I test whether the relationship between NGO activity and political protest is shaped by the quality of democracy at the local level. Where democracy is weak, do NGOs stimulate protest rather than voting? For further evidence of the conditional nature of the relationship between NGO activity and political participation, municipalities with high levels of political competition between political parties (close elections) are compared with municipalities with little or no political competition. In municipalities where one political party consistently wins by wide margins, survey evidence shows that Bolivians have less confidence in political parties, less confidence in local government, and lower overall evaluations of democracy in Bolivia. Based on this evidence, I assume here that lack of political competition signals a lack of meaningful electoral choices, not the presence of a very popular and successful political party.[10] Using political competition as a measure of local quality of democracy allows for a compelling test of the conditional hypothesis that NGOs stimulate political protest in weak democratic settings by measuring variation in the contextual variable at the local level.

NGO Data

Data on NGO activities were coded from a Bolivian government registry of NGOs published by the Vice-Ministry of Public Investment and Foreign Financing (VIPFE in Spanish acronyms). The registry has been published and

---

[10] Using political competition as a proxy for the quality of democratic institutions may not be justified in other settings. Certainly in the United States, for example, it would be difficult to make the case that only competitive congressional districts were democratic.

updated five times since 1996. Most of the data for this project were coded out of the 2003–2004 registry. The data in the registry are entered by NGO and include the official acronym, the full name of the organization, the country of origin, the department where the organization registered (Bolivia is divided into nine administrative departments), the date the NGO began activities, the date the registration was renewed, contact information, the sectors the organization is involved in, and the location of their work. All information is self-reported by the NGOs, as required by law.[11]

To make these data useful for comparing across municipalities, the numbers of NGOs in each municipality are summed to get a total number for 2004. To get a total number of NGOs for 1999, the date the NGO began activities is referenced and only those organizations that were in existence before 1999 are used.[12] These data were cross-referenced with the 1996 version of the NGO registry to identify NGOs that closed during these years.

To capture the effect of changes in numbers of NGOs, NGO counts from 1999 and 2004 are used to create a variable indicating the change in numbers of NGOs over the five-year period. Using the change in the number of NGOs helps capture changing levels of NGO activity, and allows for better causal inference. It is one thing to say that municipalities with many NGOs tend to have frequent protests (which they clearly do), but it is difficult to know if NGOs play a causal role, or whether politically engaged citizens both protest and form NGOs. Using a change variable does not entirely do away with this problem, but if change in NGOs is associated with change in protest, a causal relationship is more likely.

In most municipalities, the number of registered NGOs increased between 1999 and 2004, despite considerable differences in size and population between municipalities. This trend is consistent with the impression of experts in government and in the NGO community that the presence of NGOs in the municipalities in Bolivia has continued to increase. The maximum increase occurred in the capital city of La Paz, which gained 139 organizations, bringing the total from 55 in 1999 to 194 in 2004. The minimum is a loss of 8 NGOs. One hundred and thirty of the municipalities have no recorded NGOs in either year.

Where Do NGOs Locate?

One concern in comparing the effect of NGOs on political participation across different municipalities in Bolivia is whether NGOs tend to locate in municipalities with disproportionately high social problems, which might explain both

---

[11] This registry is available as a published book or as a PDF file on VIPFE's website (VIPFE 2004, 2006).

[12] One challenge in sorting the data was matching the locations listed by the NGO in their registration with known municipalities. To get a complete list of all the municipalities in Bolivia, I referenced Salvador Romero Ballivian's authoritative *Geographia Electoral de Bolivia* (2003) and the list of municipalities from the 2001 census (INE 2001). Several municipalities have more than one commonly used name. A complete list is available on request.

the high numbers of NGOs and high political activism. To address this concern, I offer some background on the involvement of NGOs in Bolivia, some data on where they are located, and evidence from interviews with leaders of NGOs about the decision-making process that NGOs go through to select locations for projects. In sum, because many NGOs are focused on providing services to underserved communities, they do tend to cluster in less developed areas. But reaching people who need their services is just one of several considerations – NGOs also tend to cluster in areas with higher population density, accessible roads and infrastructure, and in places where people in the organization have personal contacts. Thus the distribution of NGOs across municipalities in Bolivia is not exactly random, but we have good reason to believe that it is not tightly correlated with factors that would predict protest either.

This description of the NGO scene in Bolivia is backed by interview evidence. In 2004 and 2007, I conducted interviews with multiple leaders of mid-size NGOs in La Paz, Cochabamba, and Santa Cruz with the intention of learning as much as possible about the decisions NGOs make about where to locate projects. Most of the people I spoke with gave similar responses: NGOs locate where they think they can reach the most people who need help. Although objective need might be the highest in the most remote areas, the logistical challenges of reaching them make those places inefficient choices for NGO projects. Most people also recognized that personal contacts play a role. For example, the head of a large NGO in Santa Cruz explained that the first project was in his hometown (a small city in rural Santa Cruz department).[13] As the NGO became successful at securing grants from foreign donors, they expanded operations to other towns with similar demographics – none more than a day's travel from Santa Cruz. In his words, "there is a contradiction in how projects and locations are chosen, and the contradiction comes from the donors – they want projects that target the most people, and the most poverty, but many of the smallest municipalities have the highest percentage of poor people. So the organization strikes a balance out of self-preservation."

Data on the distribution of NGOs across municipalities support this idea that NGOs locate based on calculations of a number of factors, not simply where need or grievances are the highest. To illustrate, I point to two maps of the distribution of NGOs across municipalities in Bolivia. Figure 3.2 shows NGO activity by poverty levels. Although there are a large number of NGOs in poor municipalities in Bolivia, there are also NGOs in wealthier areas. Similarly, Figure 3.3 shows the distribution of NGOs by education levels. Both figures clearly show the wide reach of NGOs in Bolivia. They have a presence in every region and almost every municipality around the country.

---

[13] Carew Boulding, interview with the director of a mid-size NGO, Santa Cruz, Bolivia, January 2007.

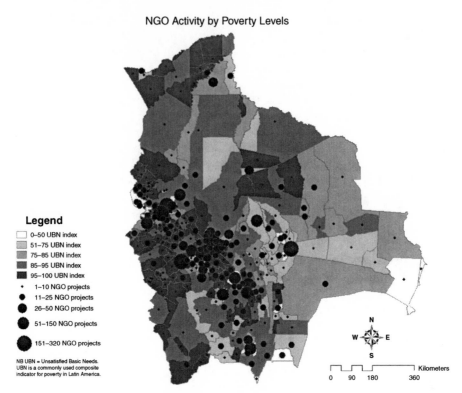

FIGURE 3.2. Map of NGO distribution in Bolivia by poverty level, 2005.

Voter Turnout Data

Municipal level data on voter turnout is available from the Bolivian national election court (Corte Nacional Electoral de Bolivia), which publishes election results down to the individual table where the votes were cast (Kohl 2003b). Bolivia held nationwide municipal elections to elect mayors and city councils in 1999 and 2004. Voters choose between political parties, not individual candidates. Seats on the city council are assigned proportionally to the votes each party receives, and the party that wins the plurality of seats on the council appoints the mayor. The municipal elections of 1999 and 2004 were chosen because they were the first two regularly scheduled elections following the reforms of the Law of Popular Participation, which opened up a more formal advisory role for many NGOs in municipal governance. Both elections were also held before Evo Morales came to power in 2005. Since 2005 was by all accounts an unusual and extreme election, looking at the two previous municipal elections allows for better inference into the role that NGOs might be playing.

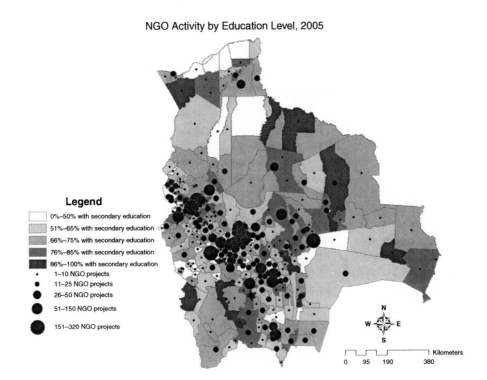

FIGURE 3.3. Map of NGO distribution in Bolivia by education, 2005.

Voting is compulsory, but there is a wide range of variation in voter turnout across the municipalities, ranging from 5 percent to 93 percent turnout. Voter turnout is calculated as the percentage of registered voters that submitted ballots. The total number of ballots submitted was used instead of the number of valid ballots because casting blank or invalid ballots is often an intentional way of expressing discontent with the choices presented under mandatory voting rules. Measuring voter turnout in Bolivia is complicated by the low reliability of voter registration lists. Salvador Romero Ballivián, a noted Bolivian expert on voter turnout and former head of the National Electoral Court, points out that inflation of registration lists has often led to false claims of increasing participation rates when that actual number of voters remains the same (Romero Ballivián 2003). The results presented below are robust to different specifications of voter turnout, including change in voter turnout calculated as the percentage of the population instead of the percentage of registered voters and change in voter turnout calculated as the change in votes cast (which may be less affected by inflation of the voter registration lists). For the best causal inference and for ease of comparison between the models of voter participation and protest participation, the dependent variable used is change in voter turn-out between 1999 and 2004.

Protest Data

Data on protest were coded from Spanish-language newspapers and English-language wire stories, using the search engines Lexis-Nexis (for English-language sources) and Factiva (for Spanish language).[14] For the years 1999 and 2004, all articles containing the search word "Bolivia" were reviewed for any mention of political violence, protests, demonstrations, riots, labor unrest, roadblocks, marches, or other forms of political protest. The English-language and Spanish-language coding were cross-referenced against each other to minimize overlap and maximize the number of observations. Although the original coding includes information on the numbers of protesters involved, the dates of the protests, the numbers injured or killed, the state response, and various other information, for the purposes of this project, the data were aggregated into simple event counts by municipality, by year. Protests that lasted multiple days are counted once for each day.

I chose the years 1999 and 2004 as a difficult test of my hypotheses. Given that NGOs have increased a great deal in most municipalities over the last decade, and that there were well-known periods of high protest mobilization in 2000 and 2003, I intentionally chose two years outside of those flashpoint events in order to explore whether NGOs facilitate political protest more systematically. Looking at 1999 and 2004 helps us capture protest as a daily phenomenon of participation, not just the fallout of a few high-profile events. The largest and most visible protests did occur in cities with very high NGO activity, including Cochabamba in 2000 and La Paz in 2003, which is consistent with my argument. But the patterns presented here are not driven only by the large cities – all the models are robust to the exclusion of the largest four cities.

Protests, even in the volatile political climate of Bolivia during these years, are still relatively rare events. In 1999, the average municipality did not experience a protest incident (the mean number of protests in 1999 is 0.55). In 2004 the mean is higher at 1.01. In 1999 the town with the most protests experienced 30, which rose to 95 in 2004. Again, this project is interested in change over this period; the variable used in the regressions is the change in number of protests between 1999 and 2004.

Control Variables

The full model of political participation estimated here includes controls for election specific variables, socioeconomic variables, and indicators of past

---

[14] Data were coded according to the conventions of the Latin American Political Protest Project (LAPP) by Steve Garrison. The data are available as part of that larger project. For more details on the coding conventions, see Garrison (2001).

participation.[15] The election specific variables include the *Number of Political Parties* and *Political Competition* (measured as the difference in vote share between the two largest political parties in the 2004 election). The number of political parties in an electoral contest can affect participation either by offering more choices (in which case a large number of parties should be associated with high participation as people can vote close to their ideal points) or by affecting the clarity and decisiveness of voting (in which case fewer parties should boost turnout). Because both of these are reasonable possibilities, the raw number of parties is included in the model.[16] Likewise, political competition is an important control because participation tends to be higher in close elections. *Evo Morales' Vote Share* in the 2005 election is also included as an indicator of support for this popular and charismatic national candidate. 2004 was the first election in which the party of Evo Morales, the MAS, captured significant vote shares in many municipalities, appealing to indigenous and excluded voters. The socioeconomic variables are *Population (logged)*, *Level of Development* (measured as percentage of household with electricity), *Rural*, *Indigenous Population*, and *Adult Literacy*.

Findings: Does NGO Activity Increase Voter Turnout?

To test for a relationship between NGO activity and voter turnout, change in voter turnout between the 1999 and 2004 municipal elections is estimated as a function of changes in the numbers of NGOs working in the municipality. Given the context of poorly performing electoral institutions and popular dissatisfaction with democracy in Bolivia during these years, it is unsurprising that the relationship between increases in NGO activity and voter turnout is not a strong one. It does not appear that increases in NGO activity had any significant impact on change in voter turnout between 1999 and 2004 (see Table 3.2). Change in the number of NGOs is not a statistically significant predictor of voter turnout in either model. Model 1 shows the model of voter turnout including change in NGOs and a baseline number of NGOs from 1999. Model 2 shows results from the same model but includes a measure of political protest in 2004 since both voter turnout and political protest can be thought of as different measures of political participation. Including protest does not change the results.

Although *change* in NGOs does not affect turnout, there is some evidence that high *levels* of NGO activity in a community are associated with higher levels of voter turnout. The number of NGOs in 1999 is positively associated with increases in voter turnout in both Models 1 and 2. This result suggests

---

[15] The number of observations changes slightly between models because of missing data in the original data sources.

[16] To make the results easy to interpret, the raw count of political parties is used in the main models. It is important to note, however, that none of the findings change if effective number of parties is used instead.

TABLE 3.2. *Change in Municipal Voter Turnout, 1999–2004*

	Model 1	Model 2
NGO Activity		
Change in NGOs	0.000	0.000
	(0.00)	(0.00)
NGOs, 1999	0.002*	0.002*
	(0.00)	(0.00)
Election-Specific Variables		
Number of Political Parties	0.003*	0.003*
	(0.00)	(0.00)
Political Competition	0.005	0.005
	(0.03)	(0.03)
Evo Morales Vote Share	0.074*	0.072*
	(0.03)	(0.03)
Socioeconomic Variables		
Population (logged)	−0.020*	−0.020*
	(0.01)	(0.01)
Level of Development (Electricity)	−0.047	−0.048
	(0.03)	(0.03)
Rural	−0.040	−0.038
	(0.02)	(0.02)
Indigenous Population	0.032	0.033
	(0.02)	(0.02)
Adult Literacy	0.117*	0.119*
	(0.04)	(0.04)
Participation Variables		
Turnout, 1999	−0.693*	−0.695*
	(0.07)	(0.07)
Change in Incidences of Protest		−0.001*
		(0.00)
Constant	0.487*	0.488*
	(0.10)	(0.10)
R^2	0.628	0.629
N	307	307

Note: OLS estimation with robust standard errors in parentheses; *$P < 0.05$.

that municipalities with more NGOs to begin with were more likely to witness higher levels of voter turnout than municipalities where few NGOs were
working.[17] However, the arrival of new NGOs during the last five years has

---

[17] The finding that municipalities with more NGOs have higher turnout (but not greater *increases* in turnout) holds up in a number of different specifications. In models with the number of votes cast as the dependent variable, change in NGOs is a significant predictor of more votes cast, both in 1999 and in 2004. Modeling change in turnout using votes cast yields similar results to the main models presented here – change in NGOs is not a significant predictor of change in votes cast.

little impact on levels of turnout. The average turnout in the 1999 municipal elections was 59 percent. In 2004, that number went up to 62. Change in turnout between the two elections spanned a large range, from a loss of 51 percent, to a gain of 57 percent. The distribution of the variable is close to normal.

The other independent variables in the model give an interesting picture of electoral politics in Bolivia. First, the *Number of Political Parties* is positive and significant. Bolivian elections are multiparty elections with proportional representation on the city council. Voter turnout is higher where a larger number of political parties ran. Second, the variable that captures support for Evo Morales' MAS party is a very strong predictor of change in turnout when all observations are included. It appears that where the MAS gained new support, turnout increases. *Population* and Adult *Literacy* are also significant; turnout is higher in smaller municipalities and in more educated ones.

The main finding that change in NGOs has little effect on turnout, but high levels of NGO activity is associated with higher turnout are robust to several different specifications of the model, included in the appendix. In different variations, NGO activity is measured as NGOs per capita instead of counts (Model 1A); the effect of NGOs are estimated on *levels* of turnout in 2004 including the logged dependent variable, rather than *change* in turnout (Model 1B), and cases that might be considered outliers are excluded, in particular the largest four cities in Bolivia (Model 1C). Additionally, the inclusion or exclusion of the first period variable in the change models (NGOs in 1999) does not change the results. Overall, there is little evidence to suggest a strong connection between NGOs and voter turnout, but given the weak performance of democratic institutions in Bolivia, this is expected.

Findings: Does NGO Activity Increase Protest?

The relationship between the changes in numbers of NGOs and changes in protest is more evident. Change in NGO activity is a positive and significant predictor of increases in protests. On average, an increase of two NGOs in a municipality is associated with an increase in 1 protest event. Or, more intuitively, an increase of 10 NGOs between 1999 and 2004 predicts an average increase of around 5 major, newsworthy protests in 2004, compared with municipalities that did not witness an increase in NGO activity.

Model 3 estimates the effect of change in NGOs on changes in incidences of protest, controlling for factors related to political participation. Model 4 includes a measure of voter turnout to capture both modes of participation. Both models show very similar results (see Table 3.3). The models of voter turnout and protest are intentionally identical for ease of comparison and to reflect the conceptualization of turnout and protest as different types of the same phenomenon: participation.[18]

---

[18] These results are very stable. Several variations on the models are available in the web appendix, including measuring NGO activity as NGOs per capita (Model 3A), estimating the effects

TABLE 3.3. *Change in Incidences of Protest, 1999–2004*

	Model 3	Model 4
NGO Activity		
Change in NGOs	0.506*	0.505*
	(0.09)	(0.10)
NGOs, 1999	0.225*	0.226*
	(0.05)	(0.05)
Election-Specific Variables		
Number of Political Parties	0.088	0.089
	(0.07)	(0.07)
Political Competition	0.226	0.229
	(0.98)	(0.99)
Evo Morales Vote Share	−2.126*	−2.085*
	(0.66)	(0.67)
Socioeconomic Variables		
Population (logged)	−0.597*	−0.599*
	(0.18)	(0.18)
Level of Development (Electricity)	−0.180	−0.211
	(0.64)	(0.65)
Rural	−0.629	−0.671
	(0.77)	(0.77)
Indigenous Population	0.191	0.228
	(0.55)	(0.56)
Adult Literacy	0.285	0.296
	(1.08)	(1.09)
Participation Variables		
Incidences of Protest, 1999	−0.934*	−0.935*
	(0.12)	(0.12)
Change in Turnout		−0.361
		(0.92)
Constant	5.080*	5.085*
	(2.43)	(2.45)
R^2	0.761	0.761
N	310	307

Note: OLS estimation with robust standard errors in parentheses; *$P < 0.05$.

The number of NGOs in 1999 is positive and significant, which lends further support to the idea that NGOs are related to protest activities. Municipalities

of NGO activity on *levels* of protest (with the lagged dependent variable) as opposed to *change* in protest (Model 3B), excluding the largest four cities as possible outliers (Model 3C), and excluding the cases with the greatest increase in NGOs as possible outliers (Model 3D). Since incidences of protest are event counts, it is possible that a Poisson estimation is more appropriate for testing these relationships. Model 3E shows the results of a Poisson estimation, and the results are very similar to the OLS estimations.

with higher numbers of NGOs tend to see higher incidences of protest. The share of the votes that went to Evo Morales is negatively associated with protest, which somewhat counters the popular notion that his supporters made up the bulk of the protests during these years. More interestingly, it lends further support to the idea that participation will be channeled into electoral routes if those routes are promising; where Evo Morales had high electoral support, there was a decrease in protests, even though protests eventually helped bring Evo to power.

One concern with these findings is that it is very hard to rule out the possibility that increases in NGOs and increases in protest and voting are both indicative of a third factor, such as rising political dissatisfaction. Both the actions of forming a new NGO and marching in the streets in protest can be seen as political actions. To address this concern, I estimate a simple regression model to determine if protests in 1999 are associated with an increase in NGO activity, which would be true if both were the result of rising dissatisfaction alone. Protests in 1999 have no statistically significant effect on changes in NGO activity, controlling for levels of NGOs in 1999. However, to the extent that increases in NGO activity and increases in protest are both responding to latent demand for political change, some feedback between the two is entirely consistent with the theory that NGOs facilitate different types of participation in different settings, and that in weakly democratic contexts, political protest is one likely outcome of NGO activity. The next section provides additional evidence in support of this conditional relationship.

Findings: Local Quality of Democracy

Bolivia during the late 1990s and early 2000s makes for a good test of how national level political context influences the relationship between NGO activity and political participation. During these years, Bolivian political institutions are near the extreme of weakly functioning democratic political institutions. In 2004, Freedom House downgraded Bolivia from "free" to "partly free" due to the irregular removal of president Sánchez de Lozada from office by street protests. The crisis of Bolivia's political institutions allows for a test of how NGOs influence political participation under these conditions, and the finding that NGOs tend to boost political protest is clear. The quality of democracy, however, is not constant across the whole country, especially as it relates to the functioning of local democratic institutions such as mayoral elections, corruption, or government responsiveness. Not all municipalities in Bolivia faced equal pressure or equal institutional failures during this time. Measuring local variation in quality of democracy allows a more direct test of the conditional nature of the relationship between NGOs and participation.

To this end, I use political competition in local elections (as indicated by the margin between the two largest political parties in the 2004 municipal elections) as an indicator of local quality of democracy in order to compare how NGOs influence voting and protest in municipalities with competition between parties and municipalities with little or no competition between parties. Political competition – though by no means a perfect measure of the performance of local electoral institutions – does capture something very important about the functioning of democratic institutions. If the margin between parties is so large that there is no effective competition, even if other aspects of the institutions are functioning well (low corruption, highly responsive politicians, etc.), we can assume that elections are not seen as the critical mechanisms for voicing discontent. However, it is more likely that extremely uncompetitive elections in developing countries are also accompanied by strong clientelist systems and corruption to ensure a certain party's hold on power.[19] That is, as Cleary and Stokes have demonstrated in Argentina and Mexico, there is wide variation in the quality of local democracy, especially in younger developing-country democracies (Kohl 2003). In the absence of direct measures of local quality of democracy, political competition is a very good proxy.

It is reasonable to assume that where the difference is less than 3 percent, there was real uncertainly over the outcome of the election, and thus some level of real competition (Nardulli 2005). Where the difference in vote share is greater than 3 percent, it is likely that the largest party had a fairly strong certainty of winning a plurality in the election. Although this is an admittedly arbitrary threshold, there is an important difference between competitive and noncompetitive elections. In one, voters go to the polls thinking their vote might make a difference. In the other, the winner is known before the election. If we expect that NGOs mobilize people to participate in politics through the political actions that are most likely to be effective, it makes sense that they should have a larger effect on voting in close elections, and a larger effect on protest in uncompetitive areas. In Bolivia, the average municipality had a 15 percent gap between the two largest political parties. Of 311 municipalities with data, 77 of them were competitive at the 3 percent threshold. Hundred and five were competitive at a 5 percent threshold.

In 2004, the Latin American Public Opinion Project (LAPOP) surveyed a representative sample of Bolivians in nearly a third of the more than 300 municipalities in the country asking a variety of questions about attitudes toward democracy and confidence in government. Comparing Bolivians who live in competitive municipalities (using the 3 percent threshold) to those who live in less competitive municipalities, it is clear that political competition is associated with higher confidence in government and belief in the system being democratic. Specifically, Bolivians in competitive municipalities have more confidence in political parties and more confidence in municipal government than Bolivians in less competitive areas. When asked "In your opinion, is Bolivia very democratic, somewhat democratic, or not very democratic?" Bolivians in

---

[19] In fact, Arce and Rice find that provinces in Bolivia with higher levels of political competition experience lower levels of political protest overall (2009).

TABLE 3.4. *Attitudes toward Democracy in Competitive and Uncompetitive Municipalities*

	Competitive Municipalities	Uncompetitive Municipalities
Confidence in Political Parties	2.565*	2.401*
1 = None	(.05)	(.03)
7 = A lot	N = 750	N = 2127
Confidence in Municipal Government	3.963*	3.829*
1 = None	(.06)	(.03)
7 = A lot	N = 749	N = 2138
How Democratic is Bolivia?	2.262*	2.377*
1 = very democratic	(.74)	(.75)
2 = somewhat democratic	N = 734	N = 2077
3 = a little democratic		
4 = not democratic		

Note: Cells show mean response value with standard errors in parentheses. *Difference in means between competitive and uncompetitive municipalities $P < 0.05$ in a two-sample t test. N = number of respondents.
Data source: LAPOP 2004 Bolivia Survey.

competitive municipalities rate Bolivian democracy more positively. In simple comparison of means tests, all of these differences are statistically significant at the 0.05 level.

To compare how NGOs affect participation in these different contexts, a dummy variable for political competition at a 3 percent threshold is used (based on the 2004 municipal elections), and fully interactive models of change in turnout and change in protest are estimated (see Table 3.4). These interactive models give strong support to the idea that NGOs stimulate participation, and that participation is channeled differently depending on the political context. In noncompetitive municipalities (where there is little or no real competition between political parties), an increase in NGO activity is associated with an *increase* in protest, as are levels of NGO activity in 1999. On the other hand, an increase in NGO activity has little effect on voter turnout in noncompetitive municipalities. These results are robust to using a 5 percent threshold as a cutoff for competitiveness, and a similar pattern is observed when the relationship is modeled using an interaction between the margin of victory in percentage points and change in NGO activity, rather than a dichotomous variable for competitive versus noncompetitive: As elections become less competitive, NGOs have a stronger stimulating effect on protest (see Figure 3.4 for an illustration of the marginal effects). This is further evidence that the effect of NGO activity on participation is conditional on how well the democratic institutions are functioning. When voting is seen as ineffective or unlikely to result in any real change, newly mobilized people are more likely to protest (Table 3.5).

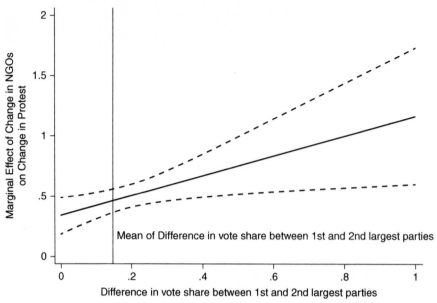

FIGURE 3.4. Effect of change in NGOs on change in protest by political competition.

CONCLUSIONS

There is good reason to expect that NGOs facilitate collective action and political participation. How that political participation is exercised, however, is contingent on the larger political context in which NGOs are operating. This chapter makes the case that NGOs do stimulate political participation, not only in terms of institutionalized methods such as voting. In weakly democratic settings where institutions are viewed with deep distrust and skepticism, new political participation can also take more contentious forms, such as political protest, demonstrations, and social movement mobilization.

These results are important for several reasons. First, together with the finding that NGOs are only weakly associated with institutional participation in the form of voter turnout, the finding that NGOs and protest are linked challenges some of the fundamental assumptions about how NGOs affect participation in weak or developing democracies. Instead of acting as training grounds for the type of citizenship we associate with developed democracies, NGOs may also be invoking much more contentious and less predictable forms of participation. Protest may well be a necessary and vital part of democratic participation, but it is rarely what advocates of civil society have in mind when they advocate for NGOs.

More importantly, this finding contributes to our understanding of how civil society works in less democratic settings and draws attention to the importance

TABLE 3.5. *OLS Change in Protest and Turnout*

Dependent Variable	Change in Protest	Change in Turnout
Noncompetitive Municipalities (Polcomp = 0)		
Change in NGOs	0.557*	−0.000
	(0.06)	(0.00)
NGOs, 1999	0.231*	0.003*
	(0.04)	(0.00)
Number of Political Parties	0.010	0.003
	(0.05)	(0.00)
Evo Morales Vote Share	−2.224*	0.072*
	(0.70)	(0.03)
Population (logged)	−0.583*	−0.025*
	(0.15)	(0.01)
Level of Development	0.084	−0.050
	(0.80)	(0.03)
Rural	−0.782	−0.065*
	(0.78)	(0.03)
Indigenous Population	0.295	0.031
	(0.58)	(0.03)
Adult Literacy	−0.646	0.099*
	(1.11)	(0.04)
Incidences of Protest, 1999	−0.960*	
	(0.11)	
Turnout, 1999		−0.718*
		(0.07)
Competitive Municipalities (Polcomp = 1)		
Polcomp * Change in NGOs	−0.542*	0.003*
	(0.09)	(0.00)
Polcomp * NGOs, 1999	−0.359*	−0.008*
	(0.13)	(0.00)
Polcomp * Number of Political Parties	0.142	−0.000
	(0.12)	(0.00)
Polcomp * Evo Morales Vote Share	1.521	0.047
	(1.46)	(0.07)
Polcomp * Population (logged)	1.020*	0.023
	(0.51)	(0.02)
Polcomp * Level of Development	−0.083	−0.023
	(1.56)	(0.07)
Polcomp * Rural	−0.278	0.072
	(2.03)	(0.05)
Polcomp * Indigenous Population	0.070	−0.022
	(1.27)	(0.06)
Polcomp * Adult Literacy	3.132	−0.017
	(2.48)	(0.09)

(*continued*)

TABLE 3.5. *(continued)*

Dependent Variable	Change in Protest	Change in Turnout
Polcomp * Incidences of Protest, 1999	1.563* (0.33)	
Polcomp * Turnout, 1999		0.116 (0.18)
Polcomp (Competitive Municipality Dummy)	−11.735* (4.58)	−0.305 (0.25)
Constant	6.246* (2.33)	0.584* (0.11)
R^2	0.814	0.644
N	310	307

Note: OLS estimation with robust standard errors in parentheses; *$P < 0.05$.

of political context. Political science tends to privilege voting as the pinnacle of political participation, when in reality voting can be a very flawed process in developing democracies. Protest, on the other hand, carries the connotation of violence and political instability, but in some circumstances may be a vital mechanism for making voices heard that would be obscured through more traditional procedures of participation.

There is ongoing debate over whether the recent protests in Bolivia represent a crisis for democracy or an advance for democracy, and it seems too early to tell for certain. Clearly, traditional mechanisms of participation were not satisfying the demands of the mostly poor protesters. The protests have succeeded in reshaping the political agenda in Bolivia to address issues of exclusion and poverty. But they have also raised questions about the stability and governability of the country. Bolivia in many ways is on the brink, and it remains to be seen if workable political compromise can be reached. Regardless of the outcome, it is important to understand civil society, and the role that NGOs play in facilitating participation, in their larger political context.

By all accounts, Bolivia is an extreme context in which to explore these issues – civil society membership is extremely high compared to other Latin American countries, and political protest has become an increasingly common tool for political participation over the last decade. Bolivia is also a country with very weak political institutions. For all these reasons, it is the "most likely" case to find a relationship between NGO activity and political protest. However, the logic of how NGOs facilitate political participation and how the context of political institutions shapes whether protest or voting is more likely to occur is by no means limited to the Bolivian context. The rest of this book explores how these relationships work across Latin America (Chapter 4) and in other parts of the world (Chapter 5) before returning to a discussion of Bolivia, civil society, and support for the democratic political system in Chapter 6.

APPENDIX 3.1. *Robustness Checks: Variations on Model 1*

Dependent Variable	Model 1A Turnout, 2004	Model 1B Change in Turnout, 1999–2004	Model 1C Turnout, 2004
Estimation	OLS	OLS	OLS
NGO Activity			
Change in NGOs per capita	−7.410		
	(14.48)		
NGOs per capita, 1999	23.360*		
	(13.26)		
Change in NGOs		0.000	0.001
		(0.00)	(0.00)
NGOs, 1999		0.003*	0.003*
		(0.00)	(0.00)
Election-Specific Variables			
Number of Political Parties	0.004*	0.004*	0.003*
	(0.00)	(0.00)	(0.00)
Political Competition	0.008	0.011	0.001
	(0.02)	(0.03)	(0.03)
Evo Morales Vote Share	0.069*	0.048	0.071*
	(0.03)	(0.03)	(0.03)
Socioeconomic Variables			
Population (logged)	−0.011	−0.030*	−0.021*
	(0.01)	(0.01)	(0.01)
Level of Development (Electricity)	−0.053	−0.068*	−0.050
	(0.03)	(0.03)	(0.03)
Rural	−0.042	−0.056*	−0.040
	(0.02)	(0.03)	(0.02)
Indigenous Population	0.034	0.041	0.032
	(0.02)	(0.03)	(0.02)
Adult Literacy	0.122*	0.151*	0.118*
	(0.04)	(0.04)	(0.04)
Participation Variables			
Turnout, 1999	−0.693*		−0.692*
	(0.07)		(0.07)
Constant	0.399*	0.752*	0.492*
	(0.09)	(0.08)	(0.10)
R^2	0.632	0.232	0.628
N	307	310	303

Note: Robust standard errors in parentheses; $*P < 0.10$.

APPENDIX 3.2. *Robustness Checks: Variations on Model 3*

Dependent Variable	Model 3A Change in Protest, 1999–2004	Model 3B Incidences of Protest, 2004	Model 3C Change in Protest, 1999–2004	Model 3D Change in Protest, 1999–2004	Model 3E Incidences of Protest, 2004
Estimation	OLS	OLS	OLS	OLS	Poisson
NGO Activity					
Change in NGOs per capita	374.705* (215.99)				
NGOs per capita, 1999	703.220 (532.59)				
Change in NGOs		0.515* (0.09)	0.183* (0.08)	0.110* (0.05)	0.027* (0.01)
NGOs, 1999		0.231* (0.05)	0.101 (0.07)	0.010 (0.04)	-0.052* (0.02)
Election-Specific Variables					
Number of Political Parties	0.216* (0.09)	0.091 (0.07)	0.114* (0.06)	0.098 (0.06)	0.208* (0.04)
Political Competition	2.956* (1.15)	0.254 (1.01)	1.347* (0.75)	0.629 (0.42)	3.059* (0.48)
Evo Morales Vote Share	-0.759 (1.45)	-2.143* (0.67)	-1.052* (0.60)	-0.275 (0.50)	-1.017 (0.79)
Socioeconomic Variables					
Population (logged)	1.040 (0.58)	-0.614* (0.17)	-0.143 (0.12)	-0.033 (0.07)	0.499* (0.13)
Level of Development	0.902 (0.80)	-0.184 (0.65)	0.736 (0.46)	0.603 (0.36)	2.220* (0.78)

Rural	1.792	−0.788	−0.581	−0.554	0.251
	(1.71)	(0.77)	(0.64)	(0.61)	(0.62)
Indigenous Population	−0.148	0.172	0.141	−0.085	0.493
	(0.66)	(0.55)	(0.42)	(0.40)	(0.92)
Adult Literacy	4.760*	0.172	0.657	0.514	2.894
	(2.11)	(1.03)	(0.71)	(0.63)	(2.04)
Participation Variables					
Protest, 1999	0.136		−0.862*	−0.957*	−0.025
	(0.74)		(0.16)	(0.10)	(0.02)
Constant	−16.579*	5.440*	0.295	−0.323	−11.253*
	(8.06)	(2.20)	(1.53)	(1.16)	(2.39)
R^2	0.136	0.844	0.468	0.584	0.762
N	310	310	306	301	310

Note: Robust standard errors in parentheses; *P < 0.10.

APPENDIX 3.3. *OLS Changes in Protest and Turnout (5% Threshold for Competitiveness)*

Dependent Variable	Change in Protest	Change in Turnout
Noncompetitive Municipalities (Polcomp = 0)		
Change in NGOs	0.565***	−0.000
	(0.06)	(0.00)
NGOs, 1999	0.221***	0.003***
	(0.04)	(0.00)
Number of Political Parties	0.016	0.003
	(0.06)	(0.00)
Evo Morales Vote Share	−2.605***	0.070
	(0.73)	(0.04)
Population (logged)	−0.586***	−0.025**
	(0.16)	(0.01)
Level of Development	0.235	−0.045
	(0.85)	(0.04)
Rural	−0.718	−0.065*
	(0.82)	(0.03)
Indigenous Population	0.564	0.032
	(0.59)	(0.03)
Adult Literacy	−0.751	0.083
	(1.23)	(0.05)
Incidences of Protest, 1999	−0.969***	
	(0.12)	
Turnout, 1999		−0.729***
		(0.08)
Competitive Municipalities (Polcomp = 1)		
Polcomp * Change in NGOs	−0.370**	0.001
	(0.13)	(0.00)
Polcomp * NGOs, 1999	−0.148	−0.004
	(0.12)	(0.00)
Polcomp * Number of Political Parties	0.093	−0.000
	(0.11)	(0.00)
Polcomp * Evo Morales Vote Share	2.322	0.032
	(1.25)	(0.06)
Polcomp * Population (logged)	0.847*	0.019
	(0.34)	(0.01)
Polcomp * Level of Development	−0.479	−0.021
	(1.31)	(0.06)
Polcomp * Rural	0.890	0.059
	(1.98)	(0.05)
Polcomp * Indigenous Population	−1.184	−0.017
	(1.15)	(0.05)
Polcomp * Adult Literacy	3.217	0.049
	(2.02)	(0.08)
Polcomp * Incidences of Protest, 1999	0.683	
	(0.53)	

Dependent Variable	Change in Protest	Change in Turnout
Polcomp * Turnout, 1999		0.131
		(0.16)
Polcomp (Competitive Municipality Dummy)	−11.452**	−0.328
	(4.26)	(0.23)
Constant	6.246*	0.584*
	(2.33)	(0.11)
R^2	0.814	0.644
N	310	307

Note: OLS estimation with robust standard errors in parentheses; $*P<0.10$, $**P<0.05$, $***P<0.01$.

APPENDIX 3.4. *Change in Incidences of Protest, 1999–2004*

	Model 7
Change in NGOs	0.340***
	(0.09)
Political Competition (Margin of Victory)	−1.473
	(0.95)
Change in NGOs * Political Competition	0.828*
	(0.41)
NGOs, 1999	0.176**
	(0.06)
Number of Political Parties	0.091
	(0.06)
Evo Morales Vote Share	−2.285**
	(0.70)
Population (logged)	−0.503**
	(0.15)
Level of Development (Electricity)	0.089
	(0.63)
Rural	−0.429
	(0.79)
Indigenous Population	0.355
	(0.53)
Adult Literacy	0.586
	(1.08)
Incidences of Protest, 1999	−0.889***
	(0.15)
Constant	4.164
	(2.31)
R^2	0.793
N	310

Note: OLS estimation with robust standard errors in parentheses; $*p < 0.10$, $**p < 0.05$, $***p < 0.01$.

APPENDIX 3.5. *Summary Statistics (Bolivia Municipal Data)*

Variable	Obs	Mean	Std. Dev.	Min	Max
Participation Variables					
Change in Turnout, 1999–2004	311	0.038	0.095	−0.513	0.573
Turnout, 2004	311	0.587	0.101	0.051	0.930
Change in Protest, 1999–2004	314	0.462	5.069	−30	74
Protest, 1999	314	0.554	2.808	0	30
NGO Activity					
Change in NGOs	314	2.424	9.598	−8	138
NGOs, 1999	314	3.803	5.341	0	56
Change in NGOs per capita, 1999–2004	314	0.0001	0.001	−0.005	.006
NGOs per capita, 1999	314	0.0004	0.0005	0	.005
Election-Specific Variables					
Number of Political Parties	314	7.933	3.615	1	21
Political Competition (Margin)	311	0.148	0.172	0	1
Political Competition (3 percent dummy)	311	0.248	0.432	0	1
Political Competition (5 percent dummy)	311	0.338	0.474	0	1
Evo Morales Votes Share	314	0.563	0.243	0.0180	0.942
Socioeconomic Variables					
Population (logged)	314	9.162	1.251	5.398	3.943
Level of Development (Electricity)	314	0.272	0.219	0	0.879
Rural	313	0.811	0.284	0.001	1
Indigenous Population	314	0.451	0.308	0.001	0.873
Adult Literacy	313	0.792	0.122	0.406	0.968

APPENDIX 3.6. *Correlation Matrix*

	Change in Protest	Change in Turnout	Change in NGOs	NGOs, 1999	Number of Political Parties	Political Competition	Evo Morales Vote share	Population (logged)	Level of Development	Rural	Indigenous Population	Literacy	Turnout, 1999
Change in Protest	1.00												
Change in Turnout	0.02	1.00											
Change in NGOs	0.77	0.05	1.00										
NGOs, 1999	0.62	0.11	0.77	1.00									
Number of Political Parties	0.27	0.17	0.36	0.52	1.00								
Political Competition	0.04	-0.03	0.06	0.06	-0.32	1.00							
Evo Morales Vote share	-0.01	0.37	0.02	0.14	0.14	0.06	1.00						
Population (logged)	0.30	0.11	0.46	0.63	0.66	-0.10	0.04	1.00					
Level of Development	0.23	-0.02	0.35	0.39	0.43	-0.05	-0.24	0.54	1.00				
Rural	-0.22	0.07	-0.35	-0.41	-0.38	0.02	0.37	-0.59	-0.80	1.00			
Indigenous Population	-0.07	0.28	-0.07	0.01	0.09	-0.01	0.79	-0.03	-0.37	0.46	1.00		
Literacy	0.13	-0.10	0.14	0.04	0.09	0.02	-0.39	-0.02	0.44	-0.46	-0.59	1.00	
Turnout, 1999	0.00	-0.72	-0.01	-0.06	-0.14	0.06	-0.19	-0.26	-0.07	0.01	-0.14	0.19	1.00

4

NGOs, Associations, Protest, and Voting in Latin America

Political protests form part of the language of participation in countries across Latin America. In Bolivia, the protests of the last decade have become one of the defining features of politics – playing a key role in changing administrations, rewriting the constitution, and shifting the political orientation of the country to the left, but protests have also had important political consequences in other countries in the region. In Ecuador, largely peaceful protests helped unseat two democratically elected presidents, Jamil Mahuad in 2000 and Lucio Gutiérrez in 2005. In Venezuela, tens of thousands of people marching in the streets, sometimes in support of President Hugo Chávez and sometimes in opposition to him, have become common events in the last decade. Similarly, in Mexico after the 2006 presidential election, the headline news was not the close election, but the mass demonstrations that followed it and the worry that the demonstrators might simply refuse to accept the results.

These recent protests are the latest in a long tradition of contentious politics in Latin America. During the wave of democratization following the dictatorships of the 1970s and 1980s, protest movements were important in bringing down dictators and demonstrating popular demand for democracy. But, by the time most countries in Latin America had transitioned to democracy, mass popular protests had become less common (Eckstein 2001). In the last decade, they have re-emerged as an important force in the politics of many countries. In some countries, such as Bolivia, Ecuador, Argentina, and Peru, protests have become a salient and sometimes effective way to press for policy change (Machado, Scartascini, and Tommasi 2009). In other countries, such as Nicaragua and El Salvador, protests remain infrequent and less of a serious factor in policymaking.

This chapter engages with the debates over the rise of political protest in Latin America, the role of civil society, and the role of non-governmental organizations (NGOs) by exploring the ways in which membership in civil society organizations and contact with NGOs influences individual-level decisions about how to participate in politics. What role do NGOs and civil society organizations play in promoting political participation in Latin America? I argue that NGOs facilitate political protest by bringing new resources to underserved communities and by creating opportunities for association, both of which make any type of participation easier. I also argue the effect of NGOs on protest is likely to be strongest under conditions of poorly functioning electoral mechanisms because motivated people are less likely to see voting as an effective means of communicating their preferences, and to the extent that organizations are directly mobilizing people, they encourage more contentious strategies.

This chapter focuses on three main empirical questions, drawing on surveys conducted by the Latinobarómetro in eighteen Latin American countries in 2005. First, how does contact with NGOs influence voting and protest behavior at the individual level? Second, how do NGOs affect participation when electoral mechanisms for participation are not working well compared to when they are working well? Finally, what is the effect of NGOs compared with other voluntary membership organizations?[1] To answer these questions systematically, I use multilevel mixed-effects statistical models, which allow for modeling individual and country-level variables to estimate the effect of contact with NGOs and membership in a variety of associations (e.g., sports clubs, religious groups, neighborhood associations) on political activities ranging from voting to rioting or participating in illegal street protests. Multilevel models then allow for exploration of how these relationships change under different country-level conditions (such as the quality of democracy, confidence in elections, or the presence of election fraud) to capture the effect of both individual factors and broader contextual factors. Using this data allows for a much more direct test of the conditional hypothesis suggested by the finding in Chapter 3 that NGOs have a greater effect in uncompetitive municipalities by directly measuring quality of democratic institutions on several important dimensions, rather than simply relying on competition as a proxy (something that may make more sense in the context of Bolivian municipalities than elsewhere).

---

[1] Non-governmental organizations are nonprofit, issue-oriented organizations engaged in either service or advocacy work, frequently with financial support from international donors. Voluntary membership organizations include a much broader set or organizations, including sports clubs, churches, professional organizations, labor unions, political parties, and consumer organizations. Though there is certainly some overlap between these two categories of organizations, NGOs have been the target of international funding for development project in a way that less issue-oriented voluntary organizations have not. In operational terms, the empirical results are based on two different sets of questions. For contact with NGOs, the question specifically asks about NGOs. For voluntary associations, the survey asks a series of questions about membership, financial donations, and participation in each of the categories listed.

The conventional wisdom from the literatures on NGOs, civil society, and social capital suggests that people who are involved in associational activity are more likely to be engaged in politics because they are better informed, have better access to information, and have better tools to overcome barriers to collective action.[2] The evidence presented here supports the claim that associational activity increases participation, but with some surprising caveats. First, across all the countries in the sample, contact with NGOs has a stronger effect on participation than membership in voluntary associations. This is a hopeful finding for those in the development policy community who have targeted funding toward NGOs in the hopes that they will strengthen civil society. However, it is a surprising finding for those who argue that NGOs are outsiders compared to more "home grown" civil society organizations that do not rely on foreign funding.

Second, NGOs do more to encourage contentious political engagement – including riots and illegal street protests as well as peaceful protests – than they do to increase voting. Given the strong consensus in the literatures on civil society, social capital, and NGOs that citizen involvement with these organizations is the bedrock of moderate civic engagement, this finding is suggestive that the conventional assumptions about NGOs and civil society in developing countries may be overly constrained by the experience of wealthy established democracies. Instead, though the effects of NGOs on participation are clear, they appear to be even stronger for contentious participation (protest) than for regularized participation (voting).

NGOs facilitate political protest through many of the same mechanisms that they facilitate more conventional participation like voting or signing petitions – by providing resources and opportunities for association, building trust among community members, and making it easier for people to obtain and evaluate political information. People who have these ties to other members of their community are better equipped to overcome collective action barriers to political involvement – they are more likely to say yes to an organizer requesting their assistance with a get out the vote campaign, or to someone suggesting participating in a demonstration.[3] In much of Latin America, however, people have little confidence that elections are a meaningful mechanism for political change. Across all eighteen countries in the Latinobarómetro sample, for example, 59.43 percent of respondents believe that elections are "rigged." In this climate, it makes sense that people who are mobilized to participate in politics explore options outside of regularized voting.

---

[2] Diamond summarizes this argument as follows: A "democracy-building function of civil society is to supplement the role of political parties in stimulating political participation, increasing the political efficacy and skill of democratic citizens, and promoting and appreciation of the obligations as well as rights of democratic citizenship" (1999: 244).

[3] This understanding of voting has its roots in the American voting literature: for example, Rosenstone and Hansen (1993), Verba, Nie, and Kim (1979), and Verba, Schlozman, and Brady (1995).

Finally, although contact with NGOs is a good predictor of political protest across all the countries in the sample, the effect is not constant. Given that confidence in elections varies widely by country – more than 70 percent of respondents believe elections are "rigged" in Bolivia, Brazil, Colombia, Ecuador, Peru, Guatemala, Honduras, Mexico, and Nicaragua, while fewer than 21 percent think elections are rigged in Chile, and fewer than 8 percent in Uruguay – this is not surprising. If we assume people pursue participatory strategies that they believe might work, they should respond to the efficacy of elections. Following this logic, NGOs have the greatest effect on protest under conditions of poorly functioning political institutions and elections. But where political institutions are functioning fairly well, and elections are viewed as reliable mechanisms for expressing preferences to the state, NGOs have more of an effect on stimulating voting. But where elections are seen as unlikely mechanisms for change, and people have little confidence in the elections themselves, NGOs have an increasing effect on contentious political participation.

Evaluating how well elections are functioning involves more than public opinion on whether elections are clean or corrupt. Citizens take into account both the fairness of the process – whether there is blatant electoral fraud, for example – but also how well the outcomes of elections serve their interests. I argue for a broad understanding of the functioning of electoral mechanisms, one that takes into account both the quality of the electoral process, and the substance of the interests represented in electoral choices, including the degree to which political parties are organized around real interests in society. Chapter 3 presents evidence of a conditional relationship between NGOs and protest using political competition as a proxy for quality of democracy. This chapter tests this conditional relationship more fully, exploring how the quality of democratic institutions – measured using the Party Institutionalization Index – changes the effect that NGOs and membership organizations have on participation. This allows for a much fuller test of the conditions under which NGO activity leads to protest and voting.

This chapter is organized as follows. First, I briefly address why Latin America is a good place to explore these issues. Second, I present the argument that contact with NGOs facilitates political participation of all kinds, and that the context of how well elections are working shapes the type of participation that is likely to result. Third, I discuss the research design and data measurement, followed by a discussion of results of tests of the direct hypotheses and conditional hypotheses. Finally, I offer some conclusions.

WHY LATIN AMERICA?

Latin America offers an opportunity to explore the relationship between civil society and political participation that is useful for several reasons. First, understanding changing political participation in Latin America is becoming increasingly important as contentious politics and street protests have become more common. Since the democratic transitions of the 1980s, most countries have remained democratic, but there has been an increase in contentious political strategies. In Mexico, for example, the 2006 presidential elections were followed by massive protests that paralyzed much of Mexico City as the election results were contested. Nearly 53 percent of respondents in the Latinobarómetro survey in Mexico claim that they "have" or "might" participate in political protests. Protests prompted the resignation of a democratically elected president in Bolivia in 2003, and have been increasingly characterized as a normal part of political life in that country. In Argentina, Bolivia, Ecuador, and Venezuela mass protests helped usher in governments that largely rejected the market-oriented policies of previous administrations in favor of left-leaning policies (Silva 2009). And, after some debate over whether the market reforms of the 1980s reduced the ability of groups to mobilize (Kurtz 2004), there is growing evidence that protest has become a common and important form of political participation in many countries (Arce and Bellinger 2007).

Protests have also become commonplace in other countries across the region as well. Across all eighteen countries, 38.7 percent of respondents reported participation in protests, and 15 percent said they have protested recently in activities including authorized demonstrations, unauthorized demonstrations, riots, land occupations, and blocking traffic. These events have been described as part of a shift toward more contentious political participation used alongside electoral participation and there is some evidence that protest is becoming a more common strategy in the countries with the weakest democratic institutions (Machado, Scartascini, and Tommasi 2009). As protest becomes a more common strategy for participation in Latin American countries, it is important to understand the determinants of protest, and how it fits with other political strategies.

Second, the role of civil society has been hotly contested in Latin America compared to other regions, with advocates claiming that civil society is the key to successful democratic consolidation and skeptics arguing that strong and mobilized civil society is bringing instability to the new democracies in the region. This is a debate that applies to developing countries the world over, but civil society historically has been very strong in Latin America, and most observers agree that the role civil society continues to play is critical for the success of democracy in the region – although there is considerable debate over what the appropriate role is (Brysk 2000; Wiarda 2003).

Finally, the role of NGOs in civil society and the differences between externally funded NGOs and local organizations is an issue that demands particular attention in Latin America. Some have argued that NGOs are part of civil society and function very similarly to other more "home-grown" civil society organizations such as churches, clubs, unions, and activist groups in that they bring people together around common interests or beliefs. The case has also been made that NGOs were critical actors in democratic transitions in Latin America (Brysk 2000; Wiarda 2003). Others, however, argue that because

NGOs tend to receive funding from international sources (through foreign aid organizations or international NGOs) they are inherently different from more domestic civil society organizations (Loveman 1991, 1995; Pearce 2000).[4] The huge proliferation of NGOs in most countries in Latin America since the 1980s raises some important questions about how these organizations, which are funded largely by development projects and foreign donors, fit into the civil societies of their host countries.

NGOS, ASSOCIATIONS, AND PARTICIPATION IN LATIN AMERICA

NGOs and civil society organizations can increase participation in political life through a variety of mechanisms. First, people who are involved in civic activities like neighborhood associations, sports clubs, or local development organizations are more likely to know and trust other people in their community. Higher interpersonal trust makes it easier for groups to act collectively because they are more likely to recognize and act on shared interests. Second, in addition to providing a forum for people to meet and get to know each other in a semistructured way, NGOs and other associations often act as information centers, either directly or indirectly through particularly active members. People who regularly attend meetings of any sort, then, are more likely to be politically informed about issues that are relevant to them – either because the organization offers analysis and information, or because an entrepreneurial fellow member does.[5] Leaders intent on mobilizing people to engage in politics also have an easier time of it when associational activity is common because members already have connections with one another. Third, NGOs provide resources that make political participation easier. Membership associations and other civil society organizations may also provide some resources, but this is an area where there are clear differences between types of organizations. NGOs as a category command much greater financial resources than other civil society organization by virtue of being externally funded through development aid programs. Financial resources can amplify the effect of NGOs: more staff, more workshops and classes, more outreach to the community, more research on relevant political issues, and so forth.

Interestingly, none of these factors require that the organization consciously or directly seek to promote political engagement, although there are certainly NGOs devoted to just those issues. Even organizations that seek to maintain strict political neutrality and avoid political issues still provide resources and opportunities for association to communities that can build trust, increase

---

[4] This debate is not without irony since most of the foreign donors and international NGOs select domestic NGO partners in large part out of belief that doing so will have benefits for domestic civil society.
[5] For a discussion of similar mechanisms in the context of the United States see Rosenstone and Hansen (1993).

access to information, and make political participation easier. The conventional wisdom has long been that this type of activity is the bedrock of moderate civil society necessary for a well-functioning electoral democracy. However, each of these factors can do as much to promote political protest as they do to promote more moderate behavior such as voting. If someone wanted to organize their neighbors to vote for a certain candidate it makes sense that it would be easier to do so under conditions of high trust, shared activities and interests, and opportunities for association. But the same is true if someone wanted to organize a political protest – it would be easier in a more trusting, more networked community. Because much of the benefit of associational activity for political participation is indirect, I argue that it serves as a general stimulus for participation, but that the actual choices about how to channel that participatory energy into action are driven in large part by the political context of how well elections function as mechanisms for change compared to more nontraditional, contentious activities.

Following this logic, I expect an observable relationship between contact with NGOs or membership in associations and willingness to engage in political protest. I expect this relationship because of two underlying mechanisms: direct mobilizing on the part of some advocacy NGOs, and the more common mechanism of indirect facilitation by providing resources and opportunities for association. Because NGOs on average have access to greater resources from external funding sources, I expect that having contact with an NGO will have an even greater positive effect on protest than associational membership.

WHO HAS CONTACT WITH NGOS? WHO JOINS ASSOCIATIONS?

NGOs and voluntary associations both have broad reach into society in Latin America. But the question remains whether contact with NGOs or membership in associations is evenly distributed across different sectors of society. There is some debate over who the target population of NGO activity really is in Latin America. Certainly there is a pro-poor emphasis to many of the programs that NGOs carry out, and also in the justification given by international donors in partnering with local NGOs. But NGOs have also been accused of being primarily elite-based organizations spending more time setting up nice offices in large cities and employing educated professionals than providing services or advocacy work in rural areas. Because there are clear examples of NGOs deeply involved in working with the poor, and urban NGOs working primarily on issues unrelated to advocacy, it is helpful to look at the overall patterns in Latin America.

Are the people who contact NGOs disproportionately poor? The clear answer is no. Using survey evidence from eighteen Latin American countries from the Latinobarómetro, it is clear that both the poor and the non-poor have

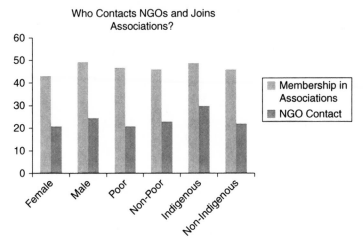

FIGURE 4.1. Contact with NGOs and associations.

similar rates of contact with NGOs.[6] In fact, as Figure 4.1 shows, the non-poor are slightly more likely to have had contact with NGOs, but the difference is quite small. Twenty-one percent of poor people across all the Latin American countries report having had contact with NGOs in the last three years, compared with 23 percent of the non-poor. Similarly, there are surprisingly few differences along gender lines in who has contact with NGOs. Twenty-one percent of women and 24 percent of men report involvement with NGOs.

There is a larger difference when it comes to ethnicity. When indigenous identity is coded by whether the respondent's first language is an indigenous language, there is a difference. Indigenous people are more likely to have had contact with NGOs by several percentage points (30 percent of indigenous people, compared with 22 percent of non-indigenous people report involvement with NGOs).

Overall, membership in voluntary organizations is much higher than contact with NGOs in the survey responses from Latinobarómetro. This is in part due to the large range of organizations included in the category of membership organizations, which includes sports and art groups, unions, professional organizations, consumer groups, international organizations, environmental groups, charity groups, leisure clubs, religious groups, political organizations (and parties), and community organizations. Again, however, membership is a common phenomenon across gender, class, and ethnic lines. Between 43 percent

---

[6] "Poor" are coded as people who do not have access to clean drinking water in their homes. "Non-poor" is the residual category of those who do have access to drinking water. This is obviously a rough cut, but gets at a major distinction in well-being that very closely correlates to income levels.

TABLE 4.1. *Who Protests?*

Country	Total	Men	Women	Rich	Poor	Non-indigenous	Indigenous
Argentina	0.41	0.44	0.39	0.26	0.43	0.41	0.00
Bolivia	0.54	0.62	0.46	0.66	0.52	0.53	0.55
Brazil	0.43	0.45	0.41	0.28	0.44	0.43	0.37
Chile	0.36	0.43	0.29	0.25	0.36	0.36	0.33
Colombia	0.43	0.51	0.36	0.45	0.42	0.43	0.40
Costa Rica	0.35	0.40	0.29	0.23	0.35	0.35	—
Dominican Republic	0.43	0.48	0.38	0.32	0.45	0.43	—
Ecuador	0.33	0.40	0.25	0.29	0.33	0.32	0.52
El Salvador	0.13	0.17	0.09	0.10	0.14	0.13	—
Guatemala	0.31	0.32	0.29	0.23	0.32	0.31	0.27
Honduras	0.37	0.39	0.35	0.39	0.37	0.37	0.23
Mexico	0.53	0.55	0.51	0.56	0.53	0.53	0.00
Nicaragua	0.26	0.32	0.21	0.21	0.27	0.26	0.33
Panama	0.30	0.36	0.24	0.24	0.30	0.30	0.19
Paraguay	0.50	0.59	0.41	0.49	0.50	0.51	0.49
Peru	0.49	0.56	0.43	0.44	0.51	0.49	0.53
Uruguay	0.40	0.48	0.34	0.29	0.42	0.40	1.00
Venezuela	0.33	0.33	0.32	0.34	0.32	0.32	0.40
Total	0.39	0.44	0.34	0.35	0.39	0.38	0.47

and 49 percent of people – regardless of gender, class, or indigenous identity – report being a member, giving money, or actively participating in at least one of these organizations.

WHO PROTESTS?

Before moving on to more direct tests of the determinants of protest, it is helpful to first look at the characteristics of the protesters, defined as those survey respondents who have or "might" participate in demonstrations. Table 4.1 shows rates of participation in protest by a number of different characteristics including gender, income, indigenous identity, employment, attitudes toward democracy, city size, and education. Overall, the demographic factors align with common expectations. Men protest more than women; the poor protest more than the wealthy; indigenous more than non-indigenous; and the unemployed protest more than those with jobs. People with education are more likely to protest than those with little education, and protest is more common in big cities than in small towns or rural areas. There is only a very small difference between those who prefer democracy and those who do not prefer democracy, which suggests that protest is not exclusively the domain of those who oppose the political system or democracy in general (Table 4.2).

TABLE 4.2. *Who Protests?* (cont'd.)

Country	Employed	Unemployed	Does not prefer Dem	Prefers Dem	City< 100,000	City> 100,000	No higher education	Some higher education
Argentina	0.41	0.45	0.38	0.43	0.49	0.35	0.38	0.54
Bolivia	0.53	0.62	0.54	0.57	0.54	0.53	0.53	0.56
Brazil	0.43	0.42	0.45	0.52	0.40	0.46	0.41	0.64
Chile	0.35	0.45	0.28	0.41	0.39	0.32	0.30	0.51
Colombia	0.42	0.49	0.45	0.45	0.44	0.39	0.38	0.58
Costa Rica	0.35	0.32	0.37	0.36	0.35	.	0.31	0.50
Dominican Republic	0.43	0.41	0.43	0.47	0.43	0.41	0.42	0.51
Ecuador	0.33	0.37	0.35	0.37	0.34	0.31	0.30	0.44
El Salvador	0.13	0.17	0.13	0.15	0.14	0.12	0.12	0.24
Guatemala	0.30	0.44	0.30	0.35	0.30	0.33	0.30	0.42
Honduras	0.36	0.45	0.38	0.40	0.34	0.43	0.36	0.55
Mexico	0.53	0.54	0.50	0.55	0.53	0.53	0.52	0.54
Nicaragua	0.26	0.34	0.30	0.30	0.27	0.24	0.25	0.46
Panama	0.29	0.36	0.28	0.34	0.30	.	0.28	0.40
Paraguay	0.49	0.62	0.46	0.59	0.49	0.52	0.48	0.64
Peru	0.49	0.56	0.53	0.51	0.48	0.54	0.46	0.62
Uruguay	0.40	0.43	0.32	0.44	0.40	.	0.37	0.58
Venezuela	0.31	0.51	0.40	0.31	0.33	0.26	0.31	0.40
Total	0.38	0.43	0.40	0.41	0.38	0.40	0.36	0.52

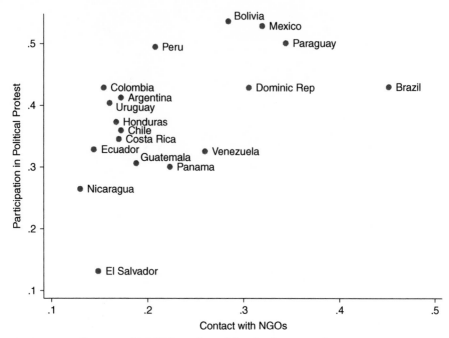

FIGURE 4.2. Contact with NGOs and participation in protest by country.

RESEARCH DESIGN

To test the effect of NGO activity and civil society membership on political participation, I estimate models of voting and protest behavior using both individual level variables from the survey responses and country level factors for eighteen countries in Latin America. Because I argue that both individual and country-level factors are important for understanding the relationships between NGOs I estimate multilevel mixed-effects logistic regression.[7] The individual level variables are drawn from responses to the 2005 Latinobarómetro Survey. Country-level variables come from a variety of sources, detailed in the text that follows.

Looking at the patterns of contact with NGOs and participation in political protest by country across the region is a useful starting point. Even at the country level, a clear pattern emerges: people in countries with high rates of contact with NGOs tend to experience higher rates of political protest (see Figure 4.2). Bolivia, Mexico, and Paraguay top the graph, with protest rates around 50 percent, and contact with NGOs between 30 and 40 percent. Brazil is unusual in

[7] For a discussion of the advantages of multilevel modeling see Steenbergen and Jones (2002).

its very high rates of NGO contact, and relatively low protest compared with Bolivia and Mexico. But overall, the pattern is clear and fairly consistent: countries in which people are more likely to contact an NGO also witness higher rates of participation in nonvoting political action.

Measuring Political Action

To measure participation, I turn to questions about participation in a variety of political actions from the Latinobarómetro survey. The first question asks whether the respondent voted in the last presidential election. The more contentious actions come from a question that asks if the respondent has participated in a range of political activities that includes signing a petition, participating in authorized demonstrations, participating in riots, occupying land buildings or factories, participating in unauthorized demonstrations, and blocking traffic.[8]

To make a comparison between institutionalized participation like voting or signing a petition, and more contentious participation like joining a demonstration or a riot, I use a summary measure of *Protest* that is coded as 1 if the respondent participated in any of the contentious political actions listed (participating in demonstrations of any sort, riots, land or building occupations, or blocking traffic). *Protest* is coded as 0 if the respondent did not participate at all. It is also coded as 0 for those who voted or signed a petition but did not participate in the more contentious forms of participation.

Figure 4.2 shows the component activities of protest and their average rates for respondents from all countries in the sample. On average in Latin America, more than 70 percent of respondents voted and over 40 percent have signed a petition. Perhaps more surprising is that nearly 35 percent of respondents report that they would participate in authorized demonstrations. Although more people vote than protest, protest is still a relatively common experience in Latin America. Figure 4.3 illustrates the variation in rates of protest and voter turnout by individual country in Latin America. Not surprisingly given the risks of protesting (and the mandatory nature of voting in some countries[9]), voting is a more common activity than protest in every country.

---

[8] I include positive responses of a hypothetical nature because of the controversial nature of political protest. Some people who have protested might be reluctant to admit doing so, especially if the protest involved violence or illegal activities or was met with repression. Asking a person "did you protest" in some cases might be taken as quite accusatory. The more hypothetical question "might you protest" in this case may be a better indicator of protest activity. All the models are estimated using both the "have" and "might" specification, with little change in the main results.

[9] Compulsory voting rules are enforced in Argentina, Brazil, Chile, Ecuador, Peru, and Uruguay, according to the Institute for Democracy and Electoral Assistance (IDEA 2010).

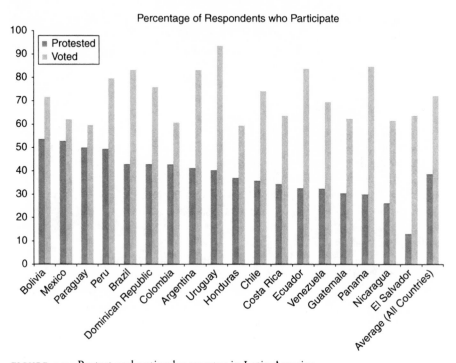

FIGURE 4.3. Protest and voting by country in Latin America.

Measuring Contact with NGOs and Associations

The measure for individual contact with NGOs comes from a survey question about contact with NGOs in the past three years. This measure captures individuals who have sought out direct contact with NGOs, not just passive encounters with NGO activity. In this sense, it measures a direct individual effect, not the broader more diffuse effects of having NGOs in a community. For this reason, it is even more surprising that such a high number of people respond yes to this question. On average across all countries in the sample, 22.48 percent of respondents have contacted NGOs, ranging from a low of 13 percent in Nicaragua to a high of 45.18 percent in Brazil. This high rate of NGO contact is consistent across recent surveys. In 2001, the only other year this question was asked, 22.82 percent of respondents contacted an NGO.

To measure broader associational activity, I construct a dichotomous measure of membership in any voluntary association from a question that lists organizations and activities and asks respondents whether they have donated money, or are active members or volunteers in each category of organization. The membership organizations include sports and recreation; artistic, musical or educational; unions; professional or business; consumer; international

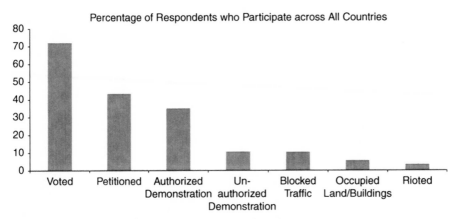

FIGURE 4.4. Varieties of participation in Latin America.

organizations for development or human rights; ecological, environmental, or animal rights; charity or social help; organizations for the elderly; religious; political parties, community organizations; and other. The average membership rates for each type of organization across Latin America are displayed in Figure 4.4.

Figure 4.5 compares rates of contact with NGOs with rates of membership in any organization by country for the eighteen countries in the sample. Combined membership rates (the percentage of respondents who are members of any of the organizations listed in Figure 4.4) are higher than the rate of contact with NGOs, with the highest rate in Argentina, where more than 75 percent of respondents are members of some organization.

To control for other individual level factors that affect political participation, I include variables for demographic factors (gender, age, education, personal income), and political attitudes (trust in government, interpersonal trust, life satisfaction, political ideology, political interest, personal experience with corruption, and political knowledge). Because I conceptualize both voting and protest as different modes on a continuum of possible political actions, I include the measure of whether a respondent voted in the last election in the protest models, and a measure of protest in the voting models as a way of getting at whether some people are just more likely to engage in all political activities than others. For ease of comparison, and in the interest of modeling participation across a broad spectrum of activities, I estimate the same models for both voting and protest.

Country-Level Factors

Several factors at the country level are important determinants of voting and protest. The main argument here is that the effect of NGOs is conditional on

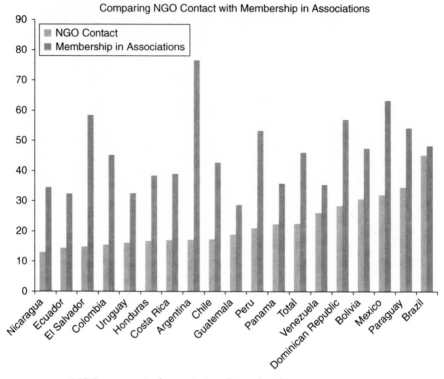

FIGURE 4.5. NGO contact and associational membership.

how well electoral mechanisms are functioning. Because elections can fail to perform well in a number of ways (both procedurally and in terms of outcomes), measuring this concept requires some careful thought. First, if political parties are not organized around the issues that are important to people, or are not stable enough to offer meaningful cues from one election to another, elections fall short. Second, fraud, corruption, voter intimidation, vote buying, or any number of other directly fraudulent actions can tarnish elections, which would impinge on an election being considered "free and fair." Finally, even if there are not obvious indications of fraud, elections can be considered less than effective if there is widespread dissatisfaction with the process of voting, or the choices available in an election. That is, even if elections appear to be running fairly regularly without blatant fraud, people are still likely to look for other venues for participation if they have little confidence that voting can accomplish their aims.

To capture this conception of variation in the effectiveness of elections as a tool for participation, I use the Party Institutionalization Index compiled by the Inter-American Development Bank (Berkman et al. 2008). This index captures all the important elements of how well elections described here are working, including the strength and issue-orientation of political parties, the degree to which the election is free and fair, and how much confidence voters have in the process. I chose the Party Institutionalization Index as the most complete measure of how well ordinary people perceive elections to be working, both procedurally and in terms of outcomes, but using other indications of the quality of democratic elections yields similar results. Specifically, the World Bank good governance indicators produce interactive effects very similar to those of the Party Institutionalization Index.[10]

Specifically, the index is composed of five measures: First is a measure of the extent to which there is a "stable, moderate and socially rooted party system to articulate and aggregate societal interests" from the Bertelsmann Transformation Index (Berkman et al. 2008: 14). Second is an indicator of confidence in political parties and elections based on the World Values Survey. Third is a measure of vote volatility, as an indicator of political competition.[11] Fourth is a measure of the extent to which the elections are considered free and fair based on elite surveys conducted by Berkman et al. (2008: 14). And fifth, the age of the political party system according to the Database of Political Institutions is included as a measure of how well political parties are able to provide continuity between elections. These five factors together give a very complete summary of how well electoral institutions are functioning for ordinary people. This index correlates at 0.70 with the Freedom House measure, so they are obviously related to other indicators or measures of quality of democracy and not merely measuring the same things.

Because there are only eighteen countries in the Latinobarómetro survey, including too many country-level variables poses a problem for estimation. However, there are several other country-level factors aside from party institutionalization that might influence the individual-level relationships we observe in the data. To address this concern, the full multilevel model is estimated with each of the following country-level variables separately, to check for the robustness of the individual-level relationships. The main result – that individuals who have contact with NGOs are more likely to participate in protest – is robust to the inclusion or exclusion of each of the following country-level variables (see Appendix 4.1 for the full models).

Freedom House

Some have argued that NGOs and civil society have very different effects depending on the level of democracy. Although all the countries in this sample are democratic, I include a measure of democracy based on political and civil

---

[10] The World Bank's good governance score averages scores on indices of Rule of Law, Control of Corruption, and Government Effectiveness (World Bank 2010).

[11] Vote volatility is calculated by taking the absolute value of the difference between votes or seats won in the current election and votes or seats won in the last election, summing the results for all parties and dividing this total by two (Berkman et al. 2008: 14). The data used in these calculations are taken from Mainwaring and Zoco (2007).

freedoms, as coded by Freedom House. I combine the scales for a 12-point scale of democratic freedoms. There is a wide range of how well they score on freedoms. The most democratic countries are Uruguay, Costa Rica, and Chile (scoring 12), and the least democratic countries are Guatemala, Nicaragua, and Venezuela (scoring 6).

The level of democracy is also an important proxy for the risks associated with participating in a demonstration or a protest. The greater the protection for democratic freedoms, the less likely a protester will face violent repression from the military or the police during a demonstration. This is important to include in the model because any individual calculation over the costs and benefits of joining in a street protest or demonstration likely include the very reasonable concern over physical safety. Protesting in a country with strong protections for democratic freedoms is not free from risk, but the chances of being shot, detained, or beaten are lower than in countries where protections for individual freedoms are less certain.

Human Development Index
Others have made the case that NGOs – and funding for NGO – direct their activities toward the highest objective levels of need (Boulding 2010; Jamal and Nooruddin 2010; Rossteutscher 2010). If NGOs consistently locate to the poorest countries with the most severe human development problems, we should not expect a constant effect for NGOs without controlling for need. Need might also be an important predictor of protest activity, as much of the grievance literature on protest suggests. In either case, it is important to include overall well-being in the model. As a measure of government performance and overall human well-being in each country, I include the Human Development Index, which is a combined index based on income, life expectancy, and literacy rates. Guatemala and Nicaragua rank the lowest, and Uruguay, Argentina, and Chile rank the highest.

Compulsory Voting
Some countries have laws that make voting compulsory, so I include a dichotomous variable for mandatory voting laws, which are enforced in Argentina, Brazil, Chile, Ecuador, Peru, and Uruguay, according to the Institute for Democracy and Electoral Assistance (IDEA 2010).

Civil Society Density
I have argued that civil society activity facilitates political participation, but that choices about how to follow through on actual participatory action are largely determined by the context of how well national level political institutions are functioning. An alternative story is that the observed differences in the effect of civil society activity on participation have less to do with the quality of governance and more to do with the nature of civil society itself. Some might argue that the density of overall civil society determines the strength of the relationship between civil society and participation – not the performance or quality

of the democratic government. Where civil society is vibrant and strong, the effect on individuals should be stronger as well (the difference between joining a strong group vs. joining a weak disinterested group). To test for this possibility, I include a measure of the average membership rates for each country as a country-level factor in the multilevel models. Surprisingly, this variable is not significant in any of the main models specified in this chapter, suggesting that individual involvement with NGOs and associations does more to explain individual behavior than the context of how dense the associational life is.

FINDINGS: THE DIRECT EFFECT OF NGOS AND MEMBERSHIP

Using these data, I first explore the hypothesis that contact with NGOs has a direct effect on political protest. The results are presented in Table 4.3. The model for voting and the model for protest are both presented in two forms, first specified with only the individual-level variables and then using multilevel mixed-effects logistic regression models based on maximum likelihood in order to include country-level factors that might influence political participation. Contact with an NGO is positively associated with both voting and participating in protest activity at a statistically significant level. Membership in associations, on the other hand, is a significant predictor of protest but is not significantly associated with having voted. This is good evidence that NGOs are not merely marginal actors compared with domestic civil society, but in fact have a more consistent impact than associations across the spectrum of political participation.

The individual variables in the model illustrate tendencies of participation in Latin America: women are less likely to protest, but no less likely to vote than men. Older people are more likely to vote, but significantly less likely to protest. More educated people participate more across the board, which is consistent with findings from studies of protests in Europe and North America, but runs counter to the characterization of protest in Latin America as a pro-poor movement made up largely of the uneducated. Interpersonal trust has no significant effect on either voting or protest, but trust in government makes people more likely to vote. Less satisfied, left-leaning people who are both interested in and knowledgeable about politics are much more likely to participate in either voting or protest than their satisfied, right-leaning counterparts with little interest in politics. Interestingly, individuals who voted in the last election are not more likely to protest than nonvoters, and likewise having protested is not a good predictor of voting.[12]

These individual-level factors are stable in the multilevel model, where the Party Institutionalization Index is included in the estimation. The index overall

---

[12] These variables make up the main model of protest and voting presented here, but there are always potential variations on the model. The results presented here are robust to the inclusion of Age-squared (to capture the nonlinear relationship between age and participation because both the very old and the very young are unlikely participants) and a measure of how frequently the respondent attempts to solve problems in their community (as a measure of political activity).

TABLE 4.3. *Contact with NGOs, Voting, and Protest in Latin America*

	Voted 1	Voted 2	Protested 1	Protested 2
Individual-Level Factors				
NGO Contact	0.183***	0.184***	0.769***	0.769***
	(0.05)	(0.05)	(0.04)	(0.04)
Membership in Associations	−0.024	−0.023	0.405***	0.405***
	(0.04)	(0.04)	(0.03)	(0.03)
Female	−0.027	−0.027	−0.299***	−0.299***
	(0.04)	(0.04)	(0.03)	(0.03)
Age	0.048***	0.048***	−0.012***	−0.012***
	(0.00)	(0.00)	(0.00)	(0.00)
Education	0.039***	0.039***	0.027***	0.027***
	(0.00)	(0.00)	(0.00)	(0.00)
Personal Income	−0.046*	−0.046*	0.000	0.000
	(0.02)	(0.02)	(0.02)	(0.02)
Trust in Government	0.060**	0.060**	0.040*	0.039*
	(0.02)	(0.02)	(0.02)	(0.02)
Interpersonal Trust	−0.048	−0.048	0.029	0.029
	(0.05)	(0.05)	(0.04)	(0.04)
Life Satisfaction	−0.018	−0.018	−0.109***	−0.109***
	(0.02)	(0.02)	(0.02)	(0.02)
Left–Right Ideology	−0.002**	−0.002**	−0.002***	−0.002***
	(0.00)	(0.00)	(0.00)	(0.00)
Political Interest	0.131***	0.131***	0.299***	0.299***
	(0.02)	(0.02)	(0.02)	(0.02)
Experience with Corruption	−0.017	−0.017	0.346***	0.346***
	(0.05)	(0.05)	(0.04)	(0.04)
Political Knowledge	0.161***	0.161***	0.150***	0.150***
	(0.02)	(0.02)	(0.02)	(0.02)
Protest	0.045	0.045		
	(0.04)	(0.04)		
Voted			0.050	0.050
			(0.04)	(0.04)
Constant	−1.364***	−2.245**	−0.958***	−1.508*
	(0.16)	(0.81)	(0.13)	(0.62)
Country-Level Factors				
Party Institutionalization		0.500		0.312
		(0.45)		(0.34)
Variance Components				
Country-Level	0.012	0.012	0.009	0.009
	(0.00)	(0.00)	(0.00)	(0.00)
Observations	18,887	18,887	18,887	18,887
No. of Countries	18	18	18	18
−2 × Log likelihood	19,551.645	19,551.645	22,391.04	22,391.04

Note: *$P < 0.10$; **$P < 0.05$; ***$P < 0.01$. Table entries are maximum likelihood estimates with estimated standard errors in parentheses generated using the command xtmelogit in Stata 10.

is a very poor predictor of protest: none of the variables are significant and only between 4 and 5 percent of the variance is explained by country-level factors, but the significance of the individual-level variables holds.[13] The individual results are also robust to the inclusion of the country-level variables discussed earlier, although only compulsory voting laws are statistically significant: countries with compulsory voting laws not surprisingly have higher voting rates as well. The weak predictive power of the country-level variables can be partly attributed to the relatively small number of countries in the sample. With only eighteen countries, and more than twenty thousand individual-level observations, only very strong cross-country relationships would likely be significant. However, the country-level factors do help us understand how the relationships between individual level factors might differ across different contexts. Including the other country-level factors does little to change the main results (for the full models including level of democracy, compulsory voting, Human Development Indicators [HDIs], and civil society density, see the Appendix 4.1).

Table 4.4 extends the analysis to more specific forms of nonvoting participation, which are collapsed in the models of protest presented in Table 4.3. The models estimate the likelihood of signing a petition, joining an unauthorized demonstration, participating in a riot, occupying land or buildings, or blocking traffic. The results support the main argument here: people who are involved in NGOs are more likely to participate in contentious political action than those who are not.

Being a member of an association or having contact with NGOs is a strong predictor of participation in each of these actions, but the effect of contact with NGOs is nearly always a larger one than membership, and is significant across all the dependent variables. Membership in voluntary associations also appears to make nonvoting participation more likely, but to a lesser degree. Drawing from these models of different types of protest, an image of the average protester emerges. Contact with NGOs, membership in associations, being male, being unsatisfied with life, being highly interested in and knowledgeable about politics, and having had personal experience with corruption are all good predictors of the individual decision to protest. Education makes most forms of participation more likely, with the exception of rioting, which is favored by the less educated.

Concerns with Endogeneity and Causality

One concern with using these specifications to estimate the effect of contact with NGOs on participation is that politically active people might be more likely to contact NGOs *and* more likely to participate in political actions, without any causal relationship between the two. If this were the case, we would

---

[13] For the model of protest, $\rho = 0.040$. For the model of voting, $\rho = 0.054$.

TABLE 4.4. *Effect of NGOs on Nonvoting Participation*

	Sign a Petition	Unauthorized Demonstration	Riot	Occupy Land or Buildings	Block Traffic
NGO Contact	0.738***	0.682***	0.458***	0.638***	0.601***
	(0.04)	(0.05)	(0.09)	(0.07)	(0.05)
Membership	0.395***	0.189***	-0.045	0.232***	0.286***
	(0.03)	(0.05)	(0.09)	(0.07)	(0.05)
Female	-0.179***	-0.270***	-0.317***	-0.357***	-0.295***
	(0.03)	(0.05)	(0.08)	(0.07)	(0.05)
Age	-0.001	-0.015***	-0.013***	-0.023***	-0.020***
	(0.00)	(0.00)	(0.00)	(0.00)	(0.00)
Education	0.060***	0.019**	-0.020	-0.017*	0.006
	(0.00)	(0.01)	(0.01)	(0.01)	(0.01)
Personal Income	0.063*	-0.001	-0.008	-0.074	-0.012
	(0.02)	(0.03)	(0.05)	(0.04)	(0.03)
Trust in Government	0.038*	-0.101***	0.070	0.083*	-0.084**
	(0.02)	(0.03)	(0.04)	(0.04)	(0.03)
Interpersonal Trust	0.008	0.199***	0.398***	0.035	0.034
	(0.04)	(0.06)	(0.09)	(0.08)	(0.06)
Life Satisfaction	-0.096***	-0.061*	-0.023	-0.074	-0.092**
	(0.02)	(0.03)	(0.05)	(0.04)	(0.03)
Left–Right Ideology	-0.001*	-0.001	-0.003	-0.003*	-0.001
	(0.00)	(0.00)	(0.00)	(0.00)	(0.00)
Political Interest	0.210***	0.289***	0.245***	0.213***	0.178***
	(0.02)	(0.03)	(0.05)	(0.04)	(0.03)
Corruption	0.379***	0.372***	0.199	0.342***	0.328***
	(0.04)	(0.06)	(0.10)	(0.08)	(0.06)

Political Knowledge	0.286***	0.150***	−0.029	−0.006	0.092**
	(0.02)	(0.03)	(0.05)	(0.04)	(0.03)
Voted	0.185***	−0.112	−0.234*	−0.242**	−0.090
	(0.04)	(0.06)	(0.09)	(0.08)	(0.06)
Constant	−2.808***	−2.867***	−2.501**	−3.103***	−1.946**
	(0.63)	(0.53)	(0.85)	(0.84)	(0.68)
Country-Level Factors					
Party Institutionalization	0.488	0.281	−0.234	0.655	0.076
	(0.35)	(0.29)	(0.46)	(0.46)	(0.37)
Observations	18,887	18,887	18,887	18,887	18,887
No. of Countries	18	18	18	18	18

Note: $*P < 0.10$; $**P < 0.05$; $***P < 0.01$. Table entries are maximum likelihood estimates with estimated standard errors in parentheses generated using the command xtmelogit in Stata 10.

still observe a positive and significant relationship between contact with NGOs and protest and voting, but not for the reasons I have presented. To the extent that this relationship still represents a serious departure from conventional characterizations of the type of the effects of NGOs, the finding is still of interest. However, the evidence presented in the text that follows suggests that the relationship does not seem to be driven primarily by active individuals, and is suggestive that NGOs do have a more causal role in the observed relationship. First, the measure of contact with an NGO is only very weakly correlated with political interest (0.16). That is, although people with high levels of interest in politics are slightly more likely to contact NGOs than those who are not at all interested in politics, the difference is minor.

More importantly, the effect of NGOs on political participation holds across different levels of political interest, ruling out the possibility that the finding is driven merely by politically engaged people contacting NGOs and participating in politics at higher levels than their less engaged counterparts. Estimating the full model of political protest from Table 4.5 for groups at different levels of political interest reveals little difference in the size or significance of the relationship between NGO contact and protest. Contact with an NGO is positive and significant across all levels of political interest (Models 1–4), including for people who respond that they have no interest in politics at all.

The same is true if the sample is split between individuals who "often" or "frequently work for issues that affect the community" (see Table 4.5 for these models). Again, NGO contact predicts protest even for those who are least politically active (Model 5), the opposite of what we would expect if these findings were driven by politically active people contacting NGOs and protesting more frequently than less politically active people. In other words, having contact with an NGO is a good predictor of political protest regardless of political interest and regardless of how politically active a person is. Splitting the sample in this way gives a very intuitive look at the differences between groups, but these results are robust to more sophisticated tests as well: estimating the full model of protest with an interaction term for NGO contact and political interest yields very similar results. The marginal effect of contact with NGOs is positive and significant for all values of political interest, including for those who have no interest in politics.

FINDINGS: THE CONDITIONAL EFFECT OF NGOS ON PARTICIPATION

People who are involved with NGOs and civil society organizations are more likely to engage in a wide range of political actions, including voting, peaceful protest, and contentious protest. However, it would be misleading to claim that the relationship between civil society and participation is constant across different contexts. In fact, there is a great deal of variation in the strength of the relationship between individual involvement with civil society and

TABLE 4.5. *Effect of NGOs on Political Protest by Level of Political Interest*

	People who are not interested in politics (Political Interest = 0)	People with some interest in politics (Political Interest = 1)	People with high interest in politics (Political Interest = 2)	People with very high interest in politics (Political Interest = 3)	People who frequently try to solve problems in their community	People who rarely try to solve problems in their community
	(1)	(2)	(3)	(4)	(5)	(6)
NGO Contact	0.744***	0.799***	0.693***	0.891***	0.612***	0.730***
	(0.069)	(0.067)	(0.084)	(0.132)	(0.075)	(0.048)
Membership	0.421***	0.420***	0.330***	0.506***	0.171*	0.377***
	(0.057)	(0.058)	(0.077)	(0.124)	(0.082)	(0.039)
Female	−0.341***	−0.296***	−0.272***	−0.199	−0.229**	−0.295***
	(0.054)	(0.055)	(0.073)	(0.119)	(0.074)	(0.037)
Age	−0.016***	−0.013***	−0.007**	−0.004	−0.007**	−0.014***
	(0.002)	(0.002)	(0.003)	(0.004)	(0.003)	(0.001)
Education	0.020*	0.029***	0.036***	0.033*	0.015	0.027***
	(0.007)	(0.008)	(0.010)	(0.015)	(0.009)	(0.005)
Income	0.002	−0.015	0.013	0.002	−0.049	0.019
	(0.033)	(0.034)	(0.045)	(0.070)	(0.045)	(0.023)
Trust in Government	0.027	0.034	0.039	0.045	0.034	0.041
	(0.030)	(0.032)	(0.041)	(0.059)	(0.040)	(0.021)
Trust in People	−0.056	0.070	−0.006	0.190	−0.049	0.037
	(0.074)	(0.072)	(0.085)	(0.137)	(0.087)	(0.048)
Life Satisfaction	−0.155***	−0.055	−0.098*	−0.193**	−0.062	−0.123***
	(0.032)	(0.035)	(0.048)	(0.072)	(0.045)	(0.023)
Ideology	−0.002*	−0.001	−0.002	−0.005*	−0.002	−0.002**
	(0.001)	(0.001)	(0.001)	(0.002)	(0.001)	(0.001)

(continued)

TABLE 4.5. *(continued)*

	People who are not interested in politics (Political Interest = 0)	People with some interest in politics (Political Interest = 1)	People with high interest in politics (Political Interest = 2)	People with very high interest in politics (Political Interest = 3)	People who frequently try to solve problems in their community	People who rarely try to solve problems in their community
	(1)	(2)	(3)	(4)	(5)	(6)
Political Interest					0.362***	0.249***
					(0.039)	(0.022)
Corruption	0.312***	0.389***	0.375***	0.292*	0.143	0.392***
	(0.074)	(0.076)	(0.094)	(0.142)	(0.088)	(0.051)
Political Knowledge	0.175***	0.074*	0.171***	0.207**	0.043	0.160***
	(0.030)	(0.036)	(0.046)	(0.065)	(0.043)	(0.022)
Voted	0.071	-0.020	0.162	-0.032	0.090	0.024
	(0.062)	(0.066)	(0.091)	(0.156)	(0.090)	(0.044)
Constant	-0.692***	-0.531**	-0.784***	-0.521	-0.158	-0.967***
	(0.178)	(0.190)	(0.238)	(0.350)	(0.226)	(0.145)
Observations	3,643	15,244	7,754	6,165	3,513	1,455
No. of Countries	18	18	18	18	18	18

Note: * P < 0.10; ** P < 0.05; *** P < 0.01. Table entries are maximum likelihood estimates with estimated standard errors in parentheses generated using the command xtmelogit in Stata 10.

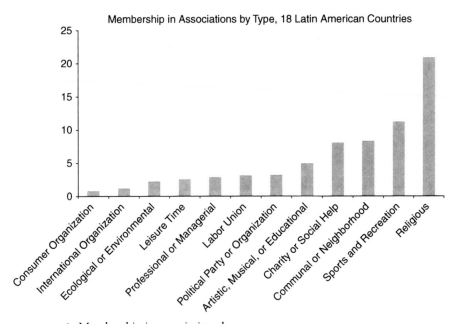

FIGURE 4.6. Membership in associations by type.

participatory action. Although in most cases contact with NGOs makes participation more likely, in some countries the effect is fairly weak. In others, it is very strong. More interesting, there is also variation in the relative impact of NGO and associative activity on individual voting versus nonvoting participation. In some cases, NGOs appear to do more to encourage voting while in others they do more to encourage political protest.

What explains the variation in the strength of the relationship between civil society and political participation across countries? What explains the relative impact on voting versus more contentious participation? In this section, I turn to the context of how well the democratic political system is working. Essentially this section explores the role that civil society plays in mobilizing political participation under conditions that are common in democracies in the developing world: democratic institutions, including regular elections, but also problems with corruption, rule of law, and poor government performance. Does civil society have the same effect on political participation under conditions of crises of the democratic process? Does civil society influence political participation differently when the government is failing in terms of providing material benefits?

Essentially, civil society activity can be thought of as a stimulant for participation, but how that participation is channeled depends on how well democratic processes are perceived to be working. When the context is one of unresponsiveness – either because of problems with the democratic process,

TABLE 4.6. *Relationship between NGOs, Associational Membership, Voting, and Protest*

Country	Effect on Protest		Effect on Voting		No. of Respondents
	NGO Contact	Membership	NGO Contact	Membership	
Argentina	+	–	–	–	1,200
Bolivia	+	+	–	–	1,200
Brazil	+	+	–	–	1,204
Chile	+	+	–	–	1,200
Colombia	+	+	–	–	1,200
Costa Rica	+	–	–	–	1,000
Dominican Republic	+	+	+	–	1,000
Ecuador	+	+	–	–	1,200
El Salvador	+	–	+	–	1,010
Guatemala	+	–	–	–	1,000
Honduras	+	–	–	–	1,000
Mexico	+	+	–	–	1,200
Nicaragua	+	+	–	–	1,000
Panama	+	+	–	–	1,008
Paraguay	+	+	+	–	1,200
Peru	+	+	–	–	1,200
Uruguay	+	+	+	–	1,200
Venezuela	+	+	–	–	1,200

Note: "+" indicates a positive and significant coefficient ($P < 0.01$) in the country-specific fully specified logistic regression with robust standard errors. "–" indicates no statistically significant relationship.

such as electoral fraud, or problems with government performance such as a chronic inability to address serious poverty – individuals involved with NGOs and associations are more likely to direct their organized energies toward contentious politics than toward standard institutional participation such as voting. Even at the extremes, civil society is only one small part of why people decide to engage politically and make the effort to participate, which is all the more reason to expect that the form of participation will be shaped by the larger political context. In cases where the government is failing to perform well either in terms of the democratic process or overall government performance, I expect NGOs to have a stronger impact on promoting protest and less of an impact on voting.

Table 4.6 illustrates the variation in the relationship between NGOs and membership associations and political participation across the Latin American countries in the Latinobarómetro sample. A few patterns stand out. First, the effect of NGO contact or associational membership on protest is much stronger and more consistent across the Latin American cases than the effect on voting. In all eighteen countries in the sample, NGO contact has a positive and significant relationship with protest. NGO contact is positively associated with voting only in the Dominican Republic, El Salvador, Paraguay, and Uruguay. Second, the effect of NGOs appears to be stronger and more consistent than other types of associational membership activities. Although NGO contact is positively associated with protest in *every* country, membership is a significant predictor of protest in most, with the exceptions of Argentina, Costa Rica, El Salvador, Guatemala, and Honduras. A similar pattern holds for voting. NGO contact is statistically significant for some countries, but those who are members of associations do not vote statistically significantly more or less than nonmembers in any country.

These patterns raise some interesting questions about the importance of the political context in shaping the relationships between NGOs, associations, and political participation. To explore the conditional effect of how well institutions are functioning, I look at the interaction between party institutionalization and contact with NGOs. In other words, I explore how the relationship between contact with NGOs and voting and political protest change under different conditions of party institutionalization. It is my contention that NGOs do more to stimulate political protest when party institutionalization is weakest. That is, where political parties are unstable, extreme, or disconnected from the needs of average citizens; where confidence in the ability of political parties to represent interests is low; and where the fairness of elections is reasonably questioned, people involved with NGOs are more likely to take to the streets instead of form orderly lines at voting booths.

To test for this conditional relationship, I estimate the models of protest and voting with a cross-level interaction term for the Party Institutionalization Index and membership. Figures 4.7 and 4.8 illustrate this conditional relationship in a more direct way, showing the marginal effect of contact with NGOs on political protest and voting at different levels of party institutionalization. Figure 4.7 shows the marginal effect of NGO contact on protest, and Figure 4.8 shows the same effect for voting. The marginal effects are based on fully specified models of protest and voting that include an interaction term between the variable for contact with NGOs and the Party Institutionalization Index. The full models with the interaction terms are in Appendix 4.2.

As party institutionalization increases, contact with NGOs has a declining effect on political protest (Figure 4.7). At low scores on the Party Institutionalization Index, NGO contact has a significant effect on protest, but the effect diminishes as elections and political parties work better. At a score of 3 or 4, NGOs no longer have a statistically significant effect on protest. The opposite is true for voting. As elections work better (and the party institutionalization index increases), NGOs have an increasing effect on voter participation (Figure 4.8). Again, at a score of 0 or 1, the effect of NGOs on voting in indistinguishable from 0 – it is not statistically significant. But beginning with a score of 2 and rising, NGOs are clearly associated with voting. This is strong

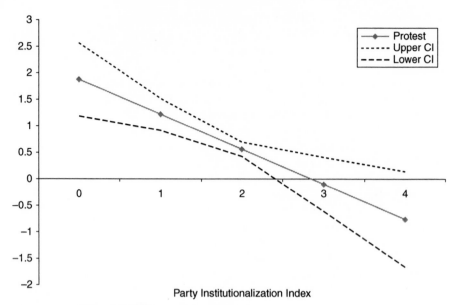

FIGURE 4.7. Effect of NGO contact on protest.

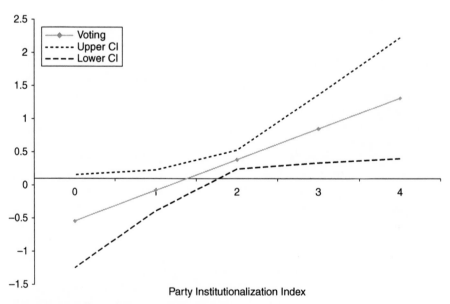

FIGURE 4.8. Effect of NGO contact on voting.

evidence that NGOs encourage political participation *of the type that is likely to make a difference* – which varies depending on the context of the effectiveness of political parties and the quality of elections.

CONCLUSIONS

The debates over civil society, associational life, social capital, and political participation are many faceted and often difficult to disentangle. But the conventional wisdom strongly suggests that engagement with community groups, membership in associations, and support for NGOs in developing countries results in higher levels of trust and social capital and a more organized, effective, and participatory citizenry. This chapter presents surprising evidence that although associational activity does seem to make voting more likely, it has a much larger effect on protest. That is, people who are actively involved in civic life are more likely to participate in all forms of political action – including very contentious political behavior along the lines of riots, illegal demonstrations, land occupations, and political protests. They are also more likely to participate in all forms of nonvoting participation, including signing petitions; joining in boycotts; and participating in legal, authorized demonstrations.

Despite the very robust finding that associational membership and contact with NGOs increases all types of political participation, there is real variation in the strength of this effect, as well as the relative influence of civil society on different types of participation. I have made the case that the form participatory action takes is determined largely by the context of how well the democratic institutions of elections and political parties are functioning. Where political parties are weak and unstable and people have little confidence in them, and where elections are viewed as fraudulent or unfair, membership in civil society organizations does more to boost protest than it does to boost voting. What this finding suggests is that civil society activity makes it easier for people to be engaged politically, and more likely that they will choose to participate. There is little to support the idea that civil society is always a moderating force. Instead, when voting is most likely to be ineffective, civil society facilitates other types of mobilization, including contentious activities such as protest.

APPENDIX 4.1. *Multilevel Models with Additional Country-Level Controls*

	Voted	Protested	Voted	Protested	Voted	Protested	Voted	Protested
NGO Contact	0.184***	0.769***	0.185***	0.769***	0.185***	0.751***	0.183***	0.769***
	(0.05)	(0.04)	(0.05)	(0.04)	(0.05)	(0.04)	(0.05)	(0.04)
Member	-0.024	0.405***	-0.025	0.405***	-0.024	0.379***	-0.023	0.405***
	(0.04)	(0.03)	(0.04)	(0.03)	(0.04)	(0.04)	(0.04)	(0.03)
Female	-0.027	-0.299***	-0.027	-0.299***	-0.033	-0.283***	-0.027	-0.299***
	(0.04)	(0.03)	(0.04)	(0.03)	(0.04)	(0.03)	(0.04)	(0.03)
Age	0.048***	-0.012***	0.048***	-0.012***	0.049***	-0.013***	0.048***	-0.012***
	(0.00)	(0.00)	(0.00)	(0.00)	(0.00)	(0.00)	(0.00)	(0.00)
Education	0.039***	0.027***	0.038***	0.027***	0.037***	0.027***	0.039***	0.027***
	(0.00)	(0.00)	(0.00)	(0.00)	(0.00)	(0.00)	(0.00)	(0.00)
Personal Income	-0.046*	0.000	-0.046*	0.000	-0.039	-0.009	-0.045*	0.000
	(0.02)	(0.02)	(0.02)	(0.02)	(0.02)	(0.02)	(0.02)	(0.02)
Trust in Government	0.060**	0.040*	0.059**	0.040*	0.066**	0.035	0.060**	0.040*
	(0.02)	(0.02)	(0.02)	(0.02)	(0.02)	(0.02)	(0.02)	(0.02)
Interpersonal Trust	-0.048	0.029	-0.048	0.029	-0.053	0.023	-0.048	0.029
	(0.05)	(0.04)	(0.05)	(0.04)	(0.05)	(0.04)	(0.05)	(0.04)
Life Satisfaction	-0.018	-0.109***	-0.016	-0.109***	-0.021	-0.095***	-0.018	-0.109***
	(0.02)	(0.02)	(0.02)	(0.02)	(0.02)	(0.02)	(0.02)	(0.02)
Left–Right Ideology	-0.002**	-0.002***	-0.002**	-0.002***	-0.001**	-0.002***	-0.002**	-0.002***
	(0.00)	(0.00)	(0.00)	(0.00)	(0.00)	(0.00)	(0.00)	(0.00)
Political Interest	0.131***	0.299***	0.131***	0.299***	0.132***	0.320***	0.131***	0.299***
	(0.02)	(0.02)	(0.02)	(0.02)	(0.02)	(0.02)	(0.02)	(0.02)
Experience with Corruption	-0.017	0.346***	-0.018	0.346***	-0.021	0.319***	-0.017	0.346***
	(0.05)	(0.04)	(0.05)	(0.04)	(0.05)	(0.05)	(0.05)	(0.04)

	(1)	(2)	(3)	(4)	(5)	(6)	(7)	(8)
Political Knowledge	0.161***	0.150***	0.161***	0.150***	0.158***	0.140***	0.161***	0.150***
	(0.02)	(0.02)	(0.02)	(0.02)	(0.02)	(0.02)	(0.02)	(0.02)
Protest	0.045		0.044		0.050		0.045	0.045
	(0.04)		(0.04)		(0.04)		(0.04)	(0.04)
Voted		0.051		0.050		0.060		0.051
		(0.04)		(0.04)		(0.04)		(0.04)
Freedom House	0.100	−0.001						
	(0.06)	(0.05)						
Compulsory Voting			0.791***	0.074				
			(0.21)	(0.21)				
HDI Index					2.659	0.263		
					(2.19)	(1.83)		
Civil Society Density							−0.919	0.282
							(1.04)	(0.79)
Constant	−2.266***	−0.948*	−1.622***	−0.982***	−3.536*	−1.122	−0.946	−1.087**
	(0.60)	(0.48)	(0.15)	(0.15)	(1.73)	(1.44)	(0.50)	(0.38)
Observations	18,887	18,887	18,887	18,887	18,887	18,887	18,887	18,887
No. of Countries	18	18	18	18	18	18	18	18

Note: $* P < 0.10$; $** P < 0.05$; $*** P < 0.01$. Table entries are maximum likelihood estimates with estimated standard errors in parentheses generated using the command xtmelogit in Stata 10.

APPENDIX 4.2. *Multilevel Models with Interactions*

	Voted	Protested 1	Protested 2
Individual-Level Factors			
NGO Contact	−0.589	1.877***	1.859**
	(0.34)	(0.35)	(0.58)
Membership in Associations	−0.024	0.384***	0.377***
	(0.04)	(0.04)	(0.04)
Female	−0.033	−0.274***	−0.283***
	(0.04)	(0.03)	(0.03)
Age	0.049***	−0.013***	−0.013***
	(0.00)	(0.00)	(0.00)
Education	0.037***	0.026***	0.027***
	(0.00)	(0.00)	(0.00)
Personal Income	−0.040	−0.004	−0.009
	(0.02)	(0.02)	(0.02)
Trust in Government	0.065**	0.011	0.034
	(0.02)	(0.02)	(0.02)
Interpersonal Trust	−0.052	0.059	0.022
	(0.05)	(0.04)	(0.04)
Life Satisfaction	−0.021	−0.092***	−0.093***
	(0.02)	(0.02)	(0.02)
Left–Right Ideology	−0.001**	−0.002***	−0.002***
	(0.00)	(0.00)	(0.00)
Political Interest	0.131***	0.321***	0.321***
	(0.02)	(0.02)	(0.02)
Experience with Corruption	−0.024	0.311***	0.321***
	(0.05)	(0.05)	(0.05)
Political Knowledge	0.158***	0.136***	0.139***
	(0.02)	(0.02)	(0.02)
Protest	0.051		
	(0.04)		
Voted		0.078	0.059
		(0.04)	(0.04)
Interactions			
NGO Contact × Party Institutionalization	0.445*	−0.659**	
	(0.20)	(0.20)	
NGO Contact × HDI			−1.398
			(0.73)
Country-Level Factors			
Party Institutionalization	0.082	1.656*	−0.190
	(0.48)	(0.72)	(0.38)

Note: *P < 0.10; **P < 0.05; ***P < 0.01. Table entries are maximum likelihood estimates with estimated standard errors in parentheses generated using the command xtmelogit in Stata 10.

APPENDIX 4.3. *Summary Statistics (Latinobarómetro 2005)*

Variable	Obs.	Mean	Std. Dev.	Min.	Max.
Participation Variables					
Voted	20222	0.721	0.448	0	1
"Has" or "Might"					
Protest	20222	0.388	0.487	0	1
Petition	20222	0.435	0.496	0	1
Authorized Demonstration	20222	0.107	0.309	0	1
Riot	20222	0.034	0.182	0	1
Occupy	20222	0.057	0.231	0	1
Block Traffic	20222	0.104	0.305	0	1
Unauthorized Demonstration	20222	0.107	0.309	0	1
"Has" only					
Protest	20222	0.150	0.357	0	1
Petition	20222	0.163	0.369	0	1
Authorized Demonstration	20222	0.131	0.337	0	1
Riot	20222	0.009	0.095	0	1
Occupy Land	20222	0.014	0.116	0	1
Unauthorized Demonstration	20222	0.034	0.181	0	1
Block Traffic	20222	0.034	0.182	0	1
Membership Variables					
NGO contact	20222	0.225	0.417	0	1
Member of Any	20222	0.461	0.498	0	1
Consumer	20222	0.008	0.091	0	1
International Organization	20222	0.012	0.111	0	1
Environmental	20222	0.022	0.148	0	1
Leisure	20222	0.026	0.159	0	1
Professional	20222	0.029	0.167	0	1
Labor	20222	0.032	0.175	0	1
Political Party	20222	0.032	0.176	0	1
Art	20222	0.049	0.217	0	1
Charity	20222	0.080	0.272	0	1
Sport	20222	0.112	0.316	0	1
Religious	20222	0.209	0.406	0	1
Control Variables					
Female	20222	0.509	0.500	0	1
Age	20222	39.283	16.376	16	96
Education Scale	20222	8.887	4.505	1	17
Income Scale	20222	2.280	0.898	0	4
Trust government	19885	1.175	0.980	0	3
Interpersonal Trust	19629	0.197	0.397	0	1
Control Variables					
Life Satisfaction	20114	1.957	0.859	0	3
Ideology	20222	24.897	37.596	0	98

(continued)

APPENDIX 4.3. *(continued)*

Variable	Obs.	Mean	Std. Dev.	Min.	Max.
Political Interest	20016	0.915	0.948	0	3
Experience with Corruption	20222	0.200	0.400	0	1
Political Knowledge	19915	1.867	0.994	0	4
Country-Level Variables					
Party Institutionalization Index	20222	2.195	0.475	1.550	3.317
Freedom House	20222	9.070	1.910	6	12
Compulsory Voting	20222	0.356	0.479	0	1
HDI Combined	19022	0.791	0.057	0.691	0.872
Civil Society Density	20222	0.461	0.125	0.286	0.766

APPENDIX 4.4. *Data Appendix (Latinobarómetro 2005)*

Individual-Level Questions from 2005 Latinobarómetro

NGO Contact	In the past three years, for you or your family, in order to solve problems that affect you in your neighborhood, have you contacted non-governmental organizations or civil society organizations? (1) Never (2) Sometimes (3) Often. This indicator was recoded dichotomously, 1 representing respondents that indicated having sometimes and often having NGO contact and 0 for individuals who responded never.
Membership in Associations	Now I am going to read out a list of organization and activities. Which do you belong to or do you not belong to any of them? To which, if any, do you donate money (do not consider membership costs)? In which one are you an active member or do you work as a volunteer? (a) Sport Organization/ club or recreational activities; (b) Artistic, musical, educational; (c) Union; (d) Professional, business; (e) Consumer organizations; (f) International organizations for Development help or human rights development; (g) Ecological, environmental protections animal rights; (h) Charity or social help; (i) Free time organizations and defense of elders retired and pensioned; (j) Religious practice/ not including religious practice; (k) Political organization or party; (l) Communal organizations and neighborhood organizations; (m) Other organizations. From this list, a dichotomous indicator for membership in associations was created with individuals who indicated having donated money and also identified themselves as active members were coded as 1 and those who indicated they did not donate money or belong to an organization are coded as 0.
Female	Sex? (0) Male; (1) Female

Education	How much and what type of education respondent completed? (1) Without education (2) 1 year, (3) 2 years, (4) 3 years, (5) 4 years, (6) 5 years, (7) 6 years, (8) 7 years, (9) 8 years, (10) 9 years, (11) 10 years, (12) 11 years, (13) 12 years, (14) Incomplete university, (15) Completed university, (16) High school/academies/Incomplete technical training, (17) High school/academies/ Complete technical training.
	From responses, dichotomous variables for education were created based on responses. Completed primary education if respondents indicated they completed 1–8 years of education, Secondary education if respondent indicated having completed 9–12 years of education, Completed some higher education if respondent indicated having incomplete university, completed university, high school/academies/ incomplete technical training, high school/academies/ complete technical training.
Personal Income	Does your salary and the total of your family's salary allow you to satisfactorily cover your needs? Which of the following situations do you find yourself in? (1) It is not sufficient, you have big problems; (2) It is not sufficient, you have problems; (3) It is just sufficient, without major problems; (4) It is sufficient, you can save.
Trust in Government	Please look at this card and tell me how much confidence you have in each of the following groups, institutions, or persons mentioned on the list: (1) a little; (2) some; and (3) a lot.
Interpersonal Trust	Generally speaking, would you say that you can trust most people, or that you can never be too careful when dealing with others? (1) You can trust most people; (0) You can never be too careful when dealing with others and no response.
Life Satisfaction	In general, would you say that you are satisfied with your life? Would you say that you are (0) Not at all satisfied; (1) Not very satisfied; (2) Fairly satisfied; (3) Very satisfied?
Left-Right Ideology	In politics, people normally speak of left and right. On a scale where 0 is left and 10 is right, where would you place yourself? (0) 0 Left; (1) 1; (2) 2; (3) 3; (4) 4; (5) 5; (6) 6; (7) 7; (8) 8; (9) 9; (10) 10 Right.
Political Interest	How interested are you in politics? (1) A little interested; (2) Fairly interested; (3) Very interested?
Experience with Corruption	Have you or someone in your family known a corruption act in the last 12 months? (0) No; (1) Yes.
Political Knowledge	How much would you say you know about political and social events in your country? Would you say you know a lot, a fair amount, a little, almost nothing or nothing about the political and social events in the country? (1) Almost nothing; (2) A little; (3) A fair amount; (4) A lot.

(*continued*)

Voting	Did you vote in the last presidential election? (0) No; (1) Yes.
Protest	If respondents indicated they had participated in an authorized demonstration, riot, land or building occupation, unauthorized demonstration, or blocked traffic, they were coded as 1 and 0 if respondents indicated they had not participated in any of these events.
Sign a Petition	I am going to read out a political activity. I would like you to tell me, if you have ever done it, if you would ever do it, or if you would never do it. Signing a petition? (1) Have done; (2) Could do; (3) Would never do; (0) Don't know/No answer.
Authorized Demonstration	I am going to read out a political activity. I would like you to tell me, if you have ever done it, if you would ever do it, or if you would never do it. Taking part in authorized demonstrations? (1) Have done; (2) Could do; (3) Would never do.
Unauthorized Demonstration	I am going to read out a political activity. I would like you to tell me, if you have ever done it, if you would ever do it, or if you would never do it. Taking part in unauthorized demonstrations? (1) Have done; (2) Could do; (3) Would never do.
Riot	I am going to read out a political activity. I would like you to tell me, if you have ever done it, if you would ever do it, or if you would never do it. Participate in riots? (1) Have done; (2) Could do; (3) Would never do.
Occupy Land or Building	I am going to read out a political activity. I would like you to tell me, if you have ever done it, if you would ever do it, or if you would never do it. Occupy land, buildings, or factories? (1) Have done; (2) Could do; (3) Would never do.
Blocking Traffic	I am going to read out a political activity. I would like you to tell me, if you have ever done it, if you would ever do it, or if you would never do it. Block the traffic? (1) Have done; (2) Could do; (3) Would never do.

Country-level Variables

Party Institutionalization	Index of five variables, compiled by Berkman et al. (2008):
	1. To what extent is there a stable, moderate, and socially rooted party system to articulate and aggregate societal interests (BTI 2006)
	2. *Confidence:* Shared Global Indicators Cross-National Database/ World Values Survey: "How much confidence do you have in the Political Parties"
	3. *Vote Volatility* (Pederson 1983)
	4. *Free and fair elections:* "To what extent are political leaders determined by general, free and fair elections?" (Profils Institutionnels 2006)
	5. *Party Age:* (Database of Political Institutions 1990–2004)

Freedom House	Freedom House political rights and civil liberties scores were combined to create a 12-point scale with 12 representing "most free." (Source: Freedom House 2010).
Compulsory Voting	Coded 1 if the country has compulsory voting rules that are enforced, 0 if voting is not compulsory or is not enforced. (Source: IDEA).
Human Development Combined Index	The Human Development Index is a composite summary index that measures human develop for a country along three dimensions: long and healthy life, access to knowledge and a decent standard of living. (Source: United Nations Development Program).
Civil Society Density	Country mean of individuals reporting having belonged to a membership organization.

5

Associational Activity and Participation in Developing Democracies

This project has shown how the services, resources, and opportunities for association provided by non-governmental organizations (NGOs) influence individual decisions about participating in political activities from voting and signing petitions to street demonstrations and riots. Although for many NGOs, encouraging political participation is a low priority compared to delivering services, there is a strong and robust relationship between contact with NGOs and higher rates of political participation. And, contrary to the expectations of many who see NGOs as the cornerstone of moderate civil society, in *every* country in Latin America NGOs do more to stimulate political protest than they do to stimulate voting. The influence of NGOs on protest is also conditional on the quality of democratic elections – where electoral institutions are working well, NGOs have a smaller effect on protest than where electoral institutions are flawed or failing.

This book has focused on the role of NGOs in civil society in Latin America, but the huge expansion of NGOs in developing countries has been a global phenomenon, not just a regional one. This chapter asks how generalizable these relationships are outside the context of Latin America. Do NGOs and voluntary associations facilitate protest in developing democracies in other regions of the world? Is their influence on participation conditional on how well elections are working as mechanisms for people to articulate demands to the state? I have argued that we can observe such a consistent relationship between NGOs and political protest in Latin America because the effect of NGOs in stimulating political participation works through both intentional activist channels and through unintended channels as a spillover effect of associational activity. That is, although some NGOs are actively trying to promote political engagement, even those that are focused solely on apolitical service provision provide resources and opportunities for association that facilitate political engagement. If this conception of NGOs and civil society organizations as spaces for associational activity is true, there is little reason to expect that similar organizations in other regions of the world would not play a similar role in mobilizing political participation.

Is the link between NGOs and protest activity unique to Latin America? Are NGOs in Latin America simply more radical, more focused on mobilization and empowerment, and more activist than NGOs and associations in other parts of the world? Certainly there is an activist tradition among Latin American NGOs, beginning with their roots in the democratization movements of many Latin American countries (Fisher 1998; Loveman 1991). But there is good evidence that NGOs have grown in numbers around the world, not just in Latin America (Werker and Ahmed 2008). There is also case-based evidence from a wide range of countries that NGOs have played a role in mobilizing protests. For example, an early work on the political consequences of NGOs in the Philippines pointed to NGOs as strategic political actors with strong links to social movements (Clarke 1998a). In Thailand, a study of local NGOs found that many NGOs became involved in antigovernment protests in the late 1990s and that the line between many Thai NGOs and social movements blurred as NGOs turned to unconventional tactics as part of their advocacy campaigns (Dechalert 1999). And in Russia, the government has seriously curtailed NGO activity out of fears that NGOs were galvanizing political opposition.

The theoretical story here, however, should apply beyond the specific context of development NGOs in Latin America. All kinds of organizations provide resources to communities and provide opportunities for association, not just NGOs. If, in fact, the causal mechanism linking NGOs and political protest includes both the direct (active mobilizing and advocacy) and the indirect (unintentional facilitation of political protest through the associational side effects of NGO activity) then it should be possible to observe similar patterns in other parts of the world, and between other types of organizations that provide opportunities for association. This chapter seeks to do just that – explore the relationship between membership in a variety of associations and engagement in different types of political action in developing-world democracies outside of Latin America.

To tease out these implications about the causal mechanisms connecting membership and protest and voting under different conditions of electoral institutions, I first look at the membership rates and demographic makeup of membership by region, using data from the 2005 wave of the World Values Survey. I then turn to the area studies literature on civil society and NGOs in Africa, Asia, Eastern Europe, and the Middle East to briefly summarize the major regional differences in the composition of civil society, its role in state–society relations, and its role in promoting political participation. With this understanding of what membership in civil society organizations looks like around the world, I then turn to the statistical analysis of how membership influences voting and protest under different conditions of confidence in electoral institutions.

Comparing membership rates and demographic patterns of membership along the lines of income, gender, and education allows for consideration of the causal mechanisms at work – and for testing of several additional hypothesis. If, for example, civil society in Latin America is made up of far more pro-poor, pro-indigenous, activist advocacy organizations compared with other developing regions, and the relationship between membership and political protest is stronger in Latin America than elsewhere, we might legitimately question the story that has been told here – that protest and voting are best understood as a function of the strength of all types of organizations (not just activist ones) and their interaction with the quality of democratic electoral institutions. Instead, it would seem much more likely that the findings are driven by direct advocacy work of the organizations. If, on the other hand, membership patterns are largely similar, both in terms of membership rates and the demographic qualities of those who join civil society organizations and we find a link between membership and protest where electoral institutions are not working well (and a link between membership and voting where they are working better), it would be good evidence that something more general than Latin American advocacy is going on.

The findings are a little more nuanced than either of the possibilities described in the preceding text. First, although there are some important differences (which I describe in more detail later), overall Latin America is not an outlier in terms of rates of membership or the composition of which groups in society tend to join organizations. Second, there is plentiful evidence from regionally based literature on NGOs and civil society that civil society plays a varying role in promoting political participation under different political contexts. Civil society organizations and NGOs around the world have been seen as having links to protest movements, especially during moments of failing confidence in elections. Finally, the statistical analysis reveals robust evidence that membership increases the likelihood of protest in nearly every country in the sample, and that the effect is strongest under conditions of weak confidence in elections, high incidence of election fraud, weak and disorganized political parties, or lack of real political competition in elections.

This chapter proceeds as follows. First, I directly address the question of whether associational membership and NGO activity is different in Latin America compared to other regions of the world, and what implications this might have for understanding the ways in which associational life influences participation in different contexts. Second, to test the relationship between civil society activity and political participation outside of Latin America more systematically, I turn to the fourth wave of the World Values Survey, carried out in 2005. Drawing from the sample of democratic countries in the developing world, but excluding the Latin American countries, this chapter explores how membership in associations affects voting and protest. I find strong evidence that people who are members of associations are more likely to protest than those who are not members. The World Values Survey was conducted in several Latin American countries as well, which I explore separately in an effort to replicate the findings from Chapter 4. The findings are quite similar, both for the Latin American cases and for countries outside of Latin America.

Third, I explore the extent to which the link between membership and protest is shaped by the quality of electoral institutions, focusing on the institutionalization of political parties, electoral fraud, and political competition. Similar to what I find in the Latin American context, the quality of electoral mechanisms is a critical factor in determining the extent of the relationship between membership and protest. Protest is most likely to result from membership under conditions of poorly functioning electoral institutions. This chapter concludes with a discussion of alternative explanations, including an analysis of how different types of membership organizations influence participation.

DEFINING THE SCOPE OF COMPARISON: DEVELOPING DEMOCRACIES

Why look at only democracies? This project is focused on the role of NGOs and membership associations as part of civil society outside of the developed West because there is growing evidence these organizations are increasingly important in the context of developing countries and their role is less well understood in contexts of poorly functioning institutions. NGOs can also plan important roles in non-democracies, but it is within the formal framework of elections that I am most interested in how they affect political participation.

Exploring the effect of membership in voluntary organizations on individual willingness to vote and protest in democratic nations in the developing world is useful for a number of reasons. Limiting the sample to countries with a minimal level of democracy allows exploration of the causes of political participation under fairly free conditions. Although voter intimidation, violence, and other forms of coercion can and do certainly occur in democracies, there is at least some minimal protection for individual rights. In non-democracies, the threat of repression and the risks associated with political participation are quite different, as participation can be interpreted either as opposition to the regime or a coerced show of support for the regime. And, as Jamal's (2007) work on social capital in authoritarian countries has shown, the role that civil society organizations play in non-democracies can be quite different than in democracies. Specifically, nondemocratic regimes tend to try to co-opt civil society organizations into the regime, using them to develop patron–client ties and to build support for the regime. Under those conditions, the question of political participation is not a free choice between alternatives, or at least the potential costs of nonparticipation or contentious participation can be much higher. Thus, in order to understand the role that associational life plays in influencing political participation in democracies, I limit the sample in this chapter to countries that are minimally democratic. Operationally, I use the Freedom House score as a cut off. Countries that score a 6 on the combined Freedom House scale of political rights and civil liberties are included.

Why look at democracies in the developing world? The empirical analysis in this chapter is also limited to developing countries, using a threshold of income per capita of $12,000 annually. This threshold is important because the analytical project here is to understand political participation outside of established, wealthy democracies. In particular, democracies in the developing world tend to be younger and have weaker political institutions – or at least there is greater concern that political institutions might fail under pressure from rapid social change or high levels of political mobilization (Huntington 1968). Although Huntington voiced this concern most strongly in the 1960s, the idea that younger, developing world democracies face particular challenges of less credible electoral competitions, corruption, lower provision of public goods, and political instability continues to find support (Keefer 2007; Keefer and Vlaicu 2008).

Limiting the sample in this way also allows for a clear comparison with the Latin American countries, which are all at least minimally democratic with incomes in this range. Some other similarities arise from setting this threshold – poor, young democracies have been fertile ground for international NGOs and foreign aid donors seeking to support local NGOs, resulting in both homegrown associations and a growing number of foreign-funded NGOs and associations. And, although NGOs are active in all these countries, there is wide variation in the quality of electoral institutions, allowing for a good test of the conditional hypothesis that NGOs have the greatest impact on protest when elections are flawed and political parties are failing to provide clear policy choices or address the salient issues in society. That is, within countries that qualify as democratic (meaning that there is minimal protection for political rights and civil liberties), there continues to be wide variation in the extent to which elections are conducted with freedom and fairness, the extent to which political parties are stable, issues-based, or coherently organized, and the extent to which elections offer real choices to people.

IS LATIN AMERICA JUST DIFFERENT?

The debates over the role that civil society plays in consolidating democracy in the developing world have not been limited to Latin America. Instead, there are active research streams on civil society, NGOs, and how they influence state–society interactions from all the regions of the developing world and Eastern Europe. This section explores how different civil society in Latin America is from civil society in other developing democracies, and what implications those differences have for our understanding of the relationship between civil society and contentious politics.

There are several important dimensions along which civil society in a country or a region can be evaluated. First, some have made the case that the overall density or strength of civil society is important for understanding the impact it is likely to have on political engagement. Where civil society organizations are abundant and active, they are much more likely to have an important influence on political life. Second, scholars point to the type of organizations that dominate the civil society scene in a country (Stolle and Rochon 1998). Are people involved mainly in very political organizations like labor unions or political parties? Or is associational life primarily organized around nonpolitical activities like church groups, sports and leisure activities, or social clubs? Are the organizations themselves very active in politics? Or is associational life quite separate from political issues?

Although there are scholars who point to the importance of civil society and associational life in every region of the world, there are also real differences in how civil society is characterized regionally. In Eastern Europe, for example, civil society organizations played a prominent role in mobilizing opposition to Communist rule and ushering in the transition to democracy (Glenn 2003). Since the transition to democracy, however, there has been a marked decline in membership in civil society organizations and today Eastern Europe is characterized as having among the lowest rates of membership in voluntary associations in the world (Howard 2003).

Recent work from both Asia and the Middle East points to the role that civil society organizations have also had in supporting authoritarian regimes, raising questions about the pro-democracy nature of civil society in those regions. For example, "significant elements supported Marcos in the early years of his dictatorship [in the Philippines]; urban groups did not oppose, and indeed welcomed, the military's seizure of power in Thailand in 1991; a substantial segment of the Indonesian middle class supported the authoritarian government of Suharto well into the 1990s" (Alagappa 2004: 7). There is also good evidence from the Middle East that civil society organizations can be important tools for authoritarian governments to maintain support in society through patron–client networks (Jamal 2007). There is also evidence comparing democracies and non-democracies around the world that membership in associations only promotes pro-democratic attitudes in already democratic countries around the world (Jamal and Nooruddin 2010).

In Africa, different scholars have characterized civil society very differently. Early work looking at the relationship between civil society in postcolonial Africa and the state saw civic organization as uniformly weak and unable to provide a counterbalance to the state. As summarized by Bratton, this literature argues, "African societies seem to possess few intermediate organizations to occupy the political space between the family ... and the state. Those civic structures that do exist are usually small in scale and local in orientation" (Bratton 1989: 411). However, Bratton makes the case that, in fact, associational life in Africa is extremely dense and politically important. He argues that voluntary organizations grew out of older societal foundations, but responded to the new pressures of urbanization and commercialization. He describes a range of associational activity in Africa, including ethnic welfare associations, prophetic movements, agricultural work parties, peasant movement, labor unions, and professional associations. And, far from being politically irrelevant, many of these organizations "became explicitly political by giving voice, first to protest at the indignities of colonial rule, and after, to the call for independence," even in some cases forming the base for political parties (1989: 411). More recent work on associational life in Africa points to very different effects for membership in different types of organization. For example, membership in religious organization is linked to lower levels of political violence, but membership in professional or business associations is linked to a heightened tendency toward violence (Backer et al. 2010).

How different is associational life in Latin America compared to these other regions in terms of the strength of civil society and the types of organizations that dominate? In brief, although there are differences in the average level of associational activity by region, and in the types of organizations that are most common, Latin America is not wildly unusual, and certainly not an outlier in a statistical sense. Figure 5.1 shows membership rates for democracies in the poorer countries of the world. The range of organizations is broad, including churches, religious groups, sports teams and clubs, recreation groups, arts organizations, music groups, educational organizations, labor unions, political parties, environmental groups, professional organizations, charitable and humanitarian groups, and consumer organizations. This broad list of clubs, organizations, and groups is intentionally wide-reaching in order to capture the many ways in which individuals organize their associational lives, from very formal types of membership (in the case of political parties) to very informal leisure-based activities such as soccer teams, book groups, prayer meetings, or choirs.

Several patterns stand out. First, associational membership in Latin America is not uniformly higher than in other regions. In fact, across all categories of organizations, membership is higher in Asia and Africa than in the Americas. Second, as the regional literature suggests, Eastern Europe shows much lower membership rates, with the exception of labor union membership, which is comparable to that in Latin America. Membership is uniformly lowest in Turkey, the only country from the North Africa/Middle East region where the World Values Survey was conducted that is included in the sample as a developing democracy. Finally, membership in religious organizations far exceeds that in all other types of organizations in the Americas, Asia, and Africa.

Another way of thinking about regional differences is to compare membership patterns by demographic groups across regions. Are there important differences in the types of people joining membership organizations in different regions? NGOs and civil society organizations in Latin America are sometimes characterized as having a strong pro-poor orientation, especially those

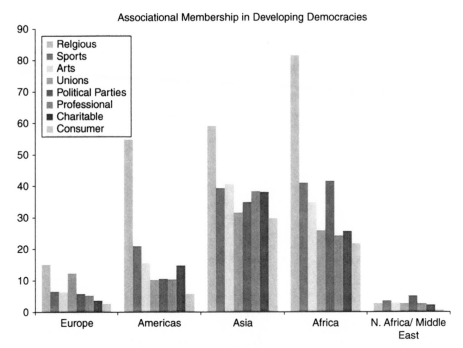

FIGURE 5.1. Membership by type and by region.
Source: World Values Survey 2005. Countries are included in the sample if they are nominally democratic (score higher than a 6 on the combined Freedom House score), and have an income below $12,000 per capita. The sample is as follows: Europe (Bulgaria, Moldova, Romania, Ukraine, 4,823 observations), Americas (Brazil, Chile, Colombia, Mexico, Peru, 8,585 observations), Asia (India, Indonesia, Thailand, 5,550 observations), Africa (Ghana, Mali, South Africa, 6,056 observations), North Africa and Middle East (Turkey, 1,346 observations).

organizations that have worked closely with excluded groups like women, indigenous groups, and the rural poor. To investigate this claim (which might explain why NGOs in Latin America seem to have such a strong effect on promoting political protest), I compare membership rates by income, gender, and educational achievement between Latin America and the world (Table 5.1). Although there are some differences, they are quite small. Membership is fairly constant across all income quintiles. Only the very wealthiest quintile shows a difference of more than 2 percent, with wealthier people participating at higher rates in Latin America.

Membership is also relatively constant across education groups, and membership is slanted toward those with more education in both the Americas and the rest of the world. The largest difference in demographic membership patterns is with respect to gender. Women in Latin America participate at a rate nearly 10 percentage points higher than women in other new democracies.

TABLE 5.1. *Are Membership Patterns Different in Latin America?*

	Americas	World	Difference
Income Quintile			
0–20	39.14	37.5	1.64
21–40	39.17	38.29	0.88
41–60	42.35	42.88	−0.53
61–80	51.35	50.68	0.67
81–100	54.33	51.95	2.38
Gender			
Women	50.81	40.82	9.99
Men	49.34	46.38	2.96
Education			
Little or none	32.49	30.84	1.65
Finished primary	42.41	37.18	5.23
Some secondary	44.15	45.48	−1.33
Finished secondary	42.82	43.07	−0.25
Some university	52.64	52.23	0.41

Men participate at nearly 3 percentage points higher, pointing to slightly higher overall membership rates.

TESTING THE EFFECT OF MEMBERSHIP ON PARTICIPATION

Although there are clearly some regional differences in the rates of membership in voluntary organizations, and in the types of organizations that have the most influence, associational organizations appear to play an important role in all developing countries around the globe. This next section turns to cross-national statistical analysis using the survey responses from the World Values Survey to explore how membership in associations affects political participation beyond just Latin America. I estimate models of voting, political protest, and all nonvoting participation using the World Values Survey data for all democratic countries in the developing world where the World Values Survey was conducted, excluding countries from Latin America.[1] As with the analysis in Chapter 4, I first explore the direct effect of membership on voting and protest. I then turn to the interaction between individual membership and the context of the quality of electoral mechanisms for participation. Overall,

[1] This sample of countries includes all democratic countries in the developing world outside of Latin America, defined as countries with incomes under $12,000 per capita and Freedom House scores higher than 6 in the combined scale of political and civil liberties. Of the countries where the World Values Survey was conducted, that leaves eleven countries: Bulgaria, Ghana, India, Indonesia, Mali, Moldova, Romania, South Africa, Thailand, Turkey, and Ukraine.

the patterns from developing democracies in the World Values Survey sample are remarkably consistent with what we see in the Latinobarómetro survey, in terms both of the direct relationship (that high rates of membership are consistently related to political protest) and of the conditional relationship (that membership has a declining effect on protest as electoral institutions improve).

Measuring Political Action with the World Values Survey

The World Values Survey does not ask a direct question about contact with NGOs, but it does include a range of questions on associational membership. Respondents are first asked whether they have done any of the listed political actions, or whether they might do it, or whether they would never under any circumstances do it. The actions listed include signing a petition, joining in boycotts, attending peaceful demonstrations, or "other." The respondents are then asked "have you or have you not done any of these activities in the last five years?" for the same list of possible political actions. A different question asked is whether the respondent voted in the last election. Using these questions, I construct dichotomous variables for voting, protest (in this case, peaceful demonstrations, which is the closest question to a protest question), joining boycotts, and signing petitions. Because there might be some reluctance to admit to participating in demonstrations, boycotts, or even signing petitions, I code one indicator that captures whether respondents answered that they "might" or "have" participated in any of these political actions, and a separate indicator based on the question of whether they have participated. I also construct a combined indicator for whether the respondent participated in any of the nonvoting political actions listed, as a way to measure participation outside of electoral channels.

Measuring Membership in Civil Society

The question about membership in voluntary organizations that best captures involvement with NGOs and civil society organization asks respondents about active membership and inactive membership in a variety of organizations. A response is recorded for each of the following organizations: church or religious organizations; sport or recreational organization; art, music, or educational organization; labor union; political party; environmental organization; professional association; humanitarian or charitable organization; consumer organization; or other. To capture involvement in this wide range of activities, I construct a measure for membership in any organization, which is coded 1 if the respondent is either an active or inactive member in any of the organizations listed. Then, to capture only those who are actively involved, I construct a measure of active membership, which includes only respondents who stated they are active members of any of the organizations.

Although associational membership includes involvement in many organizations that would not be considered NGOs, it does capture most NGO activity as well. In developing countries, where NGOs are usually defined as having some development-oriented mission, the categories here can be quite overlapping. For example, Catholic Relief Services is a worldwide NGO that is sponsored by the Catholic Church and runs a variety of service programs in most developing countries. Respondents who say that they are members of a religious association may be referring to attending church services, but they may also be referring to participating in a religious NGO. Evangelical and other Christian churches also frequently have affiliations with service NGOs in developing countries. Other categories are similarly ambiguous. An environmental advocacy group, for example, may or may not be classified as an NGO, depending on the type of activities in which it is engaged. Overall, it is important to bear in mind that these questions tap into a broad range of associational activity, but the details of each organization in the broad categories may vary widely.

FINDINGS: DOES MEMBERSHIP INCREASE PROTEST? VOTING?

Even in a simple scatterplot of the average rates of active membership and the average rates of protest by country for people who "might" or "have" participated in demonstrations, boycotts, or signed petitions, a relationship between the two is evident. Figure 5.2 plots the percentage of respondents who are active members for each country against the percentage of respondents who protested. A pattern is clearly visible: Countries with higher rates of involvement with voluntary organizations also tend to have higher rates of participation in protest activities. The pattern is similar if the measure for protest that counts only respondents who claim to have participated in demonstrations is used.

One interesting exception to the trend is Thailand, which shows very high membership rates, and relatively low protest rates. However, since 2005 when this survey was conducted, Thailand has frequently been in the news for widespread anti-government demonstrations and protests. Thailand adopted a new constitution in 1997 and in 2001 held the first democratic elections under the new rules. In 2005 the second election was held, and hopes were high for the democratic process. The candidate who won the election in 2005 was also a populist pro-poor politician, who devoted serious time and energy to building support in the poor rural areas of Thailand where NGOs have been most active in mobilizing participation. He won the election in February 2005 in a landslide. He then instituted a series of pro-poor policies, including a health program and village-level development funds, declaring that by 2009 "there would be no poor people" in Thailand. This is the year of the World Values Survey showing high levels of membership activity and low levels of political protest – a moment when the future of electoral democracy in Thailand was looking bright.

Things quickly changed – in 2006 there was a coup d'état, and the military took control of the government, ousting Prime Minister Thaksin Shinawatra.

FIGURE 5.2. Membership and protest rates by country.

A new constitution was approved in 2007, and Thailand has been in a near constant state of political upheaval since then, including a dramatic increase in the incidences of street protests. Between 2008 and 2010, protests led by a group called "Red Shirts" (frequently wearing red shirts) in support of the ousted prime minister frequently clashed with government forces, with rising fatalities. Tens of thousands have protested and dozens were killed.

It is also clear that NGOs have played a role in mobilizing protests in Thailand, even before the violent protest of the last few years. Since the 1990s, NGOs have been involved in protests at both the national and local level as an extension of their advocacy work on environmental issues, opposing dam projects, and demanding land right (Dechalert 1999). As a member of the senate explained: "The relationship between the Thai state and civil society is not always an easy one. The government often sees the NGOs as ill-informed adversaries [who constitute] an obstacle to state plans. For their part, civil society groups need to learn how to use the right to assemble and articulate their demands through the free press before resorting to acts of civil disobedience... without willingness to compromise in reasonable ways, conflict is inevitable" (Boontun Dockthaisong, second vice president of the senate, Thailand, 2000 – cited in Alagappa 2004: 2).

NGOs also played a role in negotiating the 1997 constitution, and continue to be especially active in protests around the environmental movement. Despite appearing as an outlier Figure 5.2, anecdotally at least, Thailand actually fits the model here quite well. There are strong suggestions from experts in the field that NGOs play a role in mobilizing protest activity across a range of issues, but protests have been most prevalent during times when electoral mechanisms were failing. However, because Thailand does appear as an outlier, I estimated all the models in this chapter both with and without including Thailand. And, even though the number of countries is quite small, the findings hold both with Thailand and without Thailand in the models.

Multilevel Models of Membership and Participation

To test the relationship between membership and political protest more systematically, I estimate multilevel mixed effects logistic regression models of participation in the following political actions: voting, peaceful demonstrations, signing a petition, joining a boycott, or a summary indicator of participation in any of the nonvoting political actions. The Latin American countries where the World Values Survey was conducted are not included in these models so as to make a clear comparison between Latin America and other regions.[2] Several patterns stand out. First, membership in associations is a positive and significant predictor of participation in all the nonvoting types of participation (signing a petition, joining a peaceful demonstration, or joining a boycott). The effect of membership on voting, however, is not significant. Just as we see in Latin America, involvement with civil society organizations has a larger and more consistent effect on protest behavior than it does on voter turnout in developing democracies.

The model is specified to include measures of other factors that the literature on participation has pointed to as important predictors of individual level behavior, including the demographic factors of gender, age, education, income and characteristics of the individual including overall satisfaction with life, trust in government, interpersonal trust, political ideology, and political interest. As participation in one political activity may also be a good predictor of participation in others, I also include a measure of voting in the nonvoting models, and a measure of protest in the voting model.

These factors predict voting in expected ways, with a few interesting caveats. People with a high level of interest in politics are not surprisingly more likely to vote and more likely to participate in other political actions. Likewise, more educated people are more likely to participate across all types of political action.

---

[2] Estimating the models for the Latin American countries using the World Values Survey data yields results very similar to those presented in Chapter 4 – Membership is a significant predictor of protest activity in Brazil, Chile, Colombia, Mexico, and Peru when estimated using either logistic regression by country, or using multilevel mixed-effects logistic regression, with the same control variables as in Table 5.1.

The models of nonvoting participation show some interesting differences from the model of voting, although the models are remarkably consistent across the different types of nonvoting participation. Many of the individual-level control factors actually have the opposite effect in models of nonvoting participation. For example, men and women appear to vote at roughly equal rates, but men are far more likely to protest than are women. And, though older folks are more likely to vote, younger people are more likely to participate in demonstrations, sign petitions, or join boycotts. And people on the left of the political spectrum are more likely to protest, but there is no systematic difference between those on the left versus the right in terms of voting.

The models in Table 5.2 are estimated using the measure of participation that captures those who "might" or "have" participated, but the result that membership is positively associated with every nonvoting mode of participation holds to the more stringent specification of "has" protested as well. Table 5.3 presents the same models, but using the measure based on whether a respondent has participated in the political action in the last five years. Across all three models the effect of membership in associations on attending peaceful demonstrations, signing petitions, or joining boycotts not only remains significant but the size of the coefficient also increases. The relationship between membership in associations and protest is even stronger for those who say they have protested than it is for those who say they might protest.

Because the sample includes only eleven countries from regions around the world, it is helpful to look at the relationship between membership, voting, and protest for each country as well as the aggregate patterns. Figure 5.3 summarizes the results of the full logistic regression by country for the key variables of interest. Although membership has no effect on voting or protests in two countries (Bulgaria and South Africa), in every other country in the sample membership in associations is a good predictor of participation on political protest. Interestingly, membership increases the likelihood of voting in only two countries (Romania and Thailand). Despite the small number of countries represented here, the pattern is remarkably similar to what we observe in Latin America – in almost every case membership in associations increases the likelihood of political protest, while the effect on voting is much less consistent.

FINDINGS: DOES IT MATTER HOW WELL ELECTIONS ARE WORKING?

There is good evidence that the relationship between associational membership and political protest activity is not limited to Latin America – on the contrary, it seems that membership in voluntary organizations is a strong predictor of political protest across democracies in the developing world. This finding in itself is interesting because it counters the popular notion that NGOs, civil

TABLE 5.2. *Logistic Regression: The Effect of Membership on Different Types of Participation*

	"Might" or "Has" Participated in the Following			
	Voted	Signed a Petition	Peaceful Demonstrations	Boycott
Membership	0.160	0.651***	0.703***	0.570***
	(0.100)	(0.071)	(0.071)	(0.075)
Female	0.092	−0.334***	−0.333***	−0.348***
	(0.054)	(0.042)	(0.042)	(0.044)
Age	0.056***	−0.008***	−0.015***	−0.014***
	(0.002)	(0.001)	(0.001)	(0.002)
Education	0.181**	0.473***	0.416***	0.253***
	(0.062)	(0.048)	(0.048)	(0.051)
Income	−0.037**	0.030**	0.022*	0.020
	(0.013)	(0.010)	(0.010)	(0.011)
Life Satisfaction	0.009	−0.018	−0.041***	−0.029**
	(0.012)	(0.009)	(0.010)	(0.010)
Trust in Government	−0.089**	0.100***	0.067**	0.125***
	(0.030)	(0.024)	(0.024)	(0.025)
Interpersonal Trust	0.056	−0.030	−0.048	−0.049
	(0.073)	(0.052)	(0.052)	(0.056)
Ideology	0.012	−0.020*	−0.022*	−0.023*
	(0.012)	(0.009)	(0.009)	(0.009)
Political Interest	0.251***	0.315***	0.358***	0.373***
	(0.029)	(0.022)	(0.023)	(0.024)
Peaceful Demonstration	0.140*			
	(0.056)			
Voted		0.081	0.157**	0.238***
		(0.056)	(0.056)	(0.060)
Constant	−1.071***	−1.625***	−1.090***	−1.972***
	(0.318)	(0.221)	(0.215)	(0.224)
No. of Countries	11	11	11	11
N	11015	11015	11015	11015

Note: *P < 0.10; **P < 0.05; ***P < 0.01. Table entries are maximum likelihood estimates with estimated standard errors in parentheses generated using the command xtmelogit in Stata 10. Countries are included in the sample if they are nominally democratic (score higher than a 6 on the combined Freedom House score), and have an income below $12,000 per capita. The countries included are Bulgaria, Ghana, India, Indonesia, Mali, Moldova, Romania, South Africa, Thailand, Turkey, and Ukraine.

society organizations, and other voluntary associations work as moderating forces in younger democracies. Instead, it suggests that involvement in voluntary groups does many of the things that the associational literature argues it should – members are more involved in politics than nonmembers, have higher

TABLE 5.3. *Effect of Membership on Different Types of Participation*

	"Has" Participated in the Following		
	Peaceful Demonstrations	Signed a Petition	Joined a Boycott
Membership in Association	1.132***	1.024***	0.975***
	(0.120)	(0.123)	(0.180)
Female	−0.271***	−0.207**	−0.411***
	(0.060)	(0.065)	(0.084)
Age	−0.010***	0.004	−0.006*
	(0.002)	(0.002)	(0.003)
High School Education	0.455***	0.558***	0.304***
	(0.069)	(0.074)	(0.091)
Scale of Incomes	0.022	0.068***	0.008
	(0.014)	(0.016)	(0.020)
Life Satisfaction	−0.038**	−0.009	−0.031
	(0.013)	(0.015)	(0.018)
Confidence in Government	0.103**	0.197***	0.056
	(0.033)	(0.036)	(0.045)
Interpersonal Trust	−0.056	0.115	−0.117
	(0.072)	(0.077)	(0.101)
Ideology	0.002	0.016	−0.007
	(0.012)	(0.014)	(0.017)
Political Interest	0.419***	0.382***	0.436***
	(0.033)	(0.036)	(0.046)
Voted	0.430***	0.009	0.391***
	(0.085)	(0.088)	(0.117)
Constant	−4.210***	−5.005***	−4.699***
	(0.272)	(0.410)	(0.433)
N	11015	9778	9711

Note: $*P < 0.10$; $**P < 0.05$; $***P < 0.01$. Table entries are maximum likelihood estimates with estimated standard errors in parentheses generated using the command xtmelogit in Stata 10. Countries are included in the sample if they are nominally democratic (score higher than a 6 on the combined Freedom House score), and have an income below $12,000 per capita. The countries included are Bulgaria, Ghana, India, Indonesia, Mali, Moldova, Romania, South Africa, Thailand, Turkey, and Ukraine.

rates of political interest, and more likely to participate across the political spectrum, but that participation is channeled through a variety of paths. In fact the effect of membership on voting is relatively weak when compared with the effect of membership on demonstrating, boycotting, or signing petitions. This is quite a different view of the kind of political action that civil society facilitates than much of the literature on NGOs, associational activity, and civil society would expect.

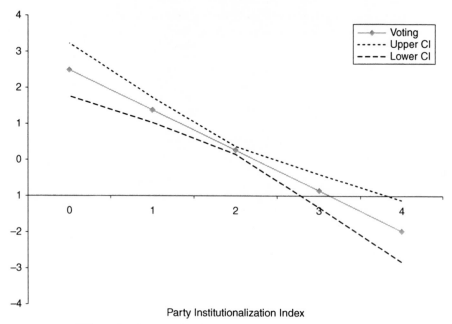

FIGURE 5.3. Effect of active membership on protest.

I have made the case that how NGO activity is translated into political action is shaped in large part by how well the democratic institutions of participation – electoral institutions and political parties in particular – are functioning. This is not to make the case that the individual activities, political leanings, or degree of activism do not matter. They quite obviously do matter. But there is also abundant evidence that the influence organizations have is not limited to their stated goals or outright activist pursuits. On the contrary – and this is the core of many of the arguments that claim that associations are the key to understanding stable civil society – organizations shape the interactions of citizens and the engagement with the state even when their stated political aims are very limited. That is, even organizations that seek a low profile, never actively engage in politics, do not offer workshops on political engagement, and so forth still bring resources into a community, and more importantly create associational space where neighbors and community members can talk (while waiting in line for a vaccine, for example, or attending a public meeting on a proposed irrigation scheme). This simple interaction, talking between neighbors in an environment with the suggestion of solving problems, facilitates political action because those neighbors who do run into each other at an NGO office are more likely to discuss shared problems and trust each other enough to try to do something about them than neighbors who have had no such opportunity.

Because this is not inherently a story about activist NGOs, understanding the political context in which NGOs are operating is crucial to understanding their likely political effects – especially how they influence individual decisions about voting and protesting. I have made the case that NGO activity stimulates political activity – it simply makes it easier for people to engage in politics. If you live in a neighborhood where many NGOs are working, your chance of knowing your neighbors, knowing something of the problems facing your community, and deciding to take some action is higher than it would be if you live in a neighborhood with no NGOs, community organizations, or voluntary associations. But the choice about how you are going to proceed – are you going to vote? Are you going to sign a petition? March to the capital? Throw rocks and break windows? – That choice is shaped by which options seem most effective. Obviously, the context of this decision is a vastly complex one involving a host of impulses, weighing costs and benefits, and practical considerations, but in general we can expect that in cases where electoral mechanisms are respected as important, effective tools for communicating discontent and pushing for policy changes, people who are motivated to participate are more likely to vote. In contrast, in cases where elections are viewed as hopelessly rigged, corrupt, or irrelevant to the real policy issues at stake, it is more likely that people will pursue other tactics.

In this chapter, I look to the data from the World Values Survey to ask whether this conditional part of the argument also applies outside of Latin America. If so, we should expect that membership in associations has more of an effect on political protest in countries where democratic institutions are struggling and where elections are viewed with suspicion. To explore how well this conditional hypothesis travels outside of Latin America, I return to the type of multilevel models used in Chapter 4 to incorporate country-level characteristics into the equation. For ease of comparison, the models shown here are very similar to the models of voting and protest earlier in this chapter and in Chapter 4. And, to capture the conditional effect of membership in civil society organizations on participation, I include an interaction term between membership and the Party Institutionalization Index.[3] This index, available from the Inter-American Development Bank, is a good measure of how well democratic institutions surrounding elections are working overall. It includes indicators of confidence in elections, party system stability, age and the extent to which political parties represent real interests in society, and electoral fraud (Berkman et al. 2008). The index ranges from 1 to 5, and indicates

---

[3] Because of the small number of countries, it is difficult to include multiple country-level factors in the same model. Because the Party Institutionalization Index captures the most important elements of how well electoral institutions are working, I present those models here. However, the individual level results hold with the inclusion of several other country-level factors, including Freedom House democracy scores, a dichotomous variable for laws on compulsory voting, the Human Development Indicators combined index, and a measure of the mean membership rates by country.

TABLE 5.4. *Relationship between Active Membership, Voting, and Protest*

Country	Effect on Protest	Effect on Voting	No. of Respondents
Bulgaria	−	−	530
Ghana	+	−	706
India	+	−	725
Indonesia	+	−	1,185
Mali	−	−	572
Moldova	+	+	765
Romania	+	−	735
South Africa	−	−	2,286
Thailand	+	+	1,475
Turkey	+	−	1,081
Ukraine	+	−	476

Note: "+" indicates a positive and significant coefficient ($P < 0.01$) in the country-specific fully specified logistic regression with robust standard errors. "−" indicates no statistically significant relationship.

the overall quality of electoral institutions based on confidence in elections, the age of the party system, the degree to which parties represent real interests in society, vote volatility, and whether the elections are considered free and fair. Low numbers indicate poor performance, and high numbers indicate good performance.

Table 5.4 presents the results of multilevel models estimated using the xtmelogit command in Stata 10 with cross-level interaction terms between individual membership and the Party Institutionalization Index. As expected with such a small number of countries (the sample includes 11 countries), the country-level factor Party Institutionalization is not significant. To get a better sense of what the model tells us about the effect of membership under different conditions of democratic functioning, I graph the marginal effects of membership on political protest at different levels of the Party Institutionalization Index. The graph shows a clear negative trend – at low levels of the Party Institutionalization Index (where confidence in elections is low, political parties are young and unstable and claim only tenuous ties to real interests in society) membership in associations has the strongest effect on protest (Table 5.5). As the Party Institutionalization Index increases, the effect of membership weakens, until it becomes insignificant at an index score of 4. In other words, when elections and political parties seem to be working well as mechanisms for communicating to the state, membership in civil society does not predict protest behavior. The marginal effect of membership on voting is not significant at any values of the Party Institutionalization Index, which is not surprising given the weak significance of the relationship between membership and voting in most of the models estimated in this chapter.

TABLE 5.5. *Interactive Models with Party Institutionalization*

	Voted	Protest
Active Membership in Association	0.516	2.499***
	(0.443)	(0.374)
Active Member × Party Institutionalization	−0.205	−1.117***
	(0.235)	(0.200)
Female	0.085	−0.339***
	(0.056)	(0.042)
Age	0.057***	−0.015***
	(0.002)	(0.001)
Education	0.174**	0.406***
	(0.063)	(0.048)
Income	−0.036**	0.020*
	(0.014)	(0.010)
Life Satisfaction	0.010	−0.045***
	(0.013)	(0.010)
Confidence in Government	−0.086**	0.070**
	(0.031)	(0.024)
Trust in People	0.074	−0.043
	(0.075)	(0.052)
Ideology	0.013	−0.023**
	(0.012)	(0.009)
Political Interest	0.233***	0.353***
	(0.030)	(0.023)
Would Likely Demonstrate	0.146***	
	(0.041)	
Voted		0.154**
		(0.056)
Country-Level Factors		
Party Institutionalization	0.484	0.519
	(0.992)	(0.696)
Variance Components		
Country-Level	.012	.010
	(0.005)	(0.004)
Observations	10538	11015
No. of Countries	11	11
−2 × Log likelihood	8456.4772	13593.5738

Notes: *P < 0.10; **P < 0.05; ***P < 0.01. Individual level models estimated using logistic regression. Multilevel models estimated using the command xtmelogit in Stata 10. Standard errors in parentheses.

ALTERNATIVE EXPLANATIONS

There are a few other alternative explanations that warrant discussion. Thus far, this chapter has made the case that the effect of civil society organizations on protest when democratic institutions are not working well is not limited to Latin America, but rather can be found in minimally democratic countries across the developing world. Here I consider three alternative explanations for this finding. First, contrary to my argument that many types of associations stimulate protest under the right conditions, it is possible that the findings mentioned in the preceding text are picking up the effect of just a few types of organizations. Second, I explore the effect of other country-level factors, including the level of democracy at the national level, compulsory voting laws, government performance at the national level (measured using the Human Development Index), and the overall density of civil society organizations in the country.

Do all types of organizations have the same effect? To explore this possibility, I look at the effect of membership in each type of organization separately. Membership in all types of organizations is positively associated with political protest, including church groups, art organizations, charity groups, consumer organizations, sports clubs, and professional organizations. Interestingly, not all organizations are associated with an increase in voting – although churches, unions, political parties, environmental groups, and professional organizations are. Breaking out the effect of membership in different types of organizations confirms the larger story that the effect on protest is largely through indirect mechanisms. It is not just unions and political parties that rally people to protest, but membership in any type of organization. Voting, on the other hand, is more influenced by membership in the more overtly political organizations such as unions and political parties.

Do the main results hold with the inclusion of other country-level factors? As with the results in Chapter 4, the individual results hold with the inclusion of several additional country-level factors, including the overall level of democracy (measured using the combined Freedom House score), compulsory voting laws, government performance (measured using the Human Development Index), and the overall density of civil society (measured using the average membership rates by country). With the exception of compulsory voting's effect on voter turnout, none of the country-level variables are statistically significant, which is unsurprising given the low number of countries. But more importantly, the individual-level results that membership encourages protest hold in each of these specifications.

CONCLUSIONS

Exploring the effect of membership in associations on political action in democratic countries from all regions of the developing world accomplishes three things. First, it allows for a test of how generalizable the findings from Latin America are to other contexts and provides strong evidence that associational life influences political participation across the developing world in predictable ways. On this count, I find strong confirmation that these relationships hold in developing democracies around the globe and that Latin America is not an exception. Using a broad measure of membership in voluntary associations, which includes many NGOs, but also includes sports clubs, community groups, professional organization, and the like, I find a relationship to political action similar to that we see for NGOs in Latin America in Chapter 4 – people who are involved in associations are more likely to demonstrate, more likely to petition, and more likely to boycott than their counterparts who are not involved with any association. This is good evidence that the relationship is a broad one, and most likely not driven by a few activist organizations, but instead reflects a broad tendency for people involved in organizations to be more involved in contentious political action.

Second, In Latin America, NGOs are associated with a pro-poor orientation, and with bringing in new voices to the political system. This chapter explores whether this is true of associations outside of Latin America, and what that means for the theory. If we can observe the same direct effect on protest, and the conditional effect that protest is more likely where institutions are not working well, and the associations involved are NOT pro-poor, that is good evidence that associational activity matters across the board – and that the context is the key factor.

Finally, looking at membership and participation outside of Latin America allows for a test of several alternative explanations for the findings presented earlier. Primarily, this chapter offers strong evidence that the relationship between NGOs and political protest cannot be attributed solely to activist NGOs in Latin America. Rather, we observe similar patterns in countries where civil society is characterized very differently. Although this relationship is strong and consistent, membership has the greatest impact on political protest in countries where elections work the worst, suggesting that the context of how well democratic institutions are functioning is an important factor in shaping how participatory energy sparked by associations will ultimately be channeled into action. In countries where elections are functioning quite well, and people have confidence in them, there is little relationship between membership and protest, as people have little reason to turn to contentious political action.

What does it mean if we find broad patterns across all these types of organizations? Finding a broader pattern linking associational activity to political protest outside of Latin America is good evidence that the mechanisms involved have less to do with the specific activities of the organization, and more to do with the broader context of institutional performance. That is, NGOs do not just motivate people to engage in contentious politics because they are directly mobilizing them to do so – they also facilitate contentious political action through other mechanisms of information, trust, and lowering barriers to collective action. This is not to say that the type of organization does not matter, but in broad trends the differences in who is a member, the type of membership, and so forth matter far less for predicting political protest than the context of how well the elections are working.

APPENDIX 5.1. *Data Appendix (World Values Survey 2005 Analysis)*
Individual-Level Questions from 2005–2006 World Values Survey

Membership in Associations	Now I am going to read off a list of voluntary organizations. For each one, could you tell me whether you are an active member, an inactive member or not a member of that type of organization?
	(a) Church or religious organization, (b) Sport or recreational organization, (c) Art, music, or educational organization, (d) Labor union, (e) Political party, (f) Environmental organization, (g) Professional association, (h) Humanitarian or charitable organization, (i) Consumer organization, (j) other.
	From this list, a dichotomous indicator for membership in associations was created with individuals who indicated having been an active member or an inactive member coded as 1 and not a member coded as 0.
Active Membership in Associations	Now I am going to read off a list of voluntary organizations. For each one, could you tell me whether you are an active member, an inactive member, or not a member of that type of organization?
	(a) Church or religious organization, (b) Sport or recreational organization, (c) Art, music, or educational organization, (d) Labor union, (e) Political party, (f) Environmental organization, (g) Professional association, (h) Humanitarian or charitable organization, (i) Consumer organization, (j) other.
	From this list, a dichotomous indicator for **active** membership in associations was created with individuals who indicated having been an active member coded as 1 and those who indicated they were an inactive member or not a member coded as 0.
Female	Sex? (0) Male, (1) Female
Education	What is the highest educational level that you have attained? 1, No formal education; 2, Incomplete primary school; 3, Complete primary school; 4, Incomplete secondary school: technical/vocational type; 5, Complete secondary school: technical/vocational type; 6, Incomplete secondary: university – preparatory type; 7, Complete secondary: university – preparatory type; 8, Some university-level education, without degree; 9, University-level education, with degree.

Income	On this card is a scale of incomes on which 1 indicates the "lowest income decile" and 10 the "highest income decile" in your country. We would like to know in what group your household is. Please specify the appropriate number, counting all wages, salaries, pensions, and other incomes that come in.
Life Satisfaction	All things considered, how satisfied are you with your life as a whole these days? Using this card on which 1 means you are "completely dissatisfied" and 10 means you are "completely satisfied" where would you put your satisfaction with your life as a whole?
Trust in Government	Could you tell me how much confidence you have in the government: 1, is it a great deal of confidence; 2, quite a lot of confidence; 3, not very much confidence; or 4, none at all.
Interpersonal Trust	Generally speaking, would you say that most people can be trusted or that you need to be very careful in dealing with people? 0, Need to be very careful; 1, Most people can be trusted.
Left–Right Ideology	In political matters, people talk of "the left" and "the right." How would you place your views on this scale, generally speaking? (0) 0 Left, (1) 1, (2) 2, (3) 3, (4) 4, (5) 5, (6) 6, (7) 7, (8) 8, (9) 9, (10) 10 Right.
Political Interest	How interested would you say you are in politics? 1, Not at all interested; 2, Not very interested; 3, Somewhat interested; 4, Very interested.
Sign a Petition	Now I'd like you to look at this card. I'm going to read out some forms of political action that people can take, and I'd like you to tell me, for each one, whether you have done any of these things, whether you might do it, or would never under any circumstances do it.
Joining in a Boycott	Now I'd like you to look at this card. I'm going to read out some forms of political action that people can take, and I'd like you to tell me, for each one, whether you have done any of these things, whether you might do it, or would never under any circumstances do it. Joining in boycotts: 1, Have; 2, Might do; 0, would never do.
Protest	Now I'd like you to look at this card. I'm going to read out some forms of political action that people can take, and I'd like you to tell me, for each one, whether you have done any of these things, whether you might do it, or would never under any circumstances do it. Attending peaceful demonstrations: 1, Have; 2, Might do; 0, Would never do.
Voting	Did you vote in your country's recent elections to the national parliament? 1, Yes; 0, No.

APPENDIX 5.1. *(continued)*

Country-Level Variables

Party Institutionalization	Index of five variables, compiled by Berkman et al. (2008): 1. To what extent is there a stable, moderate, and socially rooted party system to articulate and aggregate societal interests (BTI 2006)? 2. *Confidence:* Shared Global Indicators Cross-National Database/ World Values Survey: "How much confidence do you have in the political parties?" 3. *Vote Volatility* (Pederson 1983) 4. *Free and fair elections:* "To what extent are political leaders determined by general, free and fair elections?" (Profils Institutionnels 2006) 5. *Party Age:* (Database of Political Institutions 1990–2004)
Freedom House	Freedom House political rights and civil liberties scores were combined to create a 12-point scale with 12 representing "most free." (Source: Freedom House 2010).
Compulsory Voting	Coded 1 if the country has compulsory voting rules that are enforced, 0 if voting is not compulsory or is not enforced. (Source: IDEA).
Human Development Combined Index	The Human Development Index is a composite summary index that measures human develop for a country along three dimensions: long and healthy life, access to knowledge and a decent standard of living. (Source: United Nations Development Program).
Civil Society Density	Country mean of individuals reporting having belonged to a membership organization.
Rule of Law	An index from World Bank "capturing perceptions of the extent to which agents have confidence in and abide by the rules of society, and in particular the quality of contract enforcement, property rights, the police, and the courts, as well as the likelihood of crime and violence" (World Bank 2012).
Control of Corruption	An index from the World Bank "capturing perceptions of the extent to which public power is exercised for private gain, including both petty and grand forms of corruption, as well as "capture" of the state by elites and private interests" (World Bank 2012).
Government Effectiveness	An index from the World Bank capturing perceptions of the quality of public services, the quality of the civil service and the degree of its independence from political pressures, the quality of policy formulation and implementation, and the credibility of the government's commitment to such policies (World Bank 2012).
Good Governance	Average of scores on Rule of Law, Control of Corruption, and Government Effectiveness (World Bank 2012).

APPENDIX 5.2. *Summary Statistics (World Values Survey, 2005)*

Variable	Obs	Mean	Std. Dev.	Min.	Max.
Participation Variables					
Voted	25,173	0.800	0.400	0	1
"Might" or "Has" Participated in the Following:					
Authorized Demonstrations	26,471	0.451	0.498	0	1
Petitions	26,471	0.461	0.498	0	1
Boycott	26,471	0.252	0.434	0	1
"Has" Participated in the Following:					
Petition	20,365	0.166	0.372	0	1
Boycott	19,498	0.062	0.240	0	1
Authorized Demonstrations	26,360	0.123	0.328	0	1
Membership Variables					
Member	26,286	0.740	0.439	0	1
Active Member	26,286	0.457	0.498	0	1
Church	26,165	0.518	0.500	0	1
Sports	26,002	0.257	0.437	0	1
Arts	26,000	0.227	0.419	0	1
Union	25,948	0.181	0.385	0	1
Political	25,986	0.214	0.410	0	1
Professional	25,891	0.180	0.384	0	1
Charity	25,866	0.194	0.395	0	1
Consumer	25,658	0.135	0.342	0	1
Other	16,272	0.087	0.282	0	1
Control Variables					
Female	26,351	0.512	0.500	0	1
Age	26,235	39.964	15.933	15	97
Education	26,145	0.517	0.500	0	1
Income	24,613	4.337	2.407	1	10
Life Satisfaction	25,832	6.878	2.428	1	10
Trust in Government	25,189	2.531	0.947	1	4
Interpersonal Trust	26,361	0.180	0.384	0	1
Ideology	19,322	5.997	2.518	1	10
Political Interest	26,361	2.216	1.022	0	4
Country-Level Variables					
Party Institutionalization Index	26,467	1.844	0.208	0	3.058897
Freedom House	26,360	9.471	1.258	7	12
Compulsory Voting	26,361	0.203	0.402	0	1
HDI Combined	26,361	0.724	0.128	0.361	0.942

6

Civil Society, Protest, and Attitudes toward Democracy

How does civil society affect support for the political system in weakly democratic countries? Many have argued that civil society (made up of non-governmental organizations [NGOs] and other associational organizations) provides a bedrock of moderate, stable support for democratic political systems. Civil society organizations, by providing forums for interactions that build trust and demonstrate the value of democratic decision making, are cited as the key to making democracy work (Putnam 1993) or even a necessary precondition for democratic consolidation (Diamond 1999; Linz and Stepan 1996). Others, however, are more skeptical. Since Huntington (1968) first suggested that political mobilization may have a dark side in political instability, there has been some skepticism of civil society organizations as benevolent promoters of democratic stability. The research presented thus far in this book demonstrates that NGOs and civil society organizations do more to promote political protest in most young democracies than they do to encourage voting. This link is strongest in the weakest democracies where concerns over political instability may be higher.

This chapter explores the relationship between involvement in civil society and support for the political system at the individual level in the context of weakly democratic countries. In democratic systems where the institutions are failing, what is the relationship between associational activity and support for the political system? In the eyes of some observers, NGOs and civil society organizations earned a reputation as radical groups of agitating citizens. This view portrays civil society as undermining the stability of government – a vast departure from the rosier view that civil society fosters democracy. This view

Portions of this chapter are included in the forthcoming article "Civil Society and Support for the Political System in Times of Crisis" in *Latin American Research Review* (2014) 49 (1), co-authored with Jami Nuñez.

assumes that because civil society helps to articulate dissent against particular policies and leaders, it also erodes the deeper relationship between citizens and the democratic political system. This chapter explores the validity of these two opposing views of civil society. How does membership in civil society organizations affect the deeper level of support for the democratic political system in weakly democratic settings?

The focus here is on diffuse support for the political system rather than attitudes toward democracy or other indicators of regime legitimacy because I believe diffuse support is a good indicator of generalized support for the institutions and form of government in place, something that might be under question during times of political crises. Because discussions of democracy are often politicized on many dimensions of political debate and ideology, generalized system support is more what we are interested in. Focusing on diffuse support also allows us to compare diffuse support with more specific forms of support that are based on performance evaluations of government (Canache 2002).

Rather than seeing civil society as consistently supportive or consistently undermining of democratic political system, I argue that membership in associations can build support for the political system during times of crisis at the same time it can encourage dissatisfaction with governments that are performing poorly. Membership serves as a source of information and reduces barriers to collective action, making political participation more likely. Where civil society is playing this role of facilitating new political participation – even of contentious and critical voices – I argue that it is also likely building diffuse support for a democratic political system that allows dissent without direct repression. That is, where civil society is facilitating engagement into politics, members are more likely to be supportive of the system even if they are more critical of specific policies, politicians, or processes. This dynamic is likely to hold as long as the state does not resort to systematic repression of opposition voices or protests (i.e., as long as the regime remains minimally democratic).

This chapter approaches these questions through an exploration of the case of Bolivia during the first decade of the 21st century. First, I explore the dramatic role of political protests in shaping the upheaval of national politics in Bolivia, beginning with protests in 2000 over water privatization that grew to include widespread dissatisfaction with the incumbent government. Major political changes followed, including the resignation of Sánchez de Lozada and the election of Evo Morales. These waves of protest, which were largely mobilized through a variety of civil society organizations, were surprisingly effective both in terms of changing policies and eventually in terms of changing the government. The political changes that resulted represented a major shift in Bolivian politics toward the inclusion of the poor and indigenous majority who had long been excluded from formal political participation. The combination of protest and electoral strategies that resulted in the election of Evo Morales also seriously disrupted "politics as usual" in Bolivia, and garnered warnings of imminent democratic breakdown. Democracy, however, persisted and contentious politics remains a central strategy both for government supporters and increasingly for members of the new opposition.

Second, I turn to survey evidence from Latin American Public Opinion Project (LAPOP) to explore the relationship between membership in civil society and support for the political system during a year of particularly intense political crisis: 2004. In this year, social movements of the poor, indigenous, workers, and students regularly took to the streets to make demands on the government. The government, still reeling from the resignation of President Sanchez de Lozada under pressure from the popular protests in 2003, was paralyzed. After the violent clashes between the military and the protesters in 2003, the new president, Carlos Mesa, had promised not to use force against the social movements. Marches and demonstrations shut down roads all over the country on an almost daily basis.

I find that on average, individuals who frequently attend meetings of civil society organizations are more inclined to support the political system than those who attend only occasionally or who are not involved in civil society. Active membership is associated with higher rates of protest participation: people who are frequently involved with civil society organizations are more likely to protest *and* more likely to support the political system in times of crisis. Comparing a crisis year (2004) with a non-crisis year (2008) shows that although membership is associated with broad support for the political system in both years, it is associated with positive assessments of government only in the non-crisis year. This relationship holds even among the most dissatisfied citizens, including those who have recently protested against the government. Although this chapter focuses on Bolivia as an important case, I also consider how these results might hold in other contexts. Survey data from most similar country in crisis, Ecuador in 2010, shows very similar relationships.

Overall, this chapter gives a surprising image of the role civil society played in the political upheavals in Bolivia, and suggests that high levels of civic engagement and social mobilization are not incompatible with support for a democratic political system – even during times of political crisis in weakly democratic countries. Despite extremely high levels of mobilization, extreme dissatisfaction with government, and evidence that membership in associations actively facilitates political protest, civil society continues to be positively associated with support for the political system. Even more surprising, this relationship is not a function of wealthier, more conservative people being more likely to join organizations and more likely to support a democratic political system. The poor and indigenous are actually more active than their wealthier counterparts in Bolivia. This is good evidence that civil society can play an important stabilizing role in new democracies, even as it facilitates the articulation of serious discontents with poverty, inequality, and government policy through unconventional and contentious mechanisms.

CIVIL SOCIETY AND SUPPORT FOR WEAKLY DEMOCRATIC POLITICAL SYSTEMS

Scholars have long believed that support from the public is an integral element to the success and stability of democracy. Diamond claims "the essence of democratic consolidation is a behavioral and attitudinal embrace of democratic principles and methods" (1999: 20). Similarly, Linz and Stepan (1996) cite the requirement of attitudinal support for democracy as one of three parts of the definition of democratic consolidation. Without sufficient levels of public support, semi-democratic regimes may revert to authoritarianism and public may begin to support antisystem candidates (Hagopian and Mainwaring 2005: 320). High levels of political support, on the other hand, may help democracy run more smoothly. Positive opinions toward the political system communicate "faith in the system," which can enhance policymakers' positions in generating and implementing better policy (Chanley, Rudolph, and Rahn 2000; Weatherford 1987: 6). If there are fewer critics to assuage and more support coming from the public, policymakers have more flexibility and time to pursue better policy.

Support for the political system is thought to be particularly important in weaker democracies where it can act as insurance for the survival of democracies in times of crisis (Easton 1975; Finkel et al. 1989; Miller 1974). In addition to the literature that directly addresses support for the political system, there are strong predictions from literature on civil society, associational activity, and NGOs that involvement in any of these types of organizations should help create moderate civil society that is supportive of a democratic political system. Civil society is often mentioned as a key factor in building support for democratic political systems after transitions to democracy (Diamond 1999; Linz and Stepan 1996). In many parts of the developing world, NGOs became the visible face of civil society to foreign aid donors and development programs. A large literature developed around the role that NGOs play in developing countries, most of which focused on the benefits that NGOs had in terms of strengthening democracy (Clark 1991; Clarke 1998b; Devine 2006; Fisher 1998; Gibbs et al. 1999; Hudock 1999; Hulme and Edwards 1997; Mercer 2002; Mitlin, Hickey, and Bebbington 2007; Pearce 2000; World Bank 1989).

Although there are good reasons to expect that civil society plays some role in building support for the political system, it is much less well understood how these dynamics function under conditions of very poorly performing government institutions and high levels of social mobilization. There are many types of political crisis, but for our purposes we define a political crisis as a political situation characterized by high levels of social conflict and a high degree of uncertainty over the actions of the key actors in the conflict. In the case of Bolivia in 2004, we see evidence of political crisis in the almost daily street protests of the year, and the genuine fear that the military might crack down on the protesters as it did in October of 2003, resulting in dozens of deaths. In a very real sense, then, the crisis of 2004 was a crisis of democracy characterized by uncertainty over military intervention and the stability of the democratic system. Thus, our definition of crisis is not simply that political institutions are not working well (which would be true to some degree of any time in Bolivia since the transition to democracy), but rather a moment of extreme crisis, high uncertainty over the future, and high social mobilization.

This book has presented evidence that NGOs in developing countries can do as much – or more – to increase political protest as they do to increase voter turnout, which is quite different from conventional expectations of civil society and NGO activity. When the government is extremely unresponsive and basic needs of ordinary people are unmet, civil society can still facilitate political engagement, but the tactics used to engage the government are likely to include political protest. What is unclear is whether these protests are generally a threat to democratic stability or whether they represent the contentious articulation of interests that have often been excluded from more formal paths for participation.

Where institutions are performing poorly, civil society may actually undermine support for the political system because citizens who are members of civil society groups may have better information about government failings (Carlin 2011; Norris 1999). At one extreme, the mobilization of civil society is seen as a threat for weakly institutionalized governments, increasing the chances of civil war and regime failure as ineffective governments fail to meet the demands of citizens (Huntington 1968), or promoting undemocratic political development in certain circumstances (Berman 1997). Popular rhetoric surrounding the mass protests in Bolivia has often mirrored those concerns. In a more limited way, others worry that strong civil society may allow citizens to form more critical opinions of government failures, undermining long-term support for democracy. For example, a study of civic education programs in the Dominican Republic demonstrated that those programs actually *reduced* trust in political institutions as people became better informed (Finkel, Sabatini, and Bevis 2000).

The central purpose of this chapter is to explore this tension between those who see civil society as generally a force for building support in the political system and those who see it as a source of instability. This chapter also tests the argument that civil society may encourage criticism of government *and* build support for the political system. These two opposing viewpoints can be described as the "instability hypothesis" and the "social trust hypothesis." A third alternative, the argument presented here, is referred to as the "democratic dissent hypothesis."

The more negative instability hypothesis predicts that under conditions of weak government and poor performance active citizens mobilized through civil society organizations make demands that are impossible for the government to meet, leading to instability and even violence.

Instability Hypothesis:

*Under conditions of political crisis, involvement with civil society **decreases** support for the political system and the government.*

For proponents of civil society, involvement in associational activities builds trust, facilitates cooperation, and encourages political engagement, all of which empowers citizens to demand accountability from their government. Even if the government is unable to fully meet those demands, there is an overall net benefit to democracy in terms of both participation and performance as organized people hold the government accountable. We summarize this set of arguments as the social trust hypothesis.

Social Trust Hypothesis:

*Under conditions of political crisis, involvement with civil society **increases** support for the political system and the government.*

I argue for a third hypothesis: that where civil society is strong and is mobilizing new political participation, membership can both facilitate criticism of the government and build support for the political system – as long as the system remains minimally democratic and the state does not resort to systematic or violent repression of the opposition.

Democratic Dissent Hypothesis:

*Under conditions of political crisis, involvement with civil society **increases** support only for the political system (not the government in power).*

By facilitating dissenting political views, and boosting political participation, civil society can be a challenge to democratic systems that are not broadly inclusive or are not performing well. Civil society mobilization under conditions of crisis may look quite different from the moderate, membership associations of developed democracies – even as membership in civil society organizations builds support for the political system. In particular, if civil society organizations help build trust, share information, and facilitate collective action, there is little reason to expect they would not do so under conditions of government failures. However, the more extreme the government failures are, the more radical the interests, opinions, and preferences that civil society helps articulate may be. In fact, more engaged, networked citizens are in some ways *more* likely to accurately assess and criticize failings of the government.[1] And they are more likely to try to do something about them.

In this way, civil society membership – especially for those who are active and frequent participants in civil society – is likely to increase support for the political system at the same time that it encourages the articulation of

---

[1] It may also be the case that a healthy dose of skepticism and distrust in government is more important than blind trust in government.

dissatisfaction with particular policies, even through radical tactics such as political protest. This approach builds on recent work by Booth and Seligson (2009), who also find that protest and regime support are not incompatible. In fact, Booth and Seligson find that "citizens with high support for democracy and national institutions tend rather strongly to approve of confrontational tactics... [and] do not view the techniques of confrontational protest to be inconsistent with democracy or national institutions" (2009: 195).

More specifically, civil society is likely to have a positive effect on diffuse support for the political system even during times of crises under the following conditions: (1) membership is high and associated with political participation that is seen as effective, and (2) the regime in power is not openly or obviously repressing dissent and opposition. Under these conditions, associational activity may encourage negative evaluations of specific government policies or politicians at the same time it encourages diffuse support for the system by making political participation – even very critical dissent – easier.

PROTEST AND DEMOCRACY IN BOLIVIA, 2000–2010

Bolivia is a very interesting context in which to explore these issues for several reasons. First, Bolivia has one of the highest rates of membership in civil society organizations in the region, with more than 80 percent of the population regularly attending meetings, and nearly half attending with high frequency. If civil society is likely to matter anywhere, it is likely to matter in a place where most people are members of civil society organizations. Second, Bolivia is a highly divided society, in terms of both economic class and ethnicity: Bolivia is the poorest country in South America and one of the most unequal, with an indigenous majority who have been systematically excluded from politics since colonial times. These demographic realities mean that democracy in Bolivia faces serious challenges and that the state is limited in its ability to respond to the pressing needs of many Bolivians.

Bolivia between the years 2000 and 2010 fits the profile of rapid social change and mobilization of new groups into politics in the face of weak political institutions very well, but the question of whether Bolivia has fallen into violence and instability is rather more disputed. Certainly the massive protests that have characterized Bolivian politics in the last decade have been described as a threat to democracy. An *Economist* article in June of 2005 unequivocally called the protests in Bolivia "mob rule, not people power," with dire warnings for the future of democracy if the protesters continue to "hold an entire country to ransom." The protest movements resulted in the irregular removal of a president and provoked a constitutional crisis. As a result, both Freedom House and Polity downgraded Bolivia's democracy score. These political crises are taken as evidence of the fragility of Bolivia's democracy and the failure to overcome structural inequalities (Domingo 2005). At the extreme, critics of the Morales government claim the "attempt to revolutionize Bolivia has led to the breakdown of constitutional democracy and to the polarization of the country," which promises to continue as a "fragile stalemate at best, and at worst, a spiral into violent civil conflict" (Lehoucq 2008: 112).

Others, however, credit the protests in Bolivia with bringing about a new era in Bolivian politics that is much more inclusive of the interests of the indigenous – and largely poor – majority, including the election of Bolivia's first indigenous president Evo Morales in 2005 and again in 2009, and a landslide electoral shift toward legislators from Morales' political party, the *Movimiento al Socialismo* (MAS). These events can be seen as a victory for democratic representation (Albro 2006; Lucero 2008). Even more optimistically, Madrid (2005) argues that this political shift is likely to boost participation and acceptance of democracy while reducing party fragmentation and political violence.

The formal process of democracy in Bolivia has certainly been disrupted, but it has been disrupted largely in favor of increasing popular participation and including previously excluded groups. In thinking about the role that protest has played in Bolivian democracy in recent years, several points stand out. First, protest has been remarkably successful as a political strategy over the last decade, both for the supporters of Evo Morales and increasingly for his opponents. Second, although democracy in Bolivia has been unpredictable, contentious, and strained, it has not broken down completely. Despite political protests becoming an almost daily part of life in many parts of the country, elections continue to be held, a new constitution was drafted and ratified, regional disputes are being addressed, and – at least for the time being – Bolivia does not appear to be at the brink of civil war. Certainly the last decade has been a tumultuous one in Bolivia, but the worst-case scenario has hardly come to pass.

I argue that Bolivian democracy has been so resilient precisely because most Bolivians are part of a densely networked civil society, which helped to facilitate the protests, but also tends to encourage support for the Bolivian state and the political system in general. Even as civil society has encouraged and allowed for the articulation of interests that are very challenging to the status quo, it has not undermined respect for democracy and the political system more generally. Although the Bolivian state has responded with military force (most notably during the protests of October 2003), these crises have not resulted in a radical break with democratic processes or the systematic repression of opposition voices.

Protests have accomplished political victories that could not have been accomplished through electoral strategies alone, including removing an unpopular president, influencing the constitutional succession in favor of a more moderate interim president, overturning tax laws, and blocking legislation. These political gains for the protesters were immediate and large scale and it is difficult to imagine them occurring on the slow and steady calendar of regularly scheduled elections.

Popular protest has long been a strategy for engagement with the state in Bolivia,[2] but the influence of social movements as a force to be reckoned with launched to new levels beginning in 2000. The new century opened in Bolivia with a conflict in Cochabamba called la Guerra del Agua (the Water War). In late 1999, a law was passed to privatize the distribution of water in the rapidly growing city and agricultural valleys of Cochabamba, in central Bolivia. The contract was given to a subsidiary of Bechtel Corporation and prices were immediately raised.

In April 2000 tensions over the privatization of water and the new higher prices exploded into massive popular demonstrations led by a new organization called the *Coordinadora en Defensa de Agua y Vida* (Coalition in Defense of Water and Life). The coalition was formed out of alliances between many of the traditional actors in civil society, including NGOs, urban workers, rural peasants, students, and other citizens. The resulting demonstrations were met with police in riot gear, and violent clashes ensued. After several days, dozens were wounded and one protester was dead. In an effort to restore order, the government canceled the privatization plan. The water war was seen as a major victory of the poor against corporate globalization in Latin America (Postero 2007) and a response against the government that many people felt had failed them by exploiting natural resources, slashing social spending, and failing to bring economic equalities (Olivera 2004).

At the same time, similar conflicts were heating up all across the country as strikes, marches, and roadblocks became increasingly common events. Students, teachers, transport workers, peasant farmers, and coca growers launched a dizzying array of protests as popular unrest increased. The municipal police in La Paz even briefly went on strike, to which the military responded in a tense standoff outside the police headquarters. However, two main issues of contention took center stage as the year progressed. First, in the highlands around Lake Titicaca, an Aymara nationalist movement rooted in the *campesino* movement, the *Confederación Sindical Única de Trabajadores Campesinos de Bolivia* (CSUTCB)[3] and led by Felipe Quispe (El Mallku) launched massive demonstrations. Roads were blocked and the army was called out and the conflict turned quite violent and several people were killed.

These strikes and roadblocks were in solidarity with the other main center of protest, the coca-growing region of the Chapare. Many coca growers are Aymara and Quechua miners who lost their mining jobs and relocated following the privatization and closure of tin mines in the 1980s. The United States has long headed coca eradication projects and used their considerable foreign aid clout to pressure Bolivia to reduce coca production. In 2000, the *cocaleros*

---

[2] For a discussion of the historical roots of street protest in Bolivia see, "La Politica en las Calles" (Calderón G. 1983) and "El Poder Dual" (Zavaleta 1979)

[3] CSUTCB stands for the *Confederación Sindical Única de Trabajadores Campesinos de Bolivia* (The Federation of Syndicated Campesino Workers of Bolivia).

(coca-growers), led by the rising politician Evo Morales, launched roadblocks and protests over government intervention.

As the *campesinos* and *cocaleros* were striking, the Chiquitano Indians in eastern Santa Cruz launched a protest against a pipeline project sponsored by Enron and Shell. The Chiquitanos, working with international NGOs and *Confederación de Pueblos Indígenas del Oriente Boliviano* (CIDOB), the organization that supports the lowland indigenous movement,[4] filed lawsuits and blocked roads. Although their protest was unsuccessful, by the end of 2000, it was becoming clear that the major social movements in Bolivia were ramping up on many different issues across the country, and that the language of political protest and street blockades were becoming an integral part of the political conversation. The 2002 elections became a focal point for the social movements, and were accompanied by more protests as part of a conscious strategy by the leaders of the social movements to influence the elections. In a very close race, Sánchez de Lozada was elected president, but Evo Morales surprised many observers by coming in second place with almost 21 percent of the vote. This electoral gain, which set the foundation for future protests and the eventual electoral victory of Morales in 2005, would not have happened independently from protest mobilization. Supporters mobilized to protest and vote in support of the MAS.

Fueled by the close election of 2002, tensions between the popular sectors (many of whom supported the MAS) and the government reached new levels in 2003. Following pressure from the International Monetary Fund (IMF), President Sánchez de Lozada announced a new income tax in February. Mass protests and rioting followed, and government buildings were burnt and looted. Shocking the nation, the clashes escalated to unexpectedly violent levels, as government sharpshooters fired at the crowds in Plaza Murillo, a plaza surrounded by government buildings in a busy neighborhood of central La Paz. The next day, the COB, the major labor organization in Bolivia, organized further marches, which also ended violently.[5] In these two days, at least 31 people were killed and nearly 200 were wounded (Postero 2007: 206). In La Paz, both the COB and CSUTCB were central in mobilizing people for marches and demonstrations, but the many other organizations of Bolivian civil society also turned out in the streets, including neighborhood organizations, miners' groups, student groups, and retirees.

The crisis gathered momentum throughout the year, and in October the president's proposal to allow multinational corporations to build a pipeline to export gas through Chile to the United States and Mexico became the focal point for massive opposition, bringing together protests movements from

---

[4] CIDOB is the acronym for the *Confederacion de Pueblos Indígenas del Oriente Boliviano* (The Indigenous Federation of Eastern Bolivia).

[5] The COB, which stands for the *Central Obrera Boliviana*, is the main labor organization in Bolivia, with roots in the 1952 revolution.

several sectors. The CSUTCB, one of the main organizations of the highland indigenous movement, organized roadblocks across the altiplano. The main labor organization in Bolivia, the COB, called for an ongoing general strike against the government's economic policies. Urban neighborhood organizations launched protests in El Alto and La Paz.

The protests against the government gained new supporters after a military intervention in the town of Sorata to rescue tourists trapped by roadblocks left several dead. University students, neighborhood associations, retired miners, labor unions, and even middle class paceños joined in the demonstrations. Finally, on October 17, with nearly 80 people dead and hundreds wounded in the clashes, the president fled to Miami and resigned. His vice president, Carlos Mesa Gisbert, was sworn in. These events clearly showed that the social movements had the power to seriously disrupt "politics as usual" in Bolivia, and that the demands of the popular sectors could no longer be ignored.

These events made clear that protest was an effective tool for dramatic political change, not just an inconvenience that might put pressure on the government. Rather, protesters stopped an unpopular energy policy and forced the resignation of the president. For opponents, this was seen as tremendously threatening to the status quo. For supporters of the protests, this was seen as an energizing victory for the poor and dispossessed.

What followed was a tense year of very uneasy truce. The new president, Carlos Mesa, publicly declared that the government would not use force against the protesters in an effort to avoid further bloodshed. The protests continued on an almost daily basis. Mesa, facing rising hostility for his links to the unpopular Sánchez de Lozada, attempted to redirect popular opinion to less divisive issues with a vaguely worded referendum[6] that asked whether voters agreed with overturning the very unpopular energy law passed by Sánchez de Lozada and called for Chile (Bolivia's neighbor to the west) to return a stretch of coastline to Bolivia, which Bolivia had lost control of in the 1880s. This rather odd tactic did little to bolster public support for Mesa, and he announced that he would not complete Sánchez de Lozada's term. After a failed attempt to resign (the Congress voted to reject his resignation), and a last-minute deal to secure succession, Mesa resigned in June of 2005 and the head of the Supreme Court temporarily took the presidency until new elections in December 2005.

---

[6] The referendum consisted of five questions: "(1) Do you agree with the repeal of the 1689 Hydrocarbons Law enacted by Gonzalo Sánchez de Lozada? (2) Do you agree with the recovery of all hydrocarbons for the Bolivian state? (3) Do you agree that a state energy company should be refounded to manage energy production? (4) Do you agree with the policy of President Carlos Mesa to use gas as a strategic resource for achieving access to the Pacific Ocean? (5) Do you agree with Bolivia exporting gas within the framework of a national policy that: (a) covers the gas consumption of Bolivians, (b) promotes the industrialization of gas in the country, (c) includes oil company taxes of 50 percent of the values of the production of gas and oil for the country, and (d) allocates resources from gas exports mainly for education, health, roads and jobs?" (my translation).

Protesters again played an important role in this succession. Mesa's successor according to the Bolivian constitution should have been the head of the senate, Hormando Vaca Diez, but the protestors successfully blocked both Vaca Diez and the second in line, Mario Cossio, from succeeding Mesa until finally an agreement was reached.

In December, the new power of the social movements took an electoral turn. Evo Morales, the former *cocalero* leader and visible face of many of the street protests, was elected with the first absolute majority in Bolivian presidential election history. The election of Evo Morales marked a real turning point in the history of civil society, popular participation, and the Left in Bolivia. For some, the shift represented their worst fears that the newly vocal and newly empowered poor would loot the state and persecute the old elite with land and property seizures in a modern-day repeat of the Cuban Revolution. Others saw a tremendous victory for the poor and disenfranchised – they had clamored for inclusion, and they had brought about an historic realignment in Bolivian politics.

The effectiveness of protest did not end with the election of Evo Morales. Both supporters and the new opposition continued to mobilize protest to influence the new government and protest policies. That is, protest is not just an effective strategy for the radical Left. Instead, after Evo Morales and the MAS took power, the new opposition (made up of the old elite), increasingly turned to protest themselves as a way of putting pressure on the new government and keeping their interests as part of the conversation. This shift in strategies speaks to the perception of protest as an effective means of influencing policy and the normalization of protest participation across different sectors of society.

Pérez-Liñán (2007) argues that the irregular removal of Sánchez de Lozada is representative of a larger change in the nature of political instability in Latin America where government instability is becoming increasingly common but is not often linked to larger regime instability or democratic collapse. The point that government crises do not automatically translate into regime crises is an important one, especially when considering a democracy in which contentious participation has become increasingly normal.

The language of the new president lived up to his radical roots, but the reality was often more tempered, sometimes prompting protest from the more radical supporters of the party. Evo Morales declared his hostility to the United States by stating upon election: "I don't mind being a permanent nightmare for the United States" (McDonnell 2005). He also declared his intention to nationalize the hydrocarbons industry in Bolivia, kick out foreign companies, pursue aggressive land reform, end Bolivia's relationship with the United States Drug Enforcement Agency (which had long pursued coca eradication projects in Bolivia), and launch huge new redistributive social programs. In reality, he pursued a much more moderate path. For example, although the nationalization of the gas industries was declared in unequivocal terms, and published in domestic newspapers alongside photos of the Bolivian army outside the headquarters of foreign gas companies, the reality was closer to a renegotiation of contracts, with the government receiving a larger share of revenue (Mayorga 2006). Similarly, the new government launched several new social programs, and began pushing for a new constitution, but the most extreme fears of leftist takeover proved unfounded.

In 2006, supporters of MAS as well as representatives from the other political parties met in the city of Sucre to begin the process of writing and negotiating a new constitution. The newly empowered social movements representing indigenous people, labor unions, and the poor saw the constituent assembly as a chance to institutionalize some of the changes they saw as critical to changing Bolivia. Conservative actors and minority political parties expressed concern that the process would be biased against them, and the assembly opened amid protests and tension on both sides. Conservative delegates boycotted many of the proceedings, which had to be moved several times out of fear for safety in the tense environment of protests. Finally, the new constitution was passed without the opposition present and a yearlong battle to put the new constitution to a referendum vote began. After a postponement by the electoral court, the constitution was finally passed in January of 2009.

Gaining the majority in the legislature, the presidency, and passing a new constitution on favorable terms placed the MAS and the social movements behind it in an entirely new position as incumbents, a sharp change from their long-held role as the fiery opposition. More fundamentally, the MAS, which had built its reputation and constituency battling the Bolivian state, was now in control of the state. And the old elite – particularly landowners, the business elite, and the political elite – were uncomfortably placed in the role of opposition. Leaders from the lowland states (the "media-luna" or the "half moon" states, for the shape they make on the Bolivian map) opposed the new constitution and began mobilizing for autonomy.

The radical change in government at the national level served as a catalyst for deep regional divisions between the mostly indigenous high planes of La Paz, Oruro, and Potosí, where large majorities felt well represented by the new government, and the wealthier, more mestizo populations of the Eastern lowlands of Santa Cruz, Beni, Pando, and Tarija. This divide unfortunately corresponds to the wealth of natural resources, including newly discovered deposits of natural gas in Tarija. Leaders from those states worried that the new constitution and the new government would take disproportionately from their resources under nationalization schemes to fund social programs in the disadvantageous highlands.

Some civil society groups – most notably the neighborhood associations in conservative Santa Cruz – showed another side of civil society in Bolivia, helping to mobilize vocal opposition to the new government, strident support for regional autonomy, and increasingly radical conservative viewpoints. Interestingly, the conservative groups that had long been the established elite in Bolivia began to resort to tactics and strategies long used by the leftist opposition, including street demonstrations, road blockades, and other contentious popular mobilization.

In January of 2007, this newly mobilized force from the right organized a large street demonstration and march in Cochabamba, a department deeply divided between MAS supporters and critics. The anti-MAS protesters, armed with baseball bats and made up largely of organized youth groups from neighborhood associations, clashed with MAS supporters who had marched from the countryside armed with sticks and rocks. Two people were killed, and sympathy protests on both sides were held throughout the country. For the first time, observers and analysts began to use the language of "civil war" in discussing the future of the regional autonomy crisis.

In this new dynamic of contention, NGOs and civil society organizations found themselves in an unusual situation. For the left-leaning NGOs that had worked to represent the interests of indigenous people for decades, the new era brought previously unheard of cooperation with and support from the government. But many NGOs that rely on international funding found themselves caught between two masters, a situation felt especially by NGOs that had worked with U.S. Agency for International Development (USAID). The U.S. government, in response to Evo Morales' outright condemnation of U.S. drug policies in the region, ended many foreign assistance programs. As tensions and popular protests continued, the Peace Corps ended operations in Bolivia and evacuated all Peace Corps volunteers.

The autonomy issue came to a head when, going against the ruling of the National Electoral Court, the department of Santa Cruz carried out a vote on regional autonomy, which passed. As a response, the opposition-controlled Senate supported the recall referendum, which was carried out in eight of the nine departments (excluding Chuquisaca because it had recently elected a new prefect following the resignation of the former prefect). In the referendum, Morales was also put to a vote. Morales easily won the support needed, and two of the governors who had long been vocal opponents to Morales lost their seats. In an interesting twist, the government adopted autonomy as one of their own policies, and has since incorporated various autonomy arrangements for indigenous communities as well as departments. In December 2009, Evo Morales was re-elected in a regularly scheduled election with an even larger majority than he won in 2005, gaining the votes of 63 percent of the population.

This tumultuous decade of protests, social mobilization, and radical realignment of political power in Bolivia illustrates several key points. First, although protests in Bolivia have coincided with electoral politics, they accomplished many political victories that could not have happened through the electoral system alone. It is very hard to imagine the electoral victories of the MAS in 2004 and 2005 in the absence of the accompanying political protests. Second, although the party in power has changed, political protests continue to be common events – and an increasingly popular strategy for those who feel excluded from the new political arrangement. In this sense, protest is not limited to the radical left, but is seen as an important tool for pressuring the state to be responsive to the opposition.

Finally, although Bolivia is clearly a fragile democratic state, the high levels of social mobilization and popular protest in the last decade have not resulted in the breakdown of democracy. Instead, the dense network of civil society membership and NGO activity appears to have facilitated large-scale contentious political movements and the articulation of demands that are both important and difficult to accommodate – without pushing democracy to a breaking point.

The tensions of the last decade in Bolivia have been characterized by unusually high social mobilization and political participation rooted in a dense network of civil society organizations, including NGOs and social movements. Although some observers have worried that this mobilization poses a threat to the stability of the democratic system (Lehoucq 2008), I see little evidence that the protest has been antisystem in nature. Like Pérez-Liñán (2007), I see an important distinction between mobilization against a government and mobilization against a regime. Despite the radical changes of the last decade, Bolivia remains a democratic political system with expansive political participation rooted in civil society.

SURVEY EVIDENCE: MEMBERSHIP AND DEMOCRATIC SUPPORT

If this characterization of recent political history in Bolivia is accurate, several testable hypotheses follow. First, members of civil society should be more supportive of the democratic political system than nonmembers – even if they are actively critical of the government and even if they are engaged in contentious political activities. Second, this relationship should hold even in the context of weakly democratic countries as long as minimal requirements for democracy are met (including allowing for opposition political organizing and not directly or systematically repressing contentious dissent). This next section explores the relationship between membership in civil society organizations and support for the democratic system using survey data from Bolivia collected by the Latin American Public Opinion Project (LAPOP) at Vanderbilt University.

Research Design

The 2004 LAPOP Survey from Bolivia is an ideal survey to explore the role of civil society during times of crisis because it includes detailed questions about associational membership in different types of organizations and multiple questions about support for the political system. The sample includes 3,073 respondents from 84 municipalities in Bolivia's nine departments. Ordinary least squares (OLS) regression is used because the distribution of the index of support for the political system is normal, and robust standard errors are reported due to the presence of heteroskedasticity in the model.

Dependent Variable: Support for the Political System

A mean index of support for the political system measures support for the political system as opposed to support for particular governments, parties, or leaders. The index, initially developed by Muller and Jukam (1977), is constructed by taking the mean of responses to the following five component measures that tap attitudes toward the political system at large:

1. To what extent do you think the justice tribunals in Bolivia guarantee a fair trial?
2. To what extent do you respect the political institutions in Bolivia?
3. To what extent do you think that citizens' basic rights are well protected by the Bolivian political system?
4. To what extent do you feel proud of living under the Bolivian political system?
5. To what extent do you think that one should support the Bolivian political system?

Responses range from "not at all" (1) to "a lot" (7). On this scale, the midpoint of four represents a neutral answer.[7] Figure 6.1 displays the component parts of the support for the political system index.

Main Independent Variable: Membership in Civil Society Organizations

To measure participation in civil society organizations, membership is divided into three categories: nonmembers, members (who attend meetings of at least one organization occasionally), and active members (who frequently attend meetings of at least one organization). The LAPOP survey asks respondents whether they are active in six different civil society associations, including church groups; parents' associations; neighborhood associations; community organizations; professional associations; or territorial-based organizations, which are organizations that have the right to participate in municipal development projects.[8]

---

[7] The original support for the political system index developed by Muller and Jukam was later refined to an index of five measures by Muller et al. 1982 (see Seligson 1983 for further validation of the index). Using principal components factor analysis, we verify that this five-measure index indeed taps a primary underlying factor as has been confirmed in other research (Seligson and Carrión 2002. Several articles also use this measure, including Booth and Seligson 2005; Finkel 1987; Finkel et al. 1989; Hiskey and Seligson 2003; Muller and Jukam 1977; Muller et al. 1982; Seligson 1983; Seligson and Carrion 2001; Smith 2009.

[8] To test the robustness of our findings we use several alternative measures of membership, including (1) a mean index of participation where individuals who indicate that they frequently attend meetings for several associations have the highest scores and those who never participate in any organizations have the lowest scores; (2) a trichotomous measure of nonmembers, members,

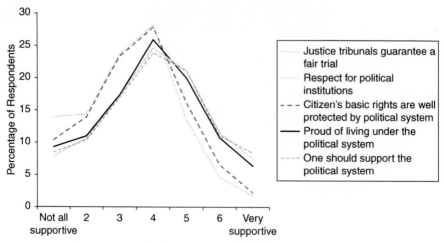

FIGURE 6.1. Components of the support for the political system index.

Control Variables

Drawing from the greater literature on attitudes toward government including trust in government and satisfaction with democracy, there are five main explanatory factors included as controls: government performance, ideology, interpersonal trust, political knowledge, and demographic factors.

GOVERNMENT PERFORMANCE. Because attitudes toward the government are likely influenced by perceptions of how well the government is performing, controls are included for perceptions of the economy, opinions of government services, perceptions of corruption, and attitudes toward the incumbent president.[9]

---

and active members; and (3) a dichotomous measure of active members versus all others. The findings presented here are robust to these different specifications of membership.

[9] These four factors were chosen based on the following literature. First, economic performance is strongly linked to positive attitudes toward the political system (Anderson and Guillory 1997; Chanley et al. 2000; Hetherington 1998; Keele 2007; Stimson 2004). Respondents rank the economic situation from very bad (0) to very good (4). Second, favorable evaluations of public services are linked to more positive attitudes toward government (Bouckeart and van de Walle 2003; Espinal et al. 2006; Hiskey and Seligson 2003) The measure used asks respondents to rate the services of the mayor's office. Third, following Mishler and Rose (2001), Anderson and Tverdova (2003), Seligson (2006), Espinal et al. (2006), and Kelleher and Wolak (2007), perceptions of corruption are included. The corruption measure is coded such that a score of three represents perceptions of widespread corruption while zero represents perceptions that corruption is minimal. Fourth, previous research indicates that more specific forms of support, such as support for policies and particular individuals, can affect more diffuse support for a regime's institutions (Norris 1999). Attitudes toward the incumbent president, who at the time of the survey is Carlos Mesa, are included.

IDEOLOGY. Ideological predispositions could be linked to support for the political system in various ways. More conservative ideology generally advocates for the maintenance of the status quo and the existing power structures but could also be linked in some contexts to less trust of large federal government. Accordingly, some scholars find conservative ideology to be positively associated with support for the political system (Anderson and Singer 2008; Hiskey and Seligson 2003) while others find a negative relationship in the U.S. context (Cook and Gronke 2005). Left-leaning ideologues may also be more supportive of the ideals of polyarchy (Carlin and Singer 2011). The president in power in Bolivia in 2004, President Carlos Mesa, was part of the Revolutionary Nationalist Movement, which had supported more neoliberal economic policies congruent with a more conservative political stance. Mesa had also made a public promise not to use force against the protesters, in sharp contrast to his predecessor, which gained him some support from the Left. To account for the political leanings of individuals, we use a measure that asks respondents to place themselves on a 10-point scale, for which the highest values are the most conservative.

INTERPERSONAL TRUST. Previous research finds that in some cases, trust in other people extends to trust in government (Brehm and Rahn 1997; Finkel et al. 2000; Keele 2007; Newton 2001). We use a four-point measure that asks respondents whether people from their communities are very trustworthy, somewhat trustworthy, not very trustworthy, or not at all trustworthy.

POLITICAL KNOWLEDGE. On one hand, political knowledge may engender greater support as individuals become more aware of the challenges of government. On the other hand, greater political knowledge could also predispose individuals to the conflict in and shortcomings of government, leading them to be more pessimistic about how the system functions. The measure is a summative index where individuals receive additional points for correct answers on the presidents of the United States, Brazil, and Argentina, as well as how many deputies are in Congress, the name of the uninominal deputy from the respondent's district, and whether candidates must belong to a political party.

DEMOGRAPHIC FACTORS. Finally, we control for a number of demographic factors: income, education, age, gender, and indigenous identity. Income is a measure derived from principal components factor analysis of various assets individuals have.[10] The education measure is a scale of the years of education that respondents were asked to view and circle. Lastly, because the indigenous identity was highly politicized in the social conflicts of the time, we include a measure of indigenous identity from a question asking if the respondent is indigenous, white, black, or mixed.

---

[10] Assets questions include a color TV, refrigerator, telephone, washing machine, microwave, electricity, drinking water, sewerage connection, and bicycle.

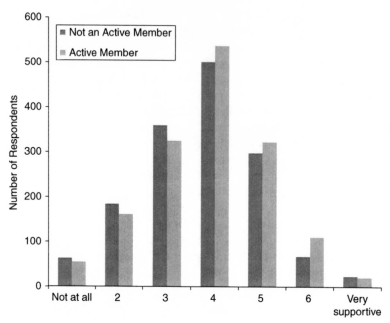

FIGURE 6.2. Civil society membership and support for the political system.

Findings

Overall, most people are dissatisfied with the political system in our sample. The average level of support for the political system is 3.782, slightly below the neutral value of 4. Figure 6.2 shows that the level of support for the political system among active members of civil society organizations is generally higher relative to nonmembers.

Table 6.1 tests this relationship more rigorously. Results indicate that contrary to the hypothesis that associations are fomenting political dissent, active membership in an association is associated with greater support for the political system. This effect is limited to those who are frequent participants in associational life; members who attend infrequently are not significantly more supportive than nonmembers.

The government performance factors lead to more sizeable effects on support for the political system. All government performance factors perform as expected in terms of sign and significance; those who have more favorable views of the economy, believe that the system is less corrupt, and indicate a high level of satisfaction with municipal services are more supportive of the political system. Next to opinions of the economic situation, political ideology makes the second largest impact on support for the political system, as individuals with the strongest leftist orientation have lower levels of support for the political system. The demographic variables yield some interesting findings. First, in 2004, non-indigenous Bolivians are no more likely than indigenous

TABLE 6.1. *Determinants of Support for the Political System*

	Model 1
Active Member of an Association	0.178**
	(0.077)
Member of an Association	−0.019
	(0.078)
Perception of the Economy	0.176***
	(0.031)
Municipal Services	0.084***
	(0.029)
Corruption	−0.103***
	(0.028)
Satisfaction with the President	0.149***
	(0.036)
Ideology	0.075***
	(0.012)
Interpersonal Trust	0.083***
	(0.027)
Political Knowledge	0.010
	(0.016)
Income	−0.118***
	(0.028)
Education	−0.012*
	(0.007)
Age	−0.004**
	(0.002)
Gender (female = 1)	0.067
	(0.048)
Indigenous	−0.026
	(0.065)
Constant	2.985***
	(0.174)
N	2,324
R^2	0.093

Note: *$P < 0.10$; **$P < 0.05$; ***$P < 0.01$. Robust standard errors in parentheses.

Bolivians to support the political system. Wealthier and younger individuals are less likely to support the political system. Higher levels of education also lead to lower levels of support for the political system. However, political knowledge appears to have no effect on support for the political system.[11]

Given the initial finding that associational participation helps build support for the political system even in a time of crisis, the question remains whether all

---

[11] The results hold using multiple imputation to account for missing data. For the full results, please see Boulding and Nuñez (2014).

associations are the same in their ability to foster stronger bonds between citizens and the political regime. As "civil society" is hardly one entity, it is helpful to explore the ways in which membership in different types of organizations affect support for the political system. Table 6.2 presents the effect of membership in each of the six association types available in the survey.

This disaggregated perspective of membership in civil society organizations presents complementary findings: most civil society organizations tend to build support for the political system. Specifically, membership in church groups, neighborhood associations, and community committees all appear to support the view that civil society builds stronger linkages between citizens and government. However, the effect approaches significance only for parent associations and does not apply for professional associations or territorial based organizations. Professional associations are likely very heterogeneous, incorporating professional organizations for the highly skilled as well as agrarian associations and labor unions. These types of organizations are often not considered to be part of the core of civil society in that they tend to span into economic society (Diamond 1999). Taken together, these findings provide evidence that the core civil society organizations function in the way that Putnam (2001) predicts, generating more positive linkages between members and government.

The question remains whether the effect of membership in civil society associations can be attributed to the people who join them, rather than an individual's participation in them. Is the effect on support for the political system merely a factor of more conservative, wealthier individuals joining associations? Or is membership dominated by a particular group that might be more supportive of the political system for another reason? Table 6.3 shows the percentages of different groups who are active members of associations.

In terms of membership in general, the differences between these segments of society are not substantial. For example, the poor are nearly as participatory as the middle class. Indigenous respondents are only slightly more likely to be members of an association than other respondents. The differences between left- and right-leaning individuals also seem immaterial. Membership by association type shows larger differences, but the degree of difference is still fairly limited. The greatest differences appear for class and education, but here the finding is not that those with more resources who tend to benefit most from the political system are more participatory. Instead, the reality in Bolivia is that generally membership in civil society organizations is high and is highest among those with lower education levels and lower socioeconomic status.[12]

---

[12] As a more rigorous test of this endogeneity problem, the relationship between civil society membership and support for the political system is modeled using a matched sample based on propensity score matching. We find very similar results, strengthening our confidence that there is a causal relationship at work. To generate the propensity scores for membership, a model of education, age, gender, ethnicity, income, and whether a respondent lives in a rural or urban context, as well as measures of political sophistication and democratic attitudes is used. Comparing members with most-similar nonmember respondents demonstrates that membership likely has an independent effect on support for the political system. For full results see Boulding and Nuñez (2014).

TABLE 6.2. *Membership in Civil Society Organizations*

	Model 2	Model 3	Model 4	Model 5	Model 6	Model 7
Member of Church Group	0.110**					
	(0.048)					
Parent Association		0.060				
		(0.047)				
Neighborhood Association			0.094**			
			(0.047)			
Community Committee				0.121**		
				(0.048)		
Professional Association					0.010	
					(0.051)	
Territorial Base Organizations						0.069
						(0.053)
Perception of the Economy	0.169***	0.169***	0.175***	0.168***	0.176***	0.173***
	(0.031)	(0.031)	(0.031)	(0.031)	(0.031)	(0.031)
Municipal Services	0.084***	0.086***	0.088***	0.087***	0.086***	0.089***
	(0.030)	(0.030)	(0.030)	(0.030)	(0.030)	(0.030)
Corruption	-0.100***	-0.099***	-0.104***	-0.109***	-0.101***	-0.104***
	(0.028	(0.029)	(0.029)	(0.029)	(0.029)	(0.029)
Satisfaction with the President	0.146***	0.155***	0.149***	0.151***	0.146***	0.150***
	(0.036	(0.036)	(0.036)	(0.037)	(0.036)	(0.036)

(continued)

TABLE 6.2. *(continued)*

	Model 2	Model 3	Model 4	Model 5	Model 6	Model 7
Ideology	0.075***	0.075***	0.075***	0.074***	0.075***	0.076***
	(0.012)	(0.012)	(0.012)	(0.012)	(0.012)	(0.012)
Interpersonal Trust	0.086***	0.087***	0.088***	0.086***	0.088***	0.085***
	(0.027)	(0.027)	(0.027)	(0.027)	(0.027)	(0.027)
Political Knowledge	0.012	0.013	0.016	0.012	0.013	0.014
	(0.016)	(0.016)	(0.016)	(0.016)	(0.016)	(0.016)
Income	-0.119***	-0.115***	-0.117***	-0.114***	-0.120***	-0.117***
	(0.028)	(0.028)	(0.028)	(0.028)	(0.028)	(0.028)
Education	-0.011	-0.012*	-0.011*	-0.010	-0.012*	-0.012*
	(0.007)	(0.007)	(0.007)	(0.007)	(0.007)	(0.007)
Age	-0.003**	-0.003**	-0.004**	-0.004**	-0.003*	-0.003**
	(0.002)	(0.002)	(0.002)	(0.002)	(0.002)	(0.002)
Gender (female = 1)	0.076	0.076	0.089*	0.083*	0.083*	0.84*
	(0.048)	(0.048)	(0.048)	(0.049)	(0.048)	(0.048)
Indigenous	-0.008	-0.017	-0.017	-0.029	-0.018	-0.018
	(0.065)	(0.065)	(0.065)	(0.065)	(0.065)	(0.065)
Constant	2.945***	2.971***	2.964***	2.990***	3.001***	2.996***
	(0.169)	(0.168)	(0.167)	(0.168)	(0.168)	(0.167)
N	2322	2313	2312	2303	2306	2308
R^2	0.088	0.087	0.089	0.088	0.087	0.088

Note: $^{*}P < 0.10$; $^{**}P < 0.05$; $^{***}P < 0.01$. Robust standard errors in parentheses.

TABLE 6.3. *Percentages of Various Groups Who Are Active Members of Civil Society Organizations*

	Active Membership	Church Group	Parent Assoc.	Neighborhood Assoc.	Community Committee	Professional Assoc.	Territorial-based Organization
Ethnicity							
Indigenous	55.05	24.59	30.23	17.05	20.33	14.29	18.92
All Others	50.02	25.37	23.50	13.80	14.77	10.78	16.89
Education							
No Education	52.54	37.29	18.97	20.69	24.14	6.78	24.14
Primary	53.87	27.99	28.27	16.31	19.43	10.83	19.01
High School	48.99	24.01	24.64	13.99	15.41	10.33	16.92
College	50.55	24.24	24.58	12.60	12.60	11.31	15.32
Postgraduate	53.19	25.64	19.83	13.62	14.72	20.17	15.74
Class							
Rich	46.68	24.58	18.84	8.70	9.70	9.50	11.13
Middle	54.38	26.48	24.81	15.37	13.87	11.91	19.17
Lower	50.41	23.42	25.04	16.22	17.06	12.42	18.83
Poor	49.29	24.33	27.58	13.88	15.03	10.14	16.28
Very Poor	51.11	27.19	26.76	15.70	20.48	12.46	18.36
Ideology							
Left-leaning	49.14	22.78	24.17	15.85	15.78	13.16	18.67
Centrist	50.40	25.76	24.50	13.61	14.08	11.45	16.69
Right-leaning	52.04	26.21	25.69	13.68	17.30	9.89	16.09

Note: The class categories are based on quintiles of the asset-based income measure.

TABLE 6.4. *Effect of Membership on Support by Participation in Protest*

	Model 8
Active Member of an Association	0.183***
	(0.060)
Active member X Protested	0.021*
	(0.092)
Protested	−0.003
	(0.066)
Perception of the Economy	0.175***
	(0.031)
Municipal Services	0.084***
	(0.029)
Corruption	−0.101***
	(0.028)
Satisfaction with the President	0.150***
	(0.036)
Ideology	0.075***
	(0.012)
Interpersonal Trust	0.084***
	(0.027)
Political Knowledge	0.009
	(0.016)
Income	−0.118***
	(0.028)
Education	−0.012*
	(0.007)
Age	−0.004**
	(0.002)
Gender (female = 1)	0.067
	(0.048)
Indigenous	−0.025
	(0.065)
Constant	2.969***
	(0.169)
N	2321
R^2	0.093

Note: *$P < 0.10$; **$P < 0.05$; ***$P < 0.01$. Robust standard errors in parentheses.

It is also possible that active membership in civil society organizations simply builds support for those who are already supportive. To test this possibility, we explore whether the effect of active membership holds even for those who have protested against the government. We use a dichotomous measure that asks if respondents have "ever participated in a demonstration or public protest."

Table 6.4 shows the results of an interactive model, in which membership in associations is interacted with the protest variable. The coefficient for

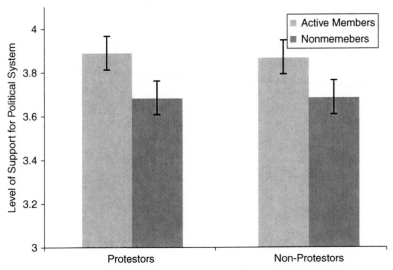

FIGURE 6.3. Effect of membership on support for protesters versus non-protesters. Confidence intervals: $P < 0.05$.

membership remains positive and significant, indicating that membership is associated with more support for the political system even for those who have recently protested. In other words, even among individuals who have taken their grievances to the street, membership in associations still exerts a positive effect on support for the political system. Figure 6.3 shows the predicted level of support for the political system for individuals who have protested and individuals who have not. In both cases, the predicted values are greater for individuals who are active members of civil society organizations. This is very direct evidence that membership in civil society is not undermining support for the political system, even among those who are most actively voicing their discontent with the leaders and policies of the time.

Figure 6.3 also shows that overall support for the political system is not vastly different between protesters and non-protesters. This is an interesting finding in itself, and further evidence that even very contentious political participation need not be at odds with support for the political system.

In fact, part of the reason active membership in associations might build support for political system even during times of crisis is that membership in this context facilitates political participation. People who are frequently involved with civil society organizations are more likely to express their discontent with government through political participation – including protest. This outlet for grievances strengthens overall support for the system even as it gives voice to serious discontent with the government. This assumption is well supported by evidence in earlier chapters, but the survey data from 2004 present another opportunity to test whether membership in associations is linked to protest participation. Because this assumption is pivotal to

TABLE 6.5. *Effect of Membership on Protest in 2004*

	Model 9
Active Member of an Association	0.661***
	(0.150)
Member of an Association	0.300*
	(0.155)
Perception of the Economy	−0.101*
	(0.059)
Municipal Services	−0.083
	(0.053)
Corruption	−0.059
	(0.055)
Satisfaction with the President	−0.057
	(0.068)
Ideology	−0.103***
	(0.022)
Interpersonal Trust	−0.145***
	(0.049)
Political Knowledge	0.111***
	(0.031)
Income	−0.008
	(0.053)
Education	0.035***
	(0.013)
Age	0.003
	(0.003)
Gender (female = 1)	−0.275***
	(0.093)
Indigenous	0.203
	(0.127)
Constant	−0.380
	(0.332)
N	2,330
R^2	0.043

Note: $*P < 0.10$; $**P < 0.05$; $***P < 0.01$. Robust standard errors in parentheses

the causal story presented here, Table 6.5 shows the results of a model that directly tests the relationship between active membership and protest participation. Active membership is indeed a significant predictor of participation in political protest.

Comparing Crisis and Non-Crisis Years

Thus far, this chapter has explored how civil society affects support for the political system in a crisis year, making the argument that members are generally more supportive of the system than nonmembers, even controlling for active dissent against the government in the form of protest. This section looks more closely at how membership influences the different components of the system support index and compare those results with results from a year in Bolivia when things are much more stable – 2008. The different questions in the index (although often used to measure general system support) actually vary in the extent to which they measure diffuse versus specific support. Questions 2, 4, and 5 that ask directly about the general political system are the best indicators of diffuse support. Questions 1 and 3 regarding guarantees of fair trial and the protection of basic rights, however, are more likely to measure evaluations of how well the government is performing.

In the midst of crisis, I argue active membership in civil society will have a stronger effect on the more diffuse aspects of support as members may be dissatisfied with government, but are more able to voice their discontent than nonmembers. Table 6.6 presents the disaggregated results. Consistent with the democratic dissent hypothesis, active membership (which is strongly associated with higher rates of participation) is a significant predictor of more diffuse support. Occasional membership, which has only a weak relationship with political participation, has no effect.

By 2008 in Bolivia, the crisis had largely abated. Social mobilization remains high, but the new administration of Evo Morales was in its third year, a new constitution had been written and put into effect, and the worst of regional tensions had been settled. In 2009, Morales won re-election with an even wider margin than in 2005. At least for the moment, the prospect of the government falling apart was put to rest. In this more stable context, I expect that active membership will be associated with all the indicators of system support, including those related to government performance. As Table 6.7 shows, the results show that both members and active members are more supportive than non-members in 2008[13] in all of the more general system support measures and also on the more specific measure of whether the system guarantees fair trials.[14]

Implications beyond Bolivia

In this section I briefly revisit the argument about *why* civil society tends to strengthen support for the political system in weakly democratic systems,

---

[13] Note that political knowledge is dropped from the 2008 model owing to fewer available measures, a high number of missing observations and a low level of variation (more than 90 percent of the sample answered three of the four base measures correctly).

[14] Extending these tests, we consider the differences between the effect of membership in 2004 and 2008 across more measures of specific support, including trust in political parties, congress, the president, the justice system, and the Bolivian Supreme Court. Our results are consistent with those in Tables 6.5 and 6.7. In 2004, neither membership nor active membership predicts any form of support, while in 2008 both membership and active membership predict all forms of specific support, with the exception of trust in the president. The full logistic regression results for these models are available in Appendixes 6.2 and 6.3.

TABLE 6.6. *Bolivia 2004 Diffuse and Specific Support*

Component Questions of the System Support Index (More diffuse questions in bold):
1. To what extent do you think the justice tribunals in Bolivia guarantee a fair trial?
2. To what extent do you respect the political institutions in Bolivia?
3. To what extent do you think that citizens' basic rights are well protected by the Bolivian political system?
4. **To what extent do you feel proud of living under the Bolivian political system?**
5. **To what extent do you think that one should support the Bolivian political system?**

	Question 1	Question 2	Question 3	Question 4	Question 5
Active Member of an Association	0.017 (0.097)	0.270** (0.116)	0.068 (0.096)	0.250** (0.108)	0.282*** (0.109)
Member of an Association	−0.118 (0.098)	−0.039 (0.117)	−0.063 (0.098)	0.066 (0.109)	0.110 (0.110)
Perception of the Economy	0.214*** (0.043)	0.144*** (0.047)	0.191*** (0.041)	0.186*** (0.046)	0.152*** (0.046)
Municipal Services	0.035 (0.040)	0.020 (0.042)	0.108*** (0.038)	0.137*** (0.044)	0.117*** (0.044)
Corruption	−0.101*** (0.039)	−0.095** (0.043)	−0.119*** (0.039)	−0.096** (0.043)	−0.128*** (0.044)
Satisfaction with the President	0.082* (0.048)	0.225*** (0.054)	0.122** (0.048)	0.120** (0.053)	0.171*** (0.056)
Ideology	0.071*** (0.016)	0.105*** (0.017)	0.064*** (0.016)	0.059*** (0.017)	0.074*** (0.018)
Interpersonal Trust	0.072** (0.035)	0.093** (0.040)	0.072** (0.035)	0.108*** (0.039)	0.074* (0.040)
Political Knowledge	−0.008 (0.021)	−0.006 (0.023)	0.005 (0.021)	0.024 (0.023)	0.038 (0.023)
Income	−0.030 (0.037)	−0.109*** (0.041)	−0.094*** (0.037)	−0.187*** (0.041)	−0.161*** (0.042)
Education	−0.014* (0.009)	−0.007 (0.010)	−0.025*** (0.009)	−0.017* (0.010)	0.004 (0.010)
Age	−0.006*** (0.002)	−0.004 (0.003)	−0.007*** (0.002)	−0.001 (0.003)	−0.002 (0.003)
Gender (female = 1)	0.091 (0.063)	0.130* (0.070)	0.028 (0.062)	0.066 (0.070)	0.016 (0.072)
Indigenous	−0.026 (0.089)	0.041 (0.093)	−0.043 (0.087)	−0.109 (0.097)	−0.018 (0.098)
Constant	3.006*** (0.234)	2.975*** (0.265)	3.173*** (0.233)	2.955*** (0.258)	2.876*** (0.262)
N	2,285	2,301	2,295	2,306	2,287
R^2	0.049	0.059	0.061	0.055	0.046

Note: $*P < 0.10$; $**P < 0.05$; $***P < 0.01$. Robust standard errors in parentheses.

TABLE 6.7. *Bolivia 2008 Diffuse and Specific Support*

Component Questions of the System Support Index (More diffuse questions in bold):
1. To what extent do you think the justice tribunals in Bolivia guarantee a fair trial?
2. To what extent do you respect the political institutions in Bolivia?
3. To what extent do you think that citizens' basic rights are well protected by the Bolivian political system?
4. **To what extent do you feel proud of living under the Bolivian political system?**
5. **To what extent do you think that one should support the Bolivian political system?**

	Question 1	Question 2	Question 3	Question 4	Question 5
Active Member of an Association	0.293*** (0.079)	0.237*** (0.089)	0.157** (0.076)	0.236*** (0.087)	0.173** (0.088)
Member of an Association	0.252*** (0.075)	0.149* (0.084)	0.034 (0.072)	0.133 (0.081)	0.249*** (0.083)
Perception of the Economy	−0.056 (0.043)	−0.129*** (0.048)	−0.100** (0.042)	−0.062 (0.046)	−0.007 (0.048)
Municipal Services	0.115*** (0.041)	0.194*** (0.045)	0.111*** (0.039)	0.042 (0.046)	0.141*** (0.043)
Corruption	−0.093** (0.041)	−0.169*** (0.045)	−0.092** (0.041)	−0.076* (0.045)	−0.049 (0.044)
Satisfaction with the President	0.069*** (0.019)	0.161*** (0.021)	0.185*** (0.018)	0.271*** (0.020)	0.279*** (0.021)
Ideology	0.080*** (0.017)	0.041** (0.018)	0.049*** (0.016)	0.049*** (0.018)	0.062*** (0.018)
Interpersonal Trust	0.157*** (0.040)	0.054 (0.044)	0.086** (0.039)	0.144*** (0.043)	0.110** (0.044)
Income	−0.074** (0.037)	0.026 (0.043)	−0.030 (0.035)	−0.095** (0.040)	−0.014 (0.041)
Education	−0.001 (0.009)	0.006 (0.010)	−0.015* (0.009)	−0.004 (0.009)	−0.007 (0.010)
Age	−0.008*** (0.002)	−0.005** (0.003)	−0.007*** (0.002)	−0.002 (0.002)	−0.006** (0.003)
Gender (female = 1)	0.021 (0.061)	0.042 (0.071)	0.042 (0.061)	−0.005 (0.069)	−0.111 (0.070)
Indigenous	0.030 (0.036)	0.020 (0.042)	−0.008 (0.049)	0.038 (0.056)	0.047 (0.055)
Constant	3.063*** (0.231)	3.781*** (0.271)	3.517*** (0.234)	3.156*** (0.256)	3.126*** (0.261)
N	1,971	2,009	1,980	2,007	1,995
R^2	0.058	0.057	0.088	0.128	0.132

Note: *$P < 0.10$; **$P < 0.05$; ***$P < 0.01$. Robust standard errors in parentheses.

and consider how our findings might hold up outside of the particular context of Bolivia. Although Bolivia is unusual, it is not unique. Civil society in
Bolivia strengthens support for the political system because membership rates
in Bolivia are high and civil society has played a strong role in mobilizing political participation into the political system. Finally, although the crisis of 2004
in Bolivia involved some violent interactions (and casualties) between the state
and mobilized citizens, the government did not respond with outright or widespread repression of opposition voices.

In general, I expect these findings to hold in countries where civil society is
strong, where civil society is mobilizing people to participate in politics and
where minimal conditions of democracy are met – that is, where the government in question has not resorted to widespread or systematic persecution
of the opposition. As a test of the validity of this argument, I replicate our
main analysis using a very similar survey conducted by LAPOP in Ecuador
in 2010. Ecuador in this year meets the criteria established from the investigation of Bolivia. First, membership rates are consistently high (63 percent of
people in the survey report membership in 2010, compared with 69 percent
for Bolivia in 2010). Second, Ecuador, like Bolivia, has experienced significant
waves of popular mobilization and protest, in which civil society has played an
important role (Feinberg, Waisman, and Zamosc 2006; Zamosc 2007). Finally,
the political crisis of 2010 represented a real threat to stability, but fell short
of resulting in widespread repression of opposition voices. During the crisis,
which began as a conflict between the police objecting to austerity measures, a
state of emergency being declared giving the military temporary powers, and a
stand-off as the president of the country, Rafael Correa, was held hostage in a
brief incident that some labeled an attempted coup.

Because of these similar conditions, I expect that the main findings – that
membership strengthens support for diffuse system support – should hold in
Ecuador. Table 6.8 presents the results, which show that membership is indeed
associated with more positive support for the political system.

CONCLUSIONS

This chapter presents the results of a difficult test of the longstanding argument that membership in civil society organizations strengthens generalized
support for the political system. The evidence here demonstrates that this relationship holds in a context where we might least expect it – a country in the
middle of a protracted political crisis of high social mobilization and poor government performance. More importantly, membership in Bolivia is associated
with more supportive attitudes *even among those who have recently protested
against the government.* And, active membership does not appear to have an
effect on more specific forms of support. In other words, membership in civil
society organizations does not seem to prevent people from criticizing their
government, protesting against government policies, or reporting high levels of

TABLE 6.8. *Effect of Membership on System Support in Ecuador, 2010*

	Model 10
Active member of an Association	0.234***
	(0.067)
Member of an Association	0.103*
	(0.060)
Perception of the Economy	0.168***
	(0.035)
Municipal Services	0.081***
	(0.031)
Corruption	−0.157***
	(0.031)
Satisfaction with the President	0.366***
	(0.031)
Ideology	0.034***
	(0.012)
Interpersonal Trust	0.061**
	(0.029)
Political Knowledge	−0.130
	(0.085)
Income	−0.012
	(0.029)
Education	−0.022***
	(0.008)
Age	−0.006***
	(0.002)
Gender (female = 1)	0.122**
	(0.052)
Indigenous	0.146
	(0.164)
Constant	3.230***
	(0.217)
N	1,809
R^2	0.173

Note: $*P < 0.10$; $**P < 0.05$; $***P < 0.01$. Robust standard errors in parentheses.

dissatisfaction and distrust of government. But membership is associated with higher levels of general system support.

This relationship between civil society and support for the political system also does not appear to be a function of who joins civil society organizations – at least in so far as it is not those with greater resources or more politically conservative views that join such organizations. In fact, in Bolivia, those with fewer resources and lower levels of education and those who are indigenous are slightly more likely to join. Moreover, the relationship between civil society membership and support for the political system cannot be attributed to more supportive people joining civil society organizations. Civil society organizations in fact boost support for the political system even among people who are actively protesting government actions. In other words, membership builds support for those who are satisfied with the political system as well as those who are not.

Overall, this study presents an optimistic view of the role that civil society can play in new democracies during times of crisis. Although civil society facilitates the articulation of interests that can be very challenging to the status quo (as in the case of Bolivia, where huge popular movements made up of the poor and indigenous mobilized against the state), they can also be a stabilizing force in terms of building support for democracy. At first this may seem like a profound contradiction, but in the context of highly unequal societies it is possible that both roles are necessary for democracy to succeed. Engaging new voices into elite-dominated political systems is unlikely to be easy, but is more likely to be successful if there is strong consensus over the rules of the game. At least in the case of Bolivia, it appears that civil society assists with both the articulation of new interests and with building support for a democratic political system.

APPENDIX 6.1. *Summary Statistics (LAPOP, 2004)*

Variable	N	Mean	Std. Dev.	Min.	Max.
Support for the Political System	2,324	3.781	1.143	1	7
Active Member of an Association	2,324	0.505	0.500	0	1
Member of an Association	2,324	0.378	0.485	0	1
Perception of the Economy	2,324	1.421	0.779	0	4
Municipal Services	2,324	1.833	0.852	0	4
Corruption	2,324	2.031	0.816	0	3
Satisfaction with the President	2,324	2.172	0.668	0	4
Ideology	2,324	4.172	2.062	0	9
Interpersonal Trust	2,324	1.478	0.897	0	3
Political Knowledge	2,324	2.168	1.680	0	6
Income	2,324	0.056	0.976	-2.053	2.418
Education	2,324	10.796	4.338	0	18
Age	2,324	36.463	14.39	18	84
Gender (female = 1)	2,324	0.467	0.499	0	1
Indigenous	2,324	0.152	0.359	0	1

APPENDIX 6.2. *Specific Forms of Support in 2004*

	Trust in Congress	Trust in Political Parties	Trust in the President	Trust in the Justice System	Trust in the Supreme Court	Trust in the National Electoral Court
Active Member of an Association	0.160	-0.023	-0.023	-0.009	0.054	0.181*
	(0.105)	(0.096)	(0.103)	(0.100)	(0.103)	(0.108)
Member of an Association	-0.010	-0.061	-0.068	-0.153	-0.061	0.020
	(0.107)	(0.096)	(0.105)	(0.101)	(0.103)	(0.110)
Perception of the Economy	0.148***	0.218***	0.272***	0.163***	0.194***	0.177***
	(0.045)	(0.042)	(0.043)	(0.043)	(0.044)	(0.044)
Municipal Services	0.099*	0.146***	0.170***	0.106**	0.086**	0.023
	(0.040)	(0.039)	(0.039)	(0.039)	(0.041)	(0.041)
Corruption	-0.146***	-0.189***	-0.118***	-0.140***	-0.142***	-0.035
	(0.041)	(0.040)	(0.041)	(0.040)	(0.041)	(0.041)
Satisfaction with the President	0.044	-0.012		0.076	0.135***	0.232***
	(0.052)	(0.047)		(0.052)	(0.050)	(0.050)
Ideology	0.086***	0.070***	0.040**	0.083***	0.103***	0.082***
	(0.017)	(0.016)	(0.016)	(0.016)	(0.016)	(0.016)
Interpersonal Trust	0.127***	0.150***	0.096***	0.112***	0.122***	0.117***
	(0.038)	(0.035)	(0.037)	(0.037)	(0.038)	(0.038)
Political Knowledge	0.009	0.070***	0.058***	0.025	0.033	0.047**
	(0.022)	(0.021)	(0.022)	(0.022)	(0.022)	(0.022)
Income	-0.173***	-0.057	0.102***	-0.070*	-0.067*	0.003
	(0.039)	(0.037)	(0.039)	(0.040)	(0.040)	(0.038)
Education	-0.024**	-0.037***	0.011	-0.020**	-0.018*	-0.008
	(0.009)	(0.009)	(0.009)	(0.009)	(0.009)	(0.009)

(*continued*)

APPENDIX 6.2. *(continued)*

	Trust in Congress	Trust in Political Parties	Trust in the President	Trust in the Justice System	Trust in the Supreme Court	Trust in the National Electoral Court
Age	-0.006**	-0.004	0.005**	-0.005**	-0.008***	-0.004
	(0.002)	(0.002)	(0.002)	(0.002)	(0.002)	(0.002)
Gender (female = 1)	0.010	0.218***	0.062	0.154**	0.079	-0.073
	(0.067)	(0.064)	(0.067)	(0.066)	(0.068)	(0.067)
Indigenous	-0.139	-0.078	-0.012	-0.093	-0.117	-0.018
	(0.093)	(0.088)	(0.090)	(0.092)	(0.091)	(0.094)
Constant	3.070***	2.137***	3.055***	2.799***	2.794***	2.806***
	(0.256)	(0.235)	(0.222)	(0.242)	(0.247)	(0.243)
N	2,288	2,320	2,331	2,300	2,289	2,305
R^2	0.066	0.076	0.057	0.054	0.065	0.046

Note: *$P < 0.10$; **$P < 0.05$; ***$P < 0.01$. Robust standard errors in parentheses.

	Trust in National Government	Trust in Congress	Trust in Political Parties	Trust in the President	Trust in the Justice System	Trust in the Supreme Court	Trust in National Electoral Court
Active Member of an Association	0.157** (0.071)	0.344*** (0.086)	0.157* (0.085)	-0.107 (0.105)	0.354*** (0.085)	0.337*** (0.083)	0.284*** (0.087)
Member of an Association	0.226*** (0.067)	0.357*** (0.079)	0.183** (0.080)	-0.088 (0.096)	0.350*** (0.079)	0.337*** (0.078)	0.209** (0.082)
Perception of the Economy	0.178*** (0.040)	-0.062 (0.047)	-0.055 (0.046)	0.864*** (0.049)	-0.107** (0.045)	-0.108** (0.044)	-0.139*** (0.048)
Municipal Services	0.026 (0.036)	0.128*** (0.045)	0.199*** (0.042)	-0.076 (0.049)	0.191*** (0.044)	0.135*** (0.043)	0.174*** (0.044)
Corruption	-0.045 (0.037)	-0.015 (0.045)	-0.078* (0.044)	-0.021 (0.052)	-0.089** (0.044)	-0.074* (0.042)	-0.077* (0.046)
Satisfaction with the President	0.621*** (0.018)	0.228*** (0.021)	0.142*** (0.020)		0.159*** (0.020)	0.226*** (0.020)	0.176*** (0.021)
Ideology	-0.024 (0.015)	0.064*** (0.017)	0.064*** (0.018)	-0.213*** (0.020)	0.091*** (0.017)	0.104*** (0.017)	0.084*** (0.017)
Interpersonal Trust	0.033 (0.033)	0.136*** (0.043)	0.182*** (0.040)	0.018 (0.049)	0.205*** (0.040)	0.084** (0.040)	0.147*** (0.042)
Income	-0.019 (0.032)	-0.027 (0.039)	-0.083** (0.038)	-0.341*** (0.046)	-0.085** (0.039)	-0.011 (0.039)	0.015 (0.039)
Education	-0.029*** (0.008)	-0.026*** (0.009)	-0.001 (0.009)	-0.031*** (0.011)	-0.012 (0.009)	-0.006 (0.009)	0.001 (0.009)
Age	-0.005*** (0.002)	-0.006** (0.002)	-0.005** (0.002)	0.003 (0.003)	-0.007*** (0.002)	-0.007*** (0.002)	-0.007*** (0.003)

(continued)

APPENDIX 6.3. *(continued)*

	Trust in National Government	Trust in Congress	Trust in Political Parties	Trust in the President	Trust in the Justice System	Trust in the Supreme Court	Trust in National Electoral Court
Gender (female = 1)	0.001	-0.074	0.051	-0.042	-0.021	-0.013	-0.101
	(0.055)	(0.067)	(0.066)	(0.080)	(0.066)	(0.065)	(0.067)
Indigenous	0.039	0.051	0.034	-0.017	0.105***	-0.016	0.077**
	(0.039)	(0.057)	(0.058)	(0.050)	(0.026)	(0.043)	(0.039)
Constant	2.382***	2.824***	1.712***	4.088***	2.654***	2.819***	3.363***
	(0.208)	(0.236)	(0.239)	(0.279)	(0.248)	(0.237)	(0.254)
N	2,024	1,968	2,012	2,040	2,011	1,969	1,983
R^2	0.564	0.116	0.073	0.265	0.102	0.109	0.076

Note: * $P < 0.10$; ** $P < 0.05$; *** $P < 0.01$. Robust standard errors in parentheses.

7

Conclusions

Articulating Democratic Discontent

Political protest makes for good news coverage. Protests are flashy, exciting, dangerous, and photogenic. The story is easy to frame: a grievance, a crowd mobilized to action, and a government forced to respond. And the stakes are high. Will the crowd go too far? Will mob violence and destruction of property ensue? Will the government response be measured and policy-oriented, or will it be violent and repressive? This tension is at the heart of the puzzle of contentious politics in weakly institutionalized democracies. For democracy to work, it is essential that active engaged citizens demand accountability and responsiveness. And, if the more institutionalized paths for participation are ineffective, taking to the streets may be one good way to make these demands. On the other hand, when democratic institutions are weak, and people have little confidence in elections, can mobilization for protest solve the problem of government responsiveness or does it just make it worse? Put differently, what happens to the dynamics of civil society when the state is unable or unwilling to respond to participatory pressure from civil society?

This book has explored these questions by looking at the role of civil society – and non-governmental organizations (NGOs) in particular – in facilitating political participation in developing democracies. The purpose of this project has been to consider the function of civil society in the context of countries that are formally democratic, but that have serious barriers to effective governance and democratic performance. There are three main findings. First, NGOs are key actors in the fabric of civil society in most democracies in the developing world and they facilitate political participation in a number of ways, both directly mobilizing people and indirectly lowering barriers to collective action. NGOs have not always been considered as the core actors in civil society because of their ties to international donors and focus on service projects, but this research shows that NGOs often have a stronger impact on political participation than more "home grown" membership associations.

More important, NGOs do as much or more to promote contentious political action as they do to promote voting. In fact, the cross-national survey evidence from Chapter 4 shows that people who have contact with NGOs are more likely to protest in every country in Latin America that is represented in the survey. People who have contact with NGOs are only more likely to vote in a handful of countries.

Second, this book demonstrates that the outcome of civil society mobilization is highly conditional on the context of democratic quality in which NGOs and other membership organizations are working. Where election fraud is common, political parties are weak, political competition is limited, or people generally have little confidence in elections, civil society mobilization is much more likely to lead people to protest than to vote in elections. Where elections are relatively fair, where political parties represent interests and issues that are important to voters, and where people have confidence in elections, on the other hand, civil society does tend to increase voter turnout. Interestingly, NGOs and membership in voluntary organizations is associated with protest across the range of quality of democracy, although the size of the effect is larger the lower the quality of democracy. That is, civil society facilitates protest in nearly all the democracies in this study, both in Latin America and in other regions of the developing world, although the relationship is strongest where democracy is most troubled. The same is not true for voting; civil society promotes voting only in the context of high-quality democratic elections. In weak democracies, people who have contact with NGOs and other organizations are no more likely to vote than people who are not involved in civil society organizations.

These findings – that NGOs and membership organization often promote contentious political action in the democracies with the weakest institutions – run counter to most of the conventional wisdom on civil society in the developing world. Usually, civil society is characterized as essential for training democratic citizens and strengthening democratic institutions by demanding accountability. Although some NGOs have long cultivated relationships with social movements, the finding that protest is a common result of NGO activity is quite surprising. To make sense of this contentious role for NGOs, I investigate how civil society affects attitudes toward democracy. Looking at the critical case of Bolivia, a country with very high social mobilization, strong links between civil society and protest movements and weakly democratic institutions, I find that membership in civil society organizations is associated with higher levels of support for the democratic political system. Although members are more likely to protest, they are also more supportive of democracy. Even among protesters, those who are members are more supportive of the democratic system than protesters who are not members. These findings hold even for a year of intense political crisis, 2004, when many observers feared that Bolivian democratic institutions were on the verge of breakdown.

Third, this book shows that civil society can facilitate democratic discontent. Where ordinary people have little confidence in elections, it makes sense that they would pursue other, more contentious, paths to express their opinions and seek to influence government. Civil society organizations, including NGOs, make this easier by providing resources and opportunities for association that lower barriers to collective action. In some cases, the grievances that people in weak democracies take to the streets are very difficult to resolve and hostility to the government can run high. Because of the unruly nature of protest participation in young democracies, analysts often worry that popular movements might overwhelm the weak institutions of democracy, resulting in regime breakdown. My research shows that this is an unlikely outcome. Instead, even in situations of very high discontent, widespread popular mobilization, and weak democratic institutions, participating in protest engages people into the democratic system by giving a voice to real criticisms against poor government performance. That is, although civil society can make it easier for grievances to be voiced in contentious ways, it also builds support for the democratic system that allows for political opposition – as long as the system itself remains minimally democratic.

Overall, this research points to the need to reconsider the role that civil society, and NGOs in particular, play in new democracies. In this conclusion I focus on several issues. First, if civil society consistently does more to promote protest than voting, what does that mean for democracy? Contentious mobilization is not incompatible with democracy. Instead, protest can be both effective and democratic as a tool for public voice. What is less clear, however, are the long-term prospects for democracy in countries where protest is consistently more effective (and arguably more democratic) than voting. What role does protest play in these democracies? Second, if civil society primarily facilitates contentious political action, what does it mean for our understanding of civil society? Finally, what are the implications of these findings for NGOs that work in developing democracies?

PROTEST AND PROSPECTS FOR DEMOCRACY

There are two very different ways of interpreting the role of protest in young democracies. Some see protest as inherently destabilizing, as a sign of the failure of democratic institutions, and as little more than "mob rule." In this view, if civil society mobilizes people to protest beyond the ability of government institutions to respond, protest can lead to political instability or even civil war (Huntington 1968). In contrast, others view protest as an essential component of participation in a democratic society, and a sign that democracy has stabilized to the point that citizens can vocally and visibly disagree with the government with little fear of violent repression. Rather than a threat to stability, protest can be a legitimate expression of interests, the "voice of the people."

Even if contentious, protest can be an important component of any healthy democracy, a sign that people are engaged, active, and not fearful of participating. In this view, "open and democratic politics ought to encourage protest, not render it obsolete" (Arce and Bellinger 2007: 100).[1]

A cursory look at the countries that became democracies in the third wave finds democracy surprisingly resilient in the face of popular protests. There is little evidence that social mobilization has led to regime breakdown in the sense that Huntington feared. Pérez-Liñan points out that although popular protests have "played a decisive role in recent presidential crises" in Latin America, these crises have almost never resulted in breakdown of the democratic regime (2007: 210). Instead, protests have removed presidents from power much the way a popular recall vote could, perhaps reducing the rigidity of presidential systems and making regime breakdown less likely (Marsteintredet and Berntzen 2008). In this view, protests are filling in the gaps where formal institutions have failed, forcing out unpopular presidents and governments, but rarely opposing the democratic system or causing regime breakdown in the way that intervention of the military would.

Survey evidence supports this view that most protesters in Latin America are not antisystem in their attitudes toward democracy. As a way of characterizing protest as system supporting (or at least compatible with support for the political system) versus system undermining or broadly antisystem, I compare the average support for a democratic political system for protesters with the average support for non-protesters. The difference between these two numbers gives an indication of how different protesters are from the general population. If protesters are much less supportive of a democratic political system than non-protesters, we might infer that the protests had an antisystem element. If, on the other hand, there is little difference between protesters and the rest of the population, there is little reason to believe that the protests are actively undermining the democratic system. For most countries in Latin America, including Bolivia, the difference between protesters and non-protesters is quite small. The measure of support for the political system is a 5-point scale,[2] ranging from 0 to 4. Most of the countries in Latin America show a difference of −0.04 or less between protesters and non-protesters. El Salvador shows the largest gap, with a difference of −0.12.

Most of the countries in Latin America show little difference between protesters and non-protesters in terms of their support for the political system. In the majority of cases in Latin America, there is little reason to suspect

---

[1] (Goldstone 2003) makes a similar point that protest can be a healthy part of the spectrum of political participation in democracies.

[2] This index is based on five questions asking respondents to evaluate: (1) the judiciary and the right to a fair trial, (2) public institutions, (3) the ability to criticize the government freely, (4) democracy in general, and (5) national pride. The index was created to closely mirror a similar index created by Muller and Jukam (1977), although the wording of the questions varies slightly.

that protest is incompatible with support for the democratic political system. Protesters are similar to non-protesters in their evaluation of the legitimacy of the system, even as they are actively protesting. Only five countries have a gap of greater than −0.05: El Salvador, Venezuela, Ecuador, Nicaragua, and Brazil. These countries, with the exception of Brazil, all fall in the bottom range of the Party Institutionalization Index. That is, in the countries with the worst performance in terms of election fraud, political party institutionalization, confidence in elections, and meaningful political competition, protesters tend to be less supportive of a democratic political system than the average non-protesting citizen.

This finding is consistent with other empirical work on protest and democratic legitimacy in Latin America that finds that protest is but one choice in a menu of options for participation, and does not tend to be antidemocratic (Booth and Seligson 2009). This finding also fits well with the argument put forth by Jamal (2007) and Jamal and Nooruddin (2010) that we cannot expect civil society organizations to have the same effects on trust or on democracy in non-democracies as they do in democratic contexts. This same variation (on a lesser scale) exists within democracies, as they vary in the extent to which elections are fraudulent, political parties are well organized and represent real interests, and elections are a meaningful vehicle for mediating between real choices in society.

In the short term, then, there is little reason to fear that popular mobilizations are overwhelming weak democratic institutions in Latin America. Popular protests do not appear to be the primary threat to democracy, even in countries like Bolivia where protests have brought down presidencies. In fact, there is growing evidence that protest is becoming a commonly accepted form of political participation in Latin America (Arce and Bellinger 2007; Booth and Seligson 2009; Moreno and Moseley 2010). It is clear that protest and voting can both be meaningful methods of voicing political opinions where democracy is working well, but in the weaker democracies civil society has little effect on voting.

Protest is not the problem, but the larger threat to democracy may be the poor performance of elections. Although elections have become a regular part of political life in Latin America, many people hold elections and political parties in low regard, and allegations of fraud and corruption are still common in many countries. Low evaluations of the quality of democracy have long concerned scholars worried about democratic stability and consolidation (Norris 1999, 2011). As Booth and Seligson (2009) show in their investigation of this "legitimacy puzzle" in Latin America, democratic legitimacy is a multifaceted concept, and low evaluations of government do not automatically undermine support for the democratic political system, especially where participation is high. Consistent problems with election fraud and corruption, however, remain troubling primarily because elections serve a necessary role in democracy that protest participation cannot replace – providing a mechanism for selecting representatives for the government. The quality of elections remains an important indicator of the quality of democracy in a country. Where elections are deeply flawed, we can also expect other problems with democracy. The positive role for civil society in facilitating support for democratic systems and encouraging political participation can be expected only in democratic countries.

This book started with the claim that both Huntington and Putnam are wrong about civil society in different ways, Huntington for seeing civil society primarily as a threat to stability and Putnam for viewing civil society as inherently democratic. Instead, I argue that the reality of citizen involvement with civil society organizations is much more complicated, especially in the context of democracies in the developing world. In democratic systems – even ones with weak institutions – civil society organizations create space for political mobilization at the same time they build support for democracy. In a sense, Huntington's prediction that social mobilization outpacing political institutionalization was a recipe for political instability holds truth. This book presents ample evidence that civil society facilitates protest in weakly institutionalized settings. In his focus on the capacity and strength of state institutions, and by explicitly discounting the importance of the form of government (democratic or communist), Huntington fails to appreciate the importance of democratic context. In democracies, political mobilization and participation may take very unruly and disruptive forms, including marches, demonstrations, blockades, sit-ins, and even riots, but this type of political instability is very different from the regime instability that Huntington envisioned. Instead of helping the masses to break down the institutions of the state, political protest in democratic countries is generally supportive of democracy because the system of democracy protects the right to speak out in contentious opposition to the government. Even at its most critical and antigovernment, political protest in democratic systems is more a call to improve democracy than a call to destroy it.

Putnam's version of civil society also holds important truths. As Putnam pointed out, membership in a wide variety of nonpolitical voluntary organizations critically shapes how people understand politics, how willing they are to engage in political life, and how likely they are to participate. And, as Putnam points out, the stronger peoples' ties with one another are, the more likely they are to overcome collective action problems and hold the government to account. Like Huntington, Putnam underplays the importance of the democratic context in shaping how associational life translates into political action. Outside of Italy and the United States, there is much wider variation in the quality of democracy. Putnam focused on how people could collectively make demands on the government to improve government performance. The capacity of government to do so is not a key part of the story. This book shows that associational life matters just as much in developing-world democracies, but that the dynamic between governments and civil society is often complicated by lack of resources. In this context, people still pressure the government, but they often resort to much more contentious means of doing so.

My research also shows that the organizations that make up civil society in developing democracies are much more powerful political actors than they are often given credit for. NGOs and membership organizations are key actors in mobilizing people for political participation. It is less clear, however, whether the impact these organizations have is primarily because of their direct activities (voter education, supporting social movements, etc.) or whether their impact is primarily indirect (providing resources and opportunities for association that activists use to mobilize people to action). To what extent does the agenda of an NGO matter compared with the mere fact of bringing resources and creating space for people to interact, share their views, and build networks?

Most of the work on civil society in Latin America focuses on the direct role for organizations as activists, organizing opposition to military rule in the 1970s and 1980s (Oxhorn 1995), and more recently supporting indigenous movements in their struggle for recognition of land rights, increased representation, and political inclusion (Feinberg, Waisman, and Zamosc 2006). Certainly, some NGOs have had a large direct effect on protest politics. Both Lucero (2008) and Yashar (2005) point to a role for NGOs in facilitating the mobilization of indigenous movements in Bolivia and Ecuador. Lucero, in particular, writes of the tremendous opportunities that NGOs like Oxfam America or DANIDA (the Danish development agency) provided to indigenous leaders to encourage networking with international NGOs and other leaders. Others have documented this role for NGOs as well, for example, Zamosc (2007) and Colloredo-Mansfeld (2009) in Ecuador and Postero (2007) in Bolivia. These activist organizations are interesting and important, but they are not the whole story – this project makes the case that a wide spectrum of NGO activity (and associational activity) influences participation. Clearly, NGOs influence participation through both direct and indirect mechanisms, but the relative importance of these mechanisms remains unknown. This project suggests that the more important role for organizations may be that they provide space for citizens to organize themselves.

References

Albro, Robert. 2006. "The Culture of Democracy and Bolivia's Indigenous Movements." *Critique of Anthropology* 26 (4) (December 1): 387–410.

Alagappa, Muthiah. 2004. *Civil Society and Political Change in Asia: Expanding and Contracting Democratic Space*. Stanford, CA: Stanford University Press.

Almond, Gabriel Abraham, and Sidney Verba. 1963. *The Civic Culture: Political Attitudes and Democracy in Five Nations*. Princeton, NJ: Princeton University Press.

Alvarez, Sonia E. 2009. "Beyond NGO-ization: Reflections from Latin America." *Development* 52 (June): 175–184.

Anderson, C., and S. Mendes. 2006. "Learning to Lose: Election Outcomes, Democratic Experience and Political Protest Potential." *British Journal of Political Science* 36 (01): 91–111.

Anderson, Christopher J., and Christine A. Guillory. 1997. "Political Institutions and Satisfaction with Democracy: A Cross-National Analysis of Consensus Majoritarian Systems." *The American Political Science Review* 91 (1): 66–81.

Anderson, Christopher J., and Matthew M. Singer. 2008. "The Sensitive Left and the Impervious Right Multilevel Models and the Politics of Inequality, Ideology, and Legitimacy in Europe." *Comparative Political Studies* 41 (4–5, April 1): 564–599.

Anderson, Leslie E. 2010. *Social Capital in Developing Democracies: Nicaragua and Argentina Compared*. Cambridge: Cambridge University Press.

Anheier, Helmut K. 2004. *Civil Society*. London: Earthscan.

Arbona, Juan Manuel. 2008. "Eso es Ser Pobre e Indio en este País: repercusiones urbanas e implicaciones sociales de la discriminación y la exclusión" *Pobreza, exclusión Social y Discriminación étno-racial en América Latina y el Caribe*. Bogotá: Siglo del Hombre, CLACSO.

Arce, Moisés, and Paul T. Bellinger. 2007. "Low-Intensity Democracy Revisited: The Effects of Economic Liberalization on Political Activity in Latin America." *World Politics* 60 (1): 97–121.

Arce, Moisés, and Roberta Rice. 2009. "Societal Protest in Post-Stabilization Bolivia." *Latin American Research Review* 44 (1): 88–101.

Armony, Ariel C. 2004. *The Dubious Link: Civic Engagement and Democratization.* Stanford, CA: Stanford University Press.

Backer, David, Ravi Bhavnani, and Christina Bodea. 2010. "Does Associational Membership Influence Political Violence in Sub-Saharan Africa?" Working Paper.

Balch, G. 1974. "Multiple Indicators in Survey Research: The Concept of 'Sense of Political Efficacy'." *Political Methodology* 37: 1–43.

Banks, Arthur S. 2010. *Cross-National Time-Series Data Archive.* Jerusalem, Israel. Retrieved from http://www.databanksinternational.com/.

Barnes, Samuel, and Max Kaase. 1979. *Political Action: Mass Participation in Five Western Democracies.* Beverly Hills, CA: SAGE.

Beaulieu, Emily. 2014. *Electoral Protest and Democracy in the Developing World.* New York: Cambridge University Press.

Bebbington, Anthony, and Graham Thiele. 1993. *Non-governmental Organizations and the State in Latin America: Rethinking Roles in Sustainable Agricultural Development.* New York: Psychology Press.

Bellinger, Paul T., and Moisés Arce. 2010. "Protest and Democracy in Latin America's Market Era." *Political Research Quarterly* 64 (3): 688–704.

Benson, Michelle, and Thomas R. Rochon. 2004. "Interpersonal Trust and the Magnitude of Protest." *Comparative Political Studies* 37 (4) (May 1): 435–457.

Berkman, Heather, Carlos Scartascini, Ernesto Stein, and Mariano Tommasi. 2008. *Political Institutions, State Capabilities, and Public Policy: An International Dataset.* Washington, DC: IDB Research Department. Retrieved from http://www.iadb.org/research/pub_desc.cfm?pub_id=DBA-012&lang=en (Accessed December 1, 2010).

Berman, Sheri. 1997. "Civil Society and Political Institutionalization." *American Behavioral Scientist* 40 (5, March 1): 562–574.

Bermeo, Nancy. 2003. *Ordinary People in Extraordinary Times: The Citizenry and the Breakdown of Democracy.* Princeton, NJ: Princeton University Press.

Blais, André, and Kees Aarts. 2006. "Electoral Systems and Turnout." *Acta Politica* 41 (2) (July): 180–196.

Blais, Andre, and R.K. Carty. 1990. "Does Proportional Representation Foster Voter Turnout?" *European Journal of Political Research* 18 (2, March): 167–181.

Blais, Andre, and A. Dobrzynska. 1998. "Turnout in Electoral Democracies." *European Journal of Political Research* 33 (2, March 1): 239–262.

Bob, Clifford. 2005. *The Marketing of Rebellion: Insurgents, Media, and International Activism.* New York: Cambridge University Press.

Booth, John A., and Patricia Bayer Richard. 1998. "Civil Society, Political Capital, and Democratization in Central America." *The Journal of Politics* 60 (3, August): 780–800.

2001. "Civil Society and Political Context in Central America." In *Beyond Tocqueville: Civil Society and the Social Capital Debate in Comparative Perspective,* ed. Bob Edwards, Michael W. Foley, and Mario Diani, 43–55. Hanover, NH: Tufts University Press.

Booth, John A., and Mitchell A. Seligson. 2009. *The Legitimacy Puzzle in Latin America: Political Support and Democracy in Eight Nations.* 1st ed. Cambridge: Cambridge University Press.

Bouckaert, Geert, and Steven van de Walle. 2003. "Comparing Measures of Citizen Trust and User Satisfaction as Indicators of 'Good Governance': Difficulties in Linking Trust and Satisfaction Indicators." *International Review of Administrative Sciences* 69 (3): 329–343.

Boulding, Carew E. 2010. "NGOs and Political Participation in Weak Democracies: Subnational Evidence on Protest and Voter Turnout from Bolivia." *The Journal of Politics* 72 (2): 456–468.

Boulding, Carew. 2012. "Dilemmas of Information and Accountability: Foreign Aid Donors and Local Development NGOs." In *The Credibility of Transnational NGOs: When Virtue Is Not Enough*, ed. Peter A. Gourevitch, David A. Lake, and Janice Gross Stein, 115–136. Cambridge: Cambridge University Press.

Boulding, Carew, and David S. Brown. 2013. "Do Political Parties Matter for Turnout? Number of Parties, Electoral Rules, and Local Elections in Brazil and Bolivia." *Party Politics* doi: 10.1177/1354068813475496.

Boulding, Carew, and Jami Nuñez. 2014. "Civil Society and Support for the Political System in Times of Crisis." *Latin American Research Review* 49 (1): 128–154.

Braithwaite, Valerie, and Margaret Levi. 2003. *Trust and Governance*. New York: Russell Sage Foundation.

Bratton, Michael. 1989. "Beyond the State: Civil Society and Associational Life in Africa." *World Politics* 41 (3, April): 407–430.

Brehm, John, and Wendy Rahn. 1997. "Individual-Level Evidence for the Causes and Consequences of Social Capital." *American Journal of Political Science* 41 (3, July): 999–1023.

Brysk, Alison. 2000. "Democratizing Civil Society in Latin America." *Journal of Democracy* 11 (3): 151–165.

Burns, Nancy, Kay Lehman Schlozman, and Sidney Verba. 2001. *The Private Roots of Public Action: Gender, Equality, and Political Participation*. Cambridge, MA: Harvard University Press.

Calderon G. Fernando. 1983. *La Politica En Las Calles. Estudios Urbanos* (Cochabamba, Bolivia); 1. Cochabamba, Bolivia: Centro de Estudios de la Realidad Economica y Social.

Canache, Damarys. 2002. *Venezuela: Public Opinion and Protest in a Fragile Democracy*. North-South Center Press at the University of Miami.

Carlin, Ryan E. 2011. "Distrusting Democrats and Political Participation in New Democracies Lessons from Chile." *Political Research Quarterly* 64 (3, September 1): 668–687.

Carroll, Thomas F. 1992. *Intermediary NGOs: The Supporting Link in Grassroots Development*. Sterling, VA: Kumarian Press.

Chanley, Virginia A., Thomas J. Rudolph, and Wendy M. Rahn. 2000. "The Origins and Consequences of Public Trust in Government: A Time Series Analysis." *Public Opinion Quarterly* 64 (3, November 1): 239–256.

Clark, John D. 1991. *Democratizing Development: The Role of Voluntary Organizations*. Sterling, VA: Kumarian Press.

Clarke, Gerard. 1998a. *The Politics of NGOs in South-East Asia*. London: Routledge.
    1998b. "Non-Governmental Organizations (NGOs) and Politics in the Developing World." *Political Studies* 46 (1): 36–52.

Coffe, Hilde, and Benny Geys. 2007. "Toward an Empirical Characterization of Bridging and Bonding Social Capital." *Nonprofit and Voluntary Sector Quarterly* 36 (1, March 1): 121–139.

Coleman, James S. 1988. "Social Capital in the Creation of Human Capital." *The American Journal of Sociology* 94: S95–S120.
    1994. *Foundations of Social Theory*. Cambridge, MA: Harvard University Press.

Colloredo-Mansfeld, Rudi. 2009. *Fighting Like a Community: Andean Civil Society in an Era of Indian Uprisings*. Chicago: University of Chicago Press.

Conway, M.M. 1991. "Political Participation in the United States." *Congressional Quarterly.*

Cook, Timothy E., and Paul Gronke. 2005. "The Skeptical American: Revisiting the Meanings of Trust in Government and Confidence in Institutions." *Journal of Politics* 67 (3): 784–803.

Covey, Jane G. 1995. "Accountability and Effectiveness in NGO Policy Alliances." In *Beyond the Magic Bullet: NGO Performance and Accountability in the Post Cold War World*, ed. David Hulme and Michael Edwards. London: Earthscan.

Craig, Stephen C. 1979. "Efficacy, Trust, and Political Behavior An Attempt to Resolve a Lingering Conceptual Dilemma." *American Politics Research* 7 (2, April 1): 225–239.

Craig, Stephen C., and Michael A. Maggiotto. 1982. "Measuring Political Efficacy." *Political Methodology* 8: 85–109.

Dechalert, Preecha. 1999. "NGOs, Advocacy, and Popular Protest: A Case Study of Thailand." *London School of Economics Center for Civil Society International Working Papers.*

Devine, Joseph. 2006. "NGOs, Politics and Grassroots Mobilisation: Evidence from Bangladesh." *Journal of South Asian Development* 1 (1, April 1): 77–99.

Diamond, Larry Jay. 1999. *Developing Democracy: Towards Consolidation.* Baltimore, MD: The Johns Hopkins University Press.

Domingo, Pilar. 2005. "Democracy and New Social Forces in Bolivia." *Social Forces* 83 (4, June 1): 1727–1743.

Downs, Anthony. 1957. "An Economic Theory of Political Action in a Democracy." *The Journal of Political Economy* 65 (2, April): 135–150.

Eckstein, Susan, ed. 2001. *Power and Popular Protest: Latin American Social Movements.* Berkeley, CA: University of California Press.

Edwards, Bob, and Michael W. Foley. 2001. "Civil Society and Social Capital: A Primer." In *Beyond Tocqueville: Civil Society and the Social Capital Debate in Comparative Perspective*, ed. Bob Edwards, Michael W. Foley, and Mario Diani. Hanover, NH: Tufts University Press.

Edwards, Bob, and John D. McCarthy. 2004. "Resources and Social Movement Mobilization." In *The Blackwell Companion to Social Movements*, ed. David A. Snow, Sarah Anne Soule, and Hanspeter Kriesi, 116–152. Oxford: Blackwell.

Edwards, Michael. 2009. *Civil Society.* Cambridge, UK: Polity Press.

Eisenstadt, Todd A. 2002. "Measuring Electoral Court Failure in Democratizing Mexico." *International Political Science Review* 23 (1, January 1): 47–68.

Eisinger, Peter K. 1973. "The Conditions of Protest Behavior in American Cities." *American Political Science Review* 67: 11–28.

Ekiert, Grzegorz, and Jan Kubik. 2001. *Rebellious Civil Society: Popular Protest and Democratic Consolidation in Poland, 1989–1993.* Ann Arbor: University of Michigan Press.

Espinal, Rosario, Jonathan Hartlyn, and Jana Morgan Kelly. 2006. "Performance Still Matters: Explaining Trust in Government in the Dominican Republic." *Comparative Political Studies* 39 (2): 200–223.

Feinberg, Richard E., Carlos Horacio Waisman, and León Zamosc, eds. 2006. *Civil Society and Democracy in Latin America.* New York: Palgrave Macmillan.

Finkel, Steven E. 1987. "The Effects of Participation on Political Efficacy and Political Support: Evidence from a West German Panel." *The Journal of Politics* 49 (2): 441–464.

Finkel, Steven E., Edward N. Muller, and Mitchell A. Seligson. 1989. "Economic Crisis, Incumbent Performance and Regime Support: A Comparison of Longitudinal Data from West Germany and Costa Rica." *British Journal of Political Science* 19 (3): 329–351.

Finkel, Steven E., Christopher A. Sabatini, and Gwendolyn G. Bevis. (2000). "Civic Education, Civil Society, and Political Mistrust in a Developing Democracy: The Case of the Dominican Republic" *World Development* 28 (11): 1851–1874.

Fisher, Julie. 1998. *Nongovernments: NGOs and the Political Development of the Third World*. Sterling, VA: Kumarian Press.

Fornos, Carolina A., Timothy J. Power, and James C. Garand. 2004. "Explaining Voter Turnout in Latin America, 1980 to 2000." *Comparative Political Studies* 37(8, October 1): 909–940.

Franklin, M.N. 1996. "Electoral Participation." In *Comparing Democracies: Elections and Voting in Global Perspective*, ed. L. LeDuc, R.G. Niemi, and P. Norris, 216–235. Thousand Oaks, CA: SAGE.

Franklin, Mark N. 2004. *Voter Turnout and the Dynamics of Electoral Competition in Established Democracies Since 1945*. Cambridge: Cambridge University Press.

Gamson, William A. 1990. *The Strategy of Social Protest*. 2nd ed. Belmont, CA: Wadsworth.

Gamson, William A., and David S. Meyer. 1996. "Framing Political Opportunity." In *Comparative Perspectives on Social Movements: Political Opportunities, Mobilizing Structures, and Cultural Framings*, ed. Doug McAdam, John D. McCarthy, and Mayer N. Zald, 275–290. Cambridge: Cambridge University Press.

Garrison, Steve. 2001. "Latin American Political Protest Project (LAPP)." Retrieved from http://faculty.mwsu.edu/politicalscience/steve.garrison/ (Accessed December 1, 2010).

Gibbs, Christopher J. N., Thomas Kuby, Claudia Fumo, and World Bank. Operations Evaluation Dept. 1999. *Nongovernmental Organizations in World Bank-supported Projects*. Washington, DC: World Bank Publications.

Gingerich, Daniel W. 2009. "Corruption and Political Decay: Evidence from Bolivia." *Quarterly Journal of Political Science* 4 (1): 1–34.

Glenn, John K. 2003. *Framing Democracy: Civil Society and Civic Movements in Eastern Europe*. Stanford, CA: Stanford University Press.

Goldstone, Jack A. 2003. *States, Parties, and Social Movements*. New York: Cambridge University Press.

Grootaert, Christiaan, and Thierry Van Bastelaer. 2002. *The Role of Social Capital in Development*. New York: Cambridge University Press.

Gurr, Ted Robert. 1970. *Why Men Rebel*. Princeton, NJ: Princeton University Press.

Hagopian, Frances, and Scott Mainwaring. 2005. *The Third Wave of Democratization in Latin America: Advances and Setbacks*. New York: Cambridge University Press.

Healy, Kevin. 2001. *Llamas, Weavings, and Organic Chocolate: Multicultural Grassroots Development in the Andes and Amazon of Bolivia*. Notre Dame, IN: University of Notre Dame Press.

Henderson, Sarah. 2002. "Selling Civil Society." *Comparative Political Studies* 35 (2, March 1): 139–167.

2003. *Building Democracy in Contemporary Russia: Western Support for Grassroots Organizations*. Ithaca, NY: Cornell University Press.

Hetherington, Marc J. 2005. *Why Trust Matters*. Princeton, NJ: Princeton University Press.

Hirschman, Albert O. 1970. *Exit, Voice, and Loyalty: Responses to Decline in Firms, Organizations, and States*. Cambridge, MA: Harvard University Press.

Hiskey, Jonathan T., and Mitchell A. Seligson. 2003. "Pitfalls of Power to the People: Decentralization, Local Government Performance, and System Support in Bolivia." *Studies in Comparative International Development* 37 (4, December 1): 64–88.

Howard, Marc Morjé. 2003. *The Weakness of Civil Society in Post-Communist Europe*. Cambridge: Cambridge University Press.

Howell, Jude, and Jenny Pearce. 2002. *Civil Society and Development: A Critical Exploration*. Boulder, CO: Lynne Rienner.

Hudock, Ann. 1999. *NGOs and Civil Society: Democracy by Proxy?* Cambridge, UK: Polity Press.

Hulme, David, and Michael Edwards. 1997. *NGOs, States and Donors: Too Close for Comfort*. New York: Palgrave Macmillan.

Huntington, Samuel P. 1968. *Political Order in Changing Societies*. New Haven, CT: Yale University Press.

   1991. *The Third Wave: Democratization in the Late Twentieth Century*. Norman, OK: University of Oklahoma Press.

IDEA. 2010. "International IDEA | Compulsory Voting." Retrieved from http://www.idea.int/vt/compulsory_voting.cfm (Accessed December 1, 2010).

INE. 2001. "Censo de Poblacion Y Vivienda-2001." *Republica de Bolivia – INE*. Retrieved from http://www.ine.gov.bo/cgi-bin/Redatam/RG4WebEngine.exe/PortalAction (Accessed January 15, 2007).

Isham, Jonathan, Thomas Kelly, and Sunder Ramaswamy. 2002. *Social Capital and Economic Development*. Cheltenham, UK: Edward Elgar Publishing.

Jamal, Amaney. 2007. *Barriers to Democracy: The Other Side of Social Capital in Palestine and the Arab World*. Princeton, NJ: Princeton University Press.

Jamal, Amaney, and Irfan Nooruddin. 2010. "The Democratic Utility of Trust: A Cross-National Analysis." *The Journal of Politics* 72 (1): 45–59.

Jenkins, J., and Michael Wallace. 1996. "The Generalized Action Potential of Protest Movements: The New Class, Social Trends, and Political Exclusion Explanations." *Sociological Forum* 11 (2, June 1): 183–207.

Kaase, Max. 1999. "Interpersonal Trust, Political Trust and Non-institutionalised Political Participation in Western Europe – West European Politics." *West European Politics* 22 (3, July): 1–21.

Kamat, Sangeeta. 2002. *Development Hegemony: NGOs and the State in India*. Oxford: Oxford University Press.

Keck, Margaret E., and Kathryn Sikkink. 1998. *Activists Beyond Borders: Advocacy Networks in International Politics*. Ithaca, NY: Cornell University Press.

Keefer, Philip. 2007. "Clientelism, Credibility, and the Policy Choices of Young Democracies." *American Journal of Political Science* 51 (4, October): 804–821.

Keefer, Philip, and Razvan Vlaicu. 2008. "Democracy, Credibility, and Clientelism." *J Law Econ Organ* 24 (2, October 1): 371–406.

Keele, Luke. 2007. "Social Capital and the Dynamics of Trust in Government." *American Journal of Political Science* 51 (2, April): 241–254.

Kelleher, Christine A., and Jennifer Wolak. 2007. "Explaining Public Confidence in the Branches of State Government." *Political Research Quarterly* 60 (4): 707–721.

King, Gary, Robert Owen Keohane, and Sidney Verba. 1994. *Designing Social Inquiry: Scientific Inference in Qualitative Research*. Princeton, NJ: Princeton University Press.

Koch, Dirk-Jan. 2007. "Blind Spots on the Map of Aid Allocations, Concentration and Complementarity of International NGO Aid." *SSRN eLibrary* (August). WIDER. Research papers, United Nations University. Retrieved from http://papers.ssrn.com/sol3/papers.cfm?abstract_id=1111950.

Kohl, Benjamin. 2003a. "Nongovernmental Organizations as Intermediaries for Decentralization in Bolivia." *Environment and Planning C: Government and Policy* 21: 317–331.

—— 2003b. "Democratizing Decentralization in Bolivia: The Law of Popular Participation." *Journal of Planning Education and Research* 23 (2, December 1): 153–164.

Kornhauser, William. 1959. *The Politics of Mass Society*. Glencoe, IL: Free Press.

Korten, David. 1990. *Getting to the 21st Century: Voluntary Action and the Global Agenda*. Sterling, VA: Kumarian Press.

Krishna, Anirudh. 2002. *Active Social Capital: Tracing the Roots of Development and Democracy*. New York: Columbia University Press.

Kuenzi, Michelle, and Gina M. S. Lambright. 2007. "Voter Turnout in Africa's Multiparty Regimes." *Comparative Political Studies* 40 (6, June 1): 665–690.

Kurtz, Marcus J. 2004. "The Dilemmas of Democracy in the Open Economy: Lessons from Latin America." *World Politics* 56 (2): 262–302.

Lambrou, Yianna. 1997. "The Changing Role of NGOs in Rural Chile After Democracy." *Bulletin of Latin American Research* 16 (1, January 1): 107–116.

Lane, Robert Edwards. 1959. *Political Life: Why People Get Involved in Politics*. Glencoe, IL: Free Press.

Lehoucq, Fabrice. 2003. "Electoral Fraud: Causes, Types, and Consequences." *Annual Review of Political Science* 6 (1): 233–256.

—— 2008. "Bolivia's Constitutional Breakdown." *Journal of Democracy* 19 (4): 110–124.

Levi, Margaret. 1996. "Social and Unsocial Capital: A Review Essay of Robert Putnam's Making Democracy Work." *Politics & Society* 24 (1, March 1): 45–55.

Lim, Chaeyoon. 2008. "Social Networks and Political Participation: How Do Networks Matter?" *Social Forces* 87 (2): 961–982.

Linz, Juan J., and Alfred Stepan. 1996. *Problems of Democratic Transition and Consolidation*. Baltimore, MD: Johns Hopkins University Press.

Lipset, Seymour Martin. 1960. *Political Man*. New York: Anchor.

Loveman, Brian. 1991. "NGOs and the Transition to Democracy." *Grass Roots Development* 15 (2): 8–19.

—— 1995. "Chilean NGOs: Forging a Role in the Transition to Democracy." In *New Paths to Democratic Development in Latin America: The Rise of NGO-municipal Collaboration*, ed. Charles Reilly, 119–144. Boulder, CO: Lynne Rienner.

Lucero, José Antonio. 2008. *Struggles of Voice: The Politics of Indigenous Representation in the Andes*. Pittsburgh: University of Pittsburgh Press.

Luong, Pauline Jones, and Erika Weinthal. 1999. "The NGO Paradox: Democratic Goals and Non-Democratic Outcomes in Kazakhstan." *Europe-Asia Studies* 51 (7, November): 1267–1284.

Machado, Fabiana, Carlos Scartascini, and Mariano Tommasi. 2009. "Political Institutions and Street Protests in Latin America." *Inter-American Development Bank* Department of Research and Chief Economist (Working Paper 110) (November).

Madrid, Raúl L. 2005. "Indigenous Parties and Democracy in Latin America." *Latin American Politics and Society* 47 (4): 161–179.

Mainwaring, Scott, and Timothy Scully. 1995. *Building Democratic Institutions: Party Systems in Latin America*. Stanford, CA: Stanford University Press.

Mainwaring, Scott, and Edurne Zoco. 2007. "Political Sequences and the Stabilization of Interparty Competition." *Party Politics* 13 (2, March 1): 155–178.

Marsteintredet, Leiv, and Einar Berntzen. 2008. "Reducing the Perils of Presidentialism in Latin America Through Presidential Interruptions." *Comparative Politics* 41 (1, October 1): 83–101.

Mayorga, Fernando. 2006. "El Gobierno De Evo Morales: Entre Nacionalismo e Indigenismo." *Nueva Sociedad* 206.

McAdam, Doug. 1999. *Political Process and the Development of Black Insurgency, 1930–1970*. Chicago: University of Chicago Press.

McAdam, Doug, and Sidney Tarrow. 2010. "Ballots and Barricades: On the Reciprocal Relationship Between Elections and Social Movements." *Perspectives on Politics* 8 (02): 529–54

McDonnell, Patrick J. 2005. "Populist Indian Leads in Bolivian Polls." *Los Angeles Times*, December 18. Retrieved from http://articles.latimes.com/2005/dec/18/world/fg-morales18 (Accessed October 3, 2008).

McVeigh, Rory, and Christian Smith. 1999. "Who Protests in America: An Analysis of Three Political Alternatives: Inaction, Institutionalized Politics, or Protest." *Sociological Forum* 14 (4, December): 685–702.

Mendelson, Sarah Elizabeth, and John K. Glenn. 2002. *The Power and Limits of NGOs: A Critical Look at Building Democracy in Eastern Europe and Eurasia*. New York: Columbia University Press.

Mercer, Claire. 2002. "NGOs, Civil Society and Democratization: A Critical Review of the Literature." *Progress in Development Studies* 2 (1, January 1): 5–22.

Meyer, Carrie A. 1995. "Northern Donors for Southern NGOs: Consequences for Local Participation and Production." *Journal of Economic Development* 20 (2, December): 7–22.

Meyer, David S. 2004. "Protest and Political Opportunities." *Annual Review of Sociology* 30 (1, August): 125–145.

Meyer, David S., and Sidney Tarrow. 1998. *The Social Movement Society: Contentious Politics for a New Century*. Lanham, MD: Rowman & Littlefield.

Mishler, William, and Richard Rose. 2001. "Political Support for Incomplete Democracies: Realist vs. Idealist Theories and Measures." *International Political Science Review/Revue Internationale de Science Politique* 22 (4, October): 303–320.

Mitlin, Diana, Sam Hickey, and Anthony Bebbington. 2007. "Reclaiming Development? NGOs and the Challenge of Alternatives." *World Development* 35 (10): 1699–1720.

Moehler, Devra C. 2008. *Distrusting Democrats*. Ann Arbor: University of Michigan Press.

Molina Monasterios, Fernando. 1997. *Historia De La Participación Popular*. La Paz, Bolivia: Ministerio de Desarrollo Humano.

Moreno, Daniel E. Moreno, and Mason W. Moseley. 2010. "The Normalization of Contentious Politics. Explaining Participation in Protests in Latin America." Presented at the Midwest Political Science Association Conference, Chicago.

Muller, Edward N., and Thomas O. Jukam. 1977. "On the Meaning of Political Support." *The American Political Science Review* 71 (4): 1561–1595.

Muller, Edward N., Thomas O. Jukam, and Mitchell A. Seligson. 1982. "Diffuse Political Support and Antisystem Political Behavior: A Comparative Analysis." *American Journal of Political Science* 26 (2): 240–264.

Murdie, Amanda, and Tavishi Bhasin. 2011. "Aiding and Abetting: Human Rights INGOs and Domestic Protest." *Journal of Conflict Resolution* 55 (2, April 1): 163–191.

Nagel, JH. 1987. *Participation*. Englewood Cliffs, NJ: Prentice Hall.

Nancy, Gilles, and Boriana Yontcheva. 2006. *Does NGO Aid Go to the Poor? Empirical Evidence from Europe*. Washington, DC: International Monetary Fund.

Nardulli, Peter F. 2005. *Popular Efficacy in the Democratic Era*. Princeton, NJ: Princeton University Press.

Newton, Kenneth. 2001. "Trust, Social Capital, Civil Society, and Democracy." *International Political Science Review/ Revue Internationale De Science Pol* 22 (2, April 1): 201–214.

Norris, Pippa. 1999. *Critical Citizens: Global Support for Democratic Government*. Oxford: Oxford University Press.

———. 2002. *Democratic Phoenix: Reinventing Political Activism*. New York: Cambridge University Press.

———. 2011. *Democratic Deficit: Critical Citizens Revisited*. Cambridge: Cambridge University Press.

Norris, Pippa, Stefaan Walgrave, and Peter Van Aelst. 2005. "Who Demonstrates? Antistate Rebels, Conventional Participants, or Everyone?" *Comparative Politics* 37 (2, January): 189–205.

O'Donnell, Guillermo A. 1973. *Modernization and Bureaucratic-Authoritarianism: Studies in South American Politics*. Institute of International Studies, University of California.

Olivera, Oscar, and Tom Lewis. 2004. *Cochabamba!: Water War in Bolivia*. Cambridge, MA: South End Press.

Olzak, Susan. 1994. *The Dynamics of Ethnic Competition and Conflict*. Stanford, CA: Stanford University Press.

Olzak, Susan, and Kiyoteru Tsutsui. 1998. "Status in the World System and Ethnic Mobilization." *The Journal of Conflict Resolution* 42 (6, December): 691–720.

Ottaway, Marina, and Thomas Carothers. 2000. *Funding Virtue*. Washington, DC: Carnegie Endowment.

Oxhorn, Philip. 1995. "From Controlled Inclusion to Coerced Marginalization: The Struggle for Civil Society in Latin America." In *Civil Society: Theory, History, Comparison*, ed. Hall, John A. Cambridge, UK: Polity Press.

Pearce, Jenny. 2000. "Development, NGOs, and Civil Society: The Debate and Its Future." In *Development, NGOs, and Civil Society*, ed. Pearce, Jenny, 15–43. Development in Practice Readers. Oxford: Oxfam GB.

Pérez-Liñán, Aníbal. 2007. *Presidential Impeachment and the New Political Instability in Latin America*. Cambridge: Cambridge University Press.

Petras, James, and Henry Veltmeyer. 2011. *Social Movements in Latin America: Neoliberalism and Popular Resistance*. New York: Palgrave Macmillan.

Postero, Nancy Grey. 2007. *Now We Are Citizens: Indigenous Politics in Postmulticultural Bolivia*. Stanford, CA: Stanford University Press.

Postero, Nancy Grey, and León Zamosc. 2004. *The Struggle for Indigenous Rights in Latin America*. East Sussex, UK: Sussex Academic Press.

Putnam, Robert D. 1994. *Making Democracy Work: Civic Traditions in Modern Italy.* Princeton, NJ: Princeton University Press.

Putnam, Robert D. 2001. *Bowling Alone.* New York: Simon and Schuster.

Reilly, Charles. 1995. *New Paths to Democratic Development in Latin America: the Rise of NGO-municipal Collaboration.* Boulder, CO: Lynne Rienner.

Romero Ballivián, Salvador. 2003. "Análisis De La Participación Electoral En Bolivia." In *Participación y Abstención Electoral En Bolivia.* La Paz, Bolivia: Friedrich Ebert Stiftung Instituto Latinoamericano de Investigaciones Sociales (FES-ILDIS).

Romero, Salvador Ballivián. 2003. *Geografía Electoral de Bolivia.* Tercera Edicion. La Paz, Bolivia: Fundemos.

Rose, Richard, and Doh Chull Shin. 2001. "Democratization Backwards: The Problem of Third-Wave Democracies." *British Journal of Political Science* 31 (2): 331–354.

Rosenstone, Steven J., and John Mark Hansen. 1993. *Mobilization, Participation, and Democracy in America.* New York: Macmillan.

Rossteutscher, Sigrid. 2010. "Social Capital Worldwide: Potential for Democratization or Stabilizer of Authoritarian Rule?" *American Behavioral Scientist* 53 (5, January 1): 737–757.

Salamon, Lester M., and H. Anheier. 2004. *Global Civil Society: Dimensions of the Nonprofit Sector.* Sterling, VA: Kumarian Press.

Sartori, Giovanni. 1976. *Parties and Party Systems: A Framework for Analysis.* Cambridge: Cambridge University Press.

Schock, Kurt. 2005. *Unarmed Insurrections: People Power Movements in Nondemocracies.* Minneapolis: University of Minnesota Press.

Schussman, Alan., and Sarah Anne Soule. 2005. "Process and Protest: Accounting for Individual Protest Participation." *Social Forces* 84 (2): 1083–1108.

Seligson, Mitchell A. 1983. "On the Measurement of Diffuse Support: Some Evidence from Mexico." *Social Indicators Research* 12 (1): 1–24.

Seligson, Mitchell A., and Julio F. Carrión. 2002. "Political Support, Political Skepticism, and Political Stability in New Democracies An Empirical Examination of Mass Support for Coups d'Etat in Peru." *Comparative Political Studies* 35 (1, February 1): 58–82.

Silva, Eduardo. 2009. *Challenging Neoliberalism in Latin America.* Cambridge: Cambridge University Press.

Snyder, Richard. 2001. "Scaling Down: The Subnational Comparative Method." *Studies in Comparative International Development (SCID)* 36 (1, March 6): 93–110.

Sobieraj, Sarah, and Deborah White. 2004. "Taxing Political Life: Reevaluating the Relationship Between Voluntary Association Membership, Political Engagement, and the State." *The Sociological Quarterly* 45 (4, August): 739–764.

Somma, Nicolás M. 2010. "How Do Voluntary Organizations Foster Protest? The Role of Organizational Involvement on Individual Protest Participation." *Sociological Quarterly* 51 (3): 384–407.

Steenbergen, Marco R., and Bradford S. Jones. 2002. "Modeling Multi-level Data Structures." *American Journal of Political Science* 46 (1, January): 218–237.

Stimson, James A. 2004. *Tides of Consent: How Public Opinion Shapes American Politics.* Cambridge: Cambridge University Press.

Stolle, Dietlind, and Thomas R. Rochon. 1998. "Are All Associations Alike?" *American Behavioral Scientist* 42 (1): 47–65.

Tarrow, Sidney. 1998. *Power in Movement: Social Movements and Contentious Politics.* Cambridge: Cambridge University Press.

Tarrow, Sidney G. 2011. *Power in Movement: Social Movements and Contentious Politics.* Cambridge: Cambridge University Press.

Tilly, Charles. 1978. *From Mobilization to Revolution.* Reading, MA: Addison-Wesley.

Tsutsui, Kiyoteru. 2004. "Global Civil Society and Ethnic Social Movements in the Contemporary World." *Sociological Forum* 19 (1, March 1): 63–87.

Tsutsui, Kiyoteru, and Christine Min Wotipka. 2004. "Global Civil Society and the International Human Rights Movement: Citizen Participation in Human Rights International Nongovernmental Organizations." *Social Forces* 83 (2): 587.

Tucker, Joshua A. 2007. "Enough! Electoral Fraud, Collective Action Problems, and Post-Communist Colored Revolutions." *Perspectives on Politics* 5 (3): 535–551.

Tusalem, Rollin F. 2007. "A Boon or a Bane? The Role of Civil Society in Third- and Fourth-Wave Democracies." *International Political Science Review* 28 (3, June 1): 361–386.

Tvedt, Terje. 1998. *Angels of Mercy or Development Diplomats?: NGOs and Foreign Aid.* Woodbridge, Suffolk, UK: James Currey.

Useem, Bert. 1980. "Solidarity Model, Breakdown Model, and the Boston Anti-Busing Movement." *American Sociological Review* 45 (3, June): 357–369.

Uvin, Peter. 1998. *Aiding Violence: The Development Enterprise in Rwanda.* Sterling, VA: Kumarian Press.

Valencia, J.F., E.H. Cohen, and D. Hermosilla. 2010. "Social Trust and Political Protest: The Mediating Role of the Value of Power Distance." *Psicología Política* (40): 61–80.

Van Cott, Donna Lee. 2000. *The Friendly Liquidation of the Past: The Politics of Diversity in Latin America.* Pittsburgh: University of Pittsburgh Press.

2005. *From Movements to Parties in Latin America: The Evolution of Ethnic Politics.* Cambridge: Cambridge University Press.

Varshney, Ashutosh. 2003. *Ethnic Conflict and Civic Life.* New Haven, CT: Yale University Press.

Verba, Sidney, and Norman H. Nie. 1987. *Participation in America.* Chicago: University of Chicago Press.

Verba, Sidney, Norman H. Nie, and Jae-on Kim. 1979. *Participation and Political Equality.* Cambridge: Cambridge University Press.

Verba, Sidney, Kay Lehman Schlozman, and Henry E. Brady. 1995. *Voice and Equality.* Cambridge, MA: Harvard University Press.

VIPFE. 2004. *Directorio Nacional de ONGs en Bolivia, 2003–2004: Registro Unico Nacional de ONGs.* La Paz, Bolivia: Viceministerio de Inversion Publica y Financiamiento Externo, Republica de Bolivia, Ministerio de Hacienda.

2006. *Directorio Nacional De ONGs En Bolivia, 2005–2006: Registro Unico Nacional De ONGs.* La Paz, Bolivia: Viceministerio de Inversion Publica y Financiamiento Externo, Republica de Bolivia, Ministerio de Hacienda.

Warren, Mark E. 2001. *Democracy and Association.* Princeton, NJ: Princeton University Press.

Werker, Eric, and Faisal Z. Ahmed. 2008. "What Do Nongovernmental Organizations Do?" *The Journal of Economic Perspectives* 22 (2): 73–92.

Weatherford, M. Stephen. 1987. "How Does Government Performance Influence Political Support?" *Political Behavior* 9 (1, March 1): 5–28.

White, Gordon. 1994. "Civil Society, Democratization and Development (I): Clearing the Analytical Ground." *Democratization* 1 (3).

Wiarda, Howard J. 2003. *Civil Society*. Boulder, CO: Westview Press.

Wilkinson, Steven I. 2006. *Votes and Violence*. Cambridge: Cambridge University Press.

Wolfinger, Raymond E., and Steven J. Rosenstone. 1980. *Who Votes*. New Haven, CT: Yale University Press.

World Bank. 1989. "Involving NGOs in Bank-supported Activities." Retrieved from http://www.gdrc.org/ngo/wb-ngo-directive.html (Accessed October 2010).

　　2006. "World Bank-Civil Society Engagement: A Review of Years 2005 and 2006." *World Bank*. Retrieved from http://go.worldbank.org/Q5VNO72MC0 (Accessed October 2010).

　　2010. "Governance & Anti-Corruption > WGI 1996–2009 Interactive > Home." Retrieved from http://info.worldbank.org/governance/wgi/index.asp (Accessed October 2010).

　　2012. "Governance & Anti-Corruption > WGI 1996–2011 Interactive > FAQ." Retrieved from http://info.worldbank.org/governance/wgi/faq.htm (Accessed October 2010).

Yashar, Deborah J. 2005. *Contesting Citizenship in Latin America: The Rise of Indigenous Movements and the Postliberal Challenge*. Cambridge: Cambridge University Press.

Zald, Mayer N. 1992. "Looking Backward to Look Forward: Reflections on the Past and Future of the Resource Mobilization Research Program." In *Frontiers in Social Movement Theory*, ed. Aldon D. Morris and Carol McClurg Mueller, 326–348. New Haven, CT: Yale University Press.

Zald, Mayer N., and John D. McCarthy. 1990. *Social Movements in an Organizational Society: Collected Essays*. New Brunswick, NJ: Transaction Publishers.

Zamosc, León. 2007. "The Indian Movement and Political Democracy in Ecuador." *Latin American Politics & Society* 49 (3): 1–34.

Zavaleta, Rene. 1979. *El Poder Dual (Coleccion Minima; 65)*. 3rd ed. Siglo XXI Editores, S. A. De C. V.

Index

CPSIA information can be obtained at www.ICGtesting.com
Printed in the USA
LVOW08s1738131016

508647LV00001B/96/P